DR. MELVYN KINDER

GOING NOWHERE FAST

Step Off Life's Treadmills and Find Peace of Mind

New York   London   Toronto   Sydney   Tokyo   Singapore

Prentice Hall Press
15 Columbus Circle
New York, New York 10023

Library of Congress Cataloging-in-Publication Data

Kinder, Melvyn.
Going nowhere fast / Melvyn Kinder. — 1st Prentice Hall Press ed.
p.   cm.
ISBN 0-13-358995-1
1. Self-acceptance.   2. Social values—Psychological aspects.
I. Title.
BF575.S37K56   1990   89-48582
158'.1—dc20   CIP

Designed by Victoria Hartman
Manufactured in the United States of America

10 9 8 7 6 5 4 3 2 1

First Edition

To my late father, Jack Kinder
and
To my wife, Sara

ACKNOWLEDGMENTS

To Marilyn Abraham, my editor, my appreciation and admiration for her special skill of communicating support while at the same time challenging me to continually sharpen my observations.

To Clayton Rich, for his wise observations, pointed dialogues, and skill in helping me to focus my point of view.

To Kristin Hohenadel for her patient and good-natured assistance in preparing this manuscript.

And finally, my deep gratitude to Richard Pine, my literary agent, for his belief in me and boundless enthusiasm for this book.

CONTENTS

INTRODUCTION

I would like to share something I don't often express in my office. Like those of you who have gravitated toward this book, I, too, have pursued many life goals with relentless fervor. I, too, have felt a gnawing doubt about the frantic course of my life and have wanted to let up, yet dreaded the void that I feared would materialize. While you may believe altering the course of one's life is easier for a therapist, trust me, it's not. Stepping off life's treadmills requires the examination and peeling away of many layers of self-deception, and nobody is better at fooling themselves than therapists when, armed with enormous amounts of information and theories, we can be terribly adept at weaving our own webs of distortion.

First-time patients, filled with both hope and trepidation, inevitably broach the question, "Can people really change?" I know what they are feeling. Naturally, they want me to respond affirmatively, but they also fear such optimism. Because the actual prospect of change is unsettling. This is especially true for those men and women to whom this book is addressed. Many of you are considered successful, even high achievers. Superficially, it seems that your life is working. But you feel a secret malaise, and a weariness, which persists even in the face of your commendable achievements. So if change were to occur, what kind of payoff are you really getting in return?

I am revealing my own struggle as a way to tell you that I understand and also to tell you there is hope for living a life that is richer. I tell my patients what I have learned myself; take a leap of faith that enables you to believe your life can be different. Know that you can choose your life. Contentment is indeed achievable, even for those of you who may have secretly given up that elusive goal.

The reality is this: Change happens when you surrender to its possibility. It is the failure to surrender that creates unseen barriers that can exist even for those who have undergone years of psychotherapy. That is why I encourage you to surrender to the message of this book. I ask you to accept the fact that you will have to mourn the loss of beliefs that you and I both know are illusions that only make you unhappy. If you recognize yourself in these pages, accept those identifications. These beliefs may have guided you for years and may have been supported by those around you, but you must reexamine their usefulness. Take as a working hypothesis that the warnings I'm issuing should be heeded, and that the guidelines I offer truly work. I'm asking you to take a leap of faith that will allow you to initiate the process of change. You will then discover that openness and receptivity necessary to step off life's treadmills and to find peace of mind.

· I ·

THE TREADMILL MENTALITY

CHAPTER ONE

BLINDLY SEARCHING FOR HAPPINESS

A string of excited, fugitive, miscellaneous pleasures is not happiness; happiness resides in an imaginative reflection and judgment, when the picture of one's life, or of human life, as it truly has been or is, satisfies the will, and is gladly accepted.

— George Santayana, philosopher

Jonathan, a forty-eight-year-old successful attorney, has come to see me at the urging of his distressed wife, Elaine, who is concerned about the quality of their marriage. "I have no idea why I'm here," he starts out, somewhat resentfully.

I answer, "Your wife is troubled by your relationship. She feels you aren't as open with her as you used to be, and that you're more irritable than ever. And she feels you won't listen to her concerns." Then I add, "Maybe that's true, maybe that's just her perception, maybe she wants too much, who knows. Why don't you tell me your view?"

Jonathan begins by telling me how he's doing better than ever, he's more successful than he dreamed, and his life is right on track. But as he continues talking, he reveals the details of what appears to be an entirely different life: long hours and a driving, even grinding existence in an effort to keep up in his rapidly expanding law firm.

When he finishes recounting, I ask him if he is satisfied with the way things are. He pauses a long while, then shrugs his shoulders. "Yeah, I think I'm happy. I'm getting what I want, I'm going in the right direction."

We look at each other without talking. We both know the truth is something else, but he can't put his finger on it, and I respect his struggle. He has worked hard all his life, taken risks, paid his dues, and, at least in his own mind, put his family's welfare on the top of his priority list. But I know he's not content, and he suspects as much but can't articulate it.

After a session or two with both of them, Jonathan asks to come in alone. "You know, I'm really not happy, I'm not feeling what I should be feeling. . . . I know something's wrong. When Elaine tells me I'm not really 'there' with the kids even when I'm with them, I get angry because I know she's right. But I don't have a clue as to what to do about this," he admits.

I nod in agreement, because I understand. I've been there myself. I know how it feels to pursue goals that seem worthy but when attained leave you with a feeling of emptiness. I know he's not alone, and I suspect that you sense that too.

A number of years ago, I began to ask myself why so many of us are secretly dissatisfied—always wanting to be "more" than we are, questing after goals that slowly and imperceptibly turn into illusions, or fool's gold, rather than anything truly precious. In these allegedly enlightened times, aren't we supposedly armed with the knowledge we need to fully realize our potential, not just cope or merely survive, but to become the best we can be? Sadly many of us seem to lack the skills to turn these dictums into more than empty clichés.

Today, I conclude that we are becoming a nation of men and women who, in the quest for happiness, all too often fall short of achieving any kind of inner peace. Instead of life's journey being an exhilarating adventure into the unknown, for many of us it is a compulsive and tiring trek, an exhausting journey where the next stop for replenishment never seems to arrive.

More than that, in my work I began to see misery of epidemic proportions, a kind of undeclared disease that I'm convinced is afflicting millions. I see countless people who are driven, often obsessed, with perfecting themselves and searching for fulfillment in ways that are not working, detached from traditional value systems and frequently based on questionable or impossible expectations. In my psychotherapy practice, I work with people who appear to have enviable lives. They are financially successful and professionally accomplished, yet they are secretly and profoundly unhappy. Although others may look up to them, they don't feel very good about themselves. These people are not "neurotic," nor are they necessarily selfish. Indeed, they are trying their best and following guidelines that most of their peers would agree are just fine. So what has gone wrong?

I find many people acting on the assumption that life is a series of self-improvements, the sum total of which is equated with happiness. But when we attempt to find happiness in this way, we engage in a never-ending quest that subtly and inevitably makes us even more unhappy! What starts out as a positive attempt to better our lives, gradually and insidiously grows negative and psychologically toxic. It seems the harder we try to achieve fulfillment, the more we are driven by the fear of not reaching these goals. We end up frustrated, going nowhere fast!

Today, when I listen to the concerns revealed by my patients, I hear more than sad or poignant personal dilemmas. As I've said, their problems are not mental illnesses, rather they are the manifestations of a pervasive social brainwashing that subtly depreciates what is natural and innate and creates exaggerated expectations about life's promises and the ease with which they are realized. And so we have become hopelessly obsessed with self-improvement. The feeling that each of us is somehow deficient is something we share, although we mask it differently.

A single woman feels torn between the "shoulds" of finding independence and a career and her powerful desires for family life. Wisely, she senses that both are essential. But she is so bombarded with conflicting opinions—from talk shows, magazine articles, friends, family, television, and movies—that she finds herself unable to enjoy considering either option!

A couple who have infrequent sexual encounters are each, candidly, quite satisfied, yet they feel abnormal because they do not feel compelled to strive for a more spectacular sex life in a time when this is considered one of the necessary qualities of a good marriage.

A young male executive, whose mind is overloaded with motivational tapes and books, frantically searches for ways to get an edge in his work and realize his particular reading of the American dream. He exemplifies the new late twenties or early thirties midlife crisis. Although he's trying therapy, he still denies the depth of his emotional fatigue, which is far more severe than his brief working years should warrant.

Although no one would regard her as anything but skinny, a young woman jogs four miles a day and works out five days a week, always seems to be on a diet. Pressured to enter therapy by a worried mother, she is finally wondering whether she is being consumed by shallow, self-destructive standards of beauty and appearance.

Each of these people is hounded by a set of "shoulds" that they identify as vital for their success and, at the same time, the cause of their unhappiness. They may be doing well, but they feel terrible. No wonder they're confused! They are not unlike the rest of us who, whether in the privacy of a therapist's office or in the course of everyday living, are plagued with the confusions that abound today.

Recently, I conducted a workshop with a group of female executives and business owners. They enthusiastically tossed around the new buzzword "balance," which means juggling your efforts so that your personal life coexists perfectly with your professional life. I'm nodding my head, thinking, "Yeah, that's nice of course, but ..." But I worry about the kind of pressure we put ourselves under. I know that the idea is right, but if the metaphor for life's journey is as precarious as a tightrope, where does that lead us? Where is it going? Are we, with gritted teeth and clenched muscles, destined to always live so stressfully?

I'm sure many of you know exactly what I'm talking about. You see it in your friends, you sense it in yourself. Viewed superficially, your life looks like it's working, but it's not. You think you'll eventually find peace of mind, but you don't. You feel a sense of having lost direction. And even more frustrating and inexplicable, the harder you try to solve your problems, the worse you feel. Your goals seem perfectly reasonable, your efforts relentless, but you aren't getting any closer to happiness. You feel as if you're on a treadmill.

OUR PSYCHOLOGICAL TERRAIN

The "treadmill" experience is baffling because it is somewhat elusive. When the externals of our lives appear orderly, it doesn't occur to us to pay attention to the valuable internal signals that clue us into the sources of our unhappiness. We don't know how to read these messages.

Clearly, the majority of us have lost contact with our inner lives. By that, I don't mean simply that we have lost the ability to experience our keen sensations, which often oscillate between excitement, anxiety, and frustration, or the all-too-common pressing feeling of having no time. More precisely, we pursue goals so frenetically and desperately that we lose sight of the interior landscape on which we travel. If we have no time in the external world, then we must have even less for the important concerns of our inner world. When we neglect the internal terrain, our very identities degenerate into an empty reflection of our external confusion.

We need to regain our inner terrain if it is to be more than a mirror of our external confusion. We need knowledge of our mountains and valleys and plateaus—our inner space and time. Without an intimate knowledge of our own internal landscape we feel only what we are told to feel and see only what we are told to see. Without a clear sense of our individual "selves," we can't make sense of our experience. We are lost inside and out.

The people I work with today lack the necessary language to describe or conceptualize their dilemma. They are simply hounded by a vague, but omnipresent, sense that something is wrong. They may be unaware that their outer pursuits and goals have defined their inner lives and eventually the two seem one and the same.

The people I counsel are on self-imposed treadmills. They are fatigued and confused. They are trying to sustain feelings of optimism, but their energy to do so is rapidly being depleted. The young single woman is so busy trying to have it all that she ends up feeling bewildered and frustrated. Jonathan, who knows he's made it, readily admits that fulfillment is a concept that eludes him. The woman who compulsively jogs is depressed more often than not, although she is unable to connect such melancholia with the fact that she has sacrificed her inner self for an obsession with her outer appearance.

When I first discovered this self-created turmoil in myself and witnessed it in others a number of years ago, I wondered, "What has happened to us? Have we all been conned, slowly and subtly, into self-loathing? Deluded into believing that seeking contentment is somehow less noble than the fierce determination to have it all?"

The individuals I've been discussing have one unfortunate thing in common. Each of them has equated the attainment of happiness with the relentless pursuit of a particular path, whether it is looking just right, being successful, or having it all. They possess the basic human need for peace of mind, but they pursue goals that never lead to it.

CAN HAPPINESS BE PURSUED?

It says in the Declaration of Independence that we have the right to life, liberty, and the pursuit of happiness. Those words are the preamble to the American dream. But more than two hundred years later, the innocent, hopeful intentions of our founding fathers have become blind and dangerous compulsions!

We have been misled by this frantic pursuit of happiness, something we regard as if it were a clearly definable entity. But we all know we can't buy happiness, and we are often surprised by what brings us happiness and frustrated by what we believe *should* make us happy.

We must step back and scrutinize our life goals and our means for pursuing them, especially in an age that is so enamored with goal setting. Happiness is the overarching goal, the goal that subsumes the rest. Success, prosperity, good relationships, and other life goals we set for ourselves are supposed to bring us happiness. Yet these goals soon become fuzzy, unclear, and elusive when we try to pin them down.

Yet we seldom examine our life goals, because we assume they are unquestionably good. When things go wrong, we suspect we aren't working hard enough, we lack dedication, or we aren't growing fast enough. We don't look at the life process we are immersed in, and in this arena of oversight our life goals can become deadly traps. It may be that happiness can't really be "pursued." Certainly we need to examine our assumptions about happiness.

"GROWTH" PSYCHOLOGY AND HAPPINESS

When I first began practicing psychotherapy almost twenty-five years ago, my profession dealt with the specific problems we called mental illness. But then things changed. In the sixties and seventies people were no longer content with just getting rid of problems, and my profession broadened its scope and became concerned with issues of happiness, well-being, contentment, and self-worth. We embraced the challenge of the "self-acceptance problem," i.e., "How can I feel good about myself?" We implicitly assumed that psychology could teach us how to be happy.

A slew of social platitudes invaded our vocabularies. Psychology focused on growth and self-realization, while society stressed having it all. Lost in the shuffle was peace of mind and unconditional self-acceptance. Lost too were the old values inherent in such maxims as Accept yourself and To thine own self be true. The tradition of American individualism—Be your own person—seemed to evaporate. Growth was the key element in a new formula for happiness.

Growth was an unquestioned good. Everyone needed to grow as part of the process of constantly bettering himself. As the romanticizing of growth evolved, it lost its organic meaning and became a metaphor for a continuous set of self-improvements that would lead to perfection. No matter how vague the concept, this idealization of self-improvement was never challenged. There was no end to it and no let up from it.

In my own practice, I began to see that the idealization and romanticizing of growth too often led people into something dark and confining, rather than illuminating. The message became if you are not growing, your life is static and stagnant. Put simply, once society's dictates tell you that you need to grow, in an odd way you begin to affirm your own inadequacy.

Those that bought into these new ways of looking at life and finding happiness received, as the price of admission, the ticket of dissatisfaction. Peace of mind or tranquility was no longer a goal and was certainly not heroic. As a result, the urge to pursue happiness came not from some foundation of contentment but rather from unhappiness, a sense of unease, a feeling of malaise. The strange twist came when the unease was valued for itself. And the new ethics of growth implied you had to be "open" about your unrest.

Remember, openness rather than intellectual thought was the new value. In the sixties and seventies, emotional truths were elevated above intellectual and spiritual truths. How you felt became more important than discovering what was true.

An incident in the early seventies—that occurred when I conducted a weekend marathon group session, a popular mode of psychotherapy at the time—reminds me of the illusions that were already taking seed. All the people in the group were asked what they wanted in life. One after another, some tearfully, some radiating a sense of inner courage, expressed what they believed were their innermost wishes: to be able to "risk joy," to be "freer to love," to "live in the now," or to "shed their ego."

One of the last to speak, a young attorney, who had been coerced by a woman friend into attending, looked around and said, "I want to be a better tennis player." Instantly, the group pounced on him with shock and righteous indignation, accusing him of being shallow and emotionally bankrupt. In fact, I thought he was probably the most well-adjusted person there. The only person who defended him was a very disturbed and painfully shy young man who turned to me and expressed his terror about being there and whispered, "They all seem like hyenas sitting on their haunches waiting to devour any feelings that might come out." The new standard of dissatisfaction and emotional turmoil was apparent.

The seventies also glorified the concept of "midlife crisis," which is often really a spiritual crisis and for many a terrifying look into the abyss of what seems a meaningless existence. But for some men, and later for independent women, such crises were unlikely badges of courage. The man who wishes to chuck it all and take off or the woman who decides she's fed up with the couch potato she lives with both have legitimate gripes and problems to solve. But rather than addressing the deep internal sources of their discontent, they may deflect any valuable revelation with abrupt and impulsive action.

As I look back, the weekend marathon group crystalized issues still bedeviling so many of us today. We equate intense emotions and sensations with being alive, while at the same time we negate self-acceptance and the need for peace of mind. This is why addictions are so prevalent and such an easy solution to the happiness problem. Addicts deaden the pain rather than face the problem.

To be absolutely clear about the terms used here, *addiction* is a physiological and emotional craving and/or dependence on a particular chemical substance. *Treadmills* take on their insidious quality not because of physical sensation, but because of cognitive meanings. Treadmills are to be distinguished from *compulsions*, which are repetitive, stereotyped, and often trivial motor actions, i.e., they are observable physical behaviors. Treadmills are not compulsions, no matter how compelling, just as my need to watch every football game on the tube is not a compulsion (although my wife might argue otherwise). Finally, *obsessions* are repetitive and insistant thoughts that are unwelcome as contrasted with treadmill ruminations, which are viewed as necessary and, therefore, are grudgingly welcomed by the patient.

I suspect that in these times many people aren't really suffering from a psychological problem, but from a spiritual one. We feel empty, disconnected from ourselves, others, and our community. We have fundamental problems with loving and giving to one another. But confronting such issues is more painful than chasing seemingly easy solutions to our happiness dilemma.

In any event, for all the good things that happened, an inadvertent legacy of the sixties and seventies was a neglect of peace of mind and a demeaning of contentment. Indeed, the new values almost suggested that self-loathing was a perfect prerequisite for becoming a new person. That's where we are today. I find it a disturbing picture.

TREADMILLS: TODAY'S DILEMMA

We are blindly and dangerously pursuing happiness without, perhaps, understanding what that is. Happiness is not about having what we want, but wanting what we have. In many ways, happiness is within us waiting to be discovered. But this message is one that most of us fail to recognize or at best realize later than is necessary. Instead of peace of mind, we've learned the language of pursuit and unceasing self-improvement.

Many of us are on life treadmills, which we mistakenly believe are paths to happiness and personal well-being. In the process of trying to look better, be healthier, prove ourselves, make more money, and have better marriages, among other things, disappointment and spiritual exhaustion set in. Because at first these treadmills appear innocuous, even appropriate, millions of us are climbing aboard and trying to stay on.

As I indicated, our choice of treadmills runs the gamut, from the frustrated "overweight" person who is starting yet another diet to the exhausted executive who is making yet another deal. We may castigate ourselves for our apparent failures and exhort ourselves to do better next time, but we never question the direction we have taken. When we first got on, we believed we were on the right path. But all too often something unexpected happens. Instead of finding an answer we become more enmeshed in our problems.

Seemingly correct paths can evolve into something else. The process of pursuit can gradually redefine one's inner life. People don't start with denial and self-deception, looking for external solutions the way an addict might. They start out with positive desires, ones that are endorsed and sanctioned by our society.

But the faster we go in pursuit, the more signals we begin to ignore. At first you ignore negative feelings. Perhaps this is the price you have to pay. Eventually isn't hard work supposed to pay off? But as you follow new and seductive external maps, you lose control of what you pay attention to. After a while, the pursuit of success, for example, becomes an end in itself. And if it doesn't, then you are invariably urged to set new goals. The problem is that nobody tells you to consult with *yourself* before you decide on these new goals. Most of us just latch on to whatever seems trendy or appropriate at the moment.

Sadly, our current paths to happiness have left us feeling lost, driven by a haunting sense we are never enough, unable to appreciate who we are and what we have. Our response to our anguish is to try harder—relentlessly striving to improve ourselves and those we love in the vain hope we will eventually find happiness.

It may be that our goals are killing us! Our highly touted solutions are making us miserable. Our paths to happiness are actually treadmills, going nowhere fast.

Fortunately, in increasing numbers, people are beginning to ask an important question: "I think I'm doing all the right things, so why do I still feel so tense, exhausted, and empty?" We need to stop, we need to hear this question, we need to reexamine our prescriptions for happiness, we need to get off our treadmills!

Treadmills are false goals that lead to dead ends. They are prescribed by society's new and seductive values, fueled by a fear of imperfection and sustained by a myopia, an inattention to other options. For example, if you believe looking better is the solution to a sense of inadequacy, the appearance treadmill beckons you. But appearance in itself is a false goal. Society has tricked us into believing it is a guarantee of self-worth. The more we believe this, the more we fail to see alternatives to this path.

A treadmill becomes a treadmill because it doesn't answer our real needs. It carries us along, gathering momentum because we're secretly feeling worse—we secretly give up hope, as feeling better seems increasingly elusive.

When we no longer have access to an inner life that takes into account who we really are, we have developed a treadmill mentality. Its legacy is anxiety, chronic dissatisfaction, exhaustion, and an even more diminished sense of worth, which only leads us to stay caught in life's treadmills.

The goal of this book is to explain how that happened, why treadmills are so powerful, what we can do to escape them, and how we can rediscover the comfort of peace of mind.

You will learn that treadmills are spurred on by two sources. The external one comes from our social and psychological maps—the tantalizing prescriptions for getting better and better and having more and more, which are solutions offered by the self-improvement industries and the media. The internal source is the vague sense felt by millions that we have lost something, that something is not right, that we are not enough, that we are inadequate. This sense of inner loss makes us highly vulnerable to the allure of treadmills, but treadmills result only in magnifying our inner emptiness. Each source insidiously feeds into the other.

Treadmills offer the illusory promise that looking better or making more money or having better kids will make us happy. The other side of this promise is the hidden agenda: "If I do this, I won't have to face my inner unhappiness." Society keeps telling us we're on the right path, and our distress keeps telling us we had better stay on that path.

Treadmills feed on anxiety and create even more. At first treadmills reduce our anguish because we believe we have made a good choice for our lives. But they end up creating more anxiety because all the while the answer to finding the self-acceptance we crave is inside us, not outside. But we don't know that because we've confused self-improvement with self-acceptance. Treadmills become terribly rigid and repetitive responses to inner problems. They become unending because they are stimulated by anxiety and create more anxiety all at the same time.

The treadmill mentality determines how we process life's experiences and explains why we are so mentally fatigued today. It causes us to pay singular attention to the treadmill. And as our attention becomes overly focused, we lose sense of time; our lives are so consumed with a frantic urgency that we never take the time to stop and reflect or open ourselves up to alternatives.

But that's one of the purposes of the treadmill. Once we're on, we try not to slow down, because we fear discovering how unhappy we may be inside. Yet residing within us are the very qualities that may allow us to appreciate ourselves. The paradox of the treadmill is that it takes us farther and farther away from that which could solve our pain.

Sadly we have lost contact with ourselves. No matter how good we might have been, our interior life can end up becoming shallow and superficial, concerned more with lifestyles rather than life. Because of the information overload in society today, we have become information processors and have given away a deeper sense of ourselves as we frantically keep information flowing along.

FINDING OURSELVES

How we see ourselves and how we should live our lives is profoundly shaped by the guidelines or maps our society gives us for making sense of the world. Our culture—families, schools, and churches—mark the trails, label the peaks, shade the valleys. As bright-eyed travelers we trust these maps to get us where we want to go, or think we should be going.

Over the years these maps change in complex ways. Sometimes the changes are for the good, and other times they leave us stranded. I believe our present maps have left us stranded. They leave out trails we need to take, places we need to rediscover. In this book I want to examine our maps, and suggest some changes.

To do this remapping I will introduce some concepts that I have found useful in understanding my life and useful in helping my patients make sense of their lives. In chapter 3, I will develop the concepts of the Imperfect Self, the Perfect Self, and the Forgotten Self. These are important tools for discovering where we are and mapping some new directions.

The other tool I want to develop is the concept of a plateau, which can become part of our inner landscape. Plateaus exemplify a period of rest, consolidation, and peace. To reach a plateau, you must dismantle your present picture of your inner life as a never-ending stairway of self-improvements and replace it with a map that leaves space for who you really are.

Ultimately, I want to show how plateaus help us to avoid being victims, brainwashed by trendy societal values, and allow us to take control of our lives. To achieve this, we must create an alternative to the treadmill mentality. Plateaus can replace treadmills; they are the foundations of satisfaction. They embody the concept of "This is who I am, and it is enough." They solve the circularity of the self-acceptance problem of "How can I accept myself when I dislike myself?"

I have found that anyone can discover his plateaus. The process starts with a leap of faith that life has many options that lead to well-being. More particularly, I let people in on a secret: Just getting off a treadmill creates the paradoxical effect of bringing them closer to what they needed in the first place. As you read about each treadmill, you will see these paradoxes in action.

Plateaus are not about resignation. You will see, for example, how letting go of unending pursuits for more success, more money, or a perfect love can be liberating. Discovering a plateau of satisfaction in life is a victory. From plateaus, further dreams and aspirations can transpire, now motivated by positive wishes rather than fear and a sense of deficiency. Only when you experience a plateau in those areas of life where you previously had no control, can you then begin living life on your own terms. It is then that you can come to believe in the elusive phrase we have heard many times, but never known: the "real you."

I know that each of you can identify your own plateaus and discover the real you if you diligently and honestly entertain the possibility that you might be a lot better off than you realize. You can recognize and enjoy the value of who you are and what you have, while still having dreams. In attempting to be happy, you don't have to make yourself miserable. I also believe the desire for coming to terms with oneself, for peace of mind, is finally becoming one of the most compelling quests for men and women today.

CHAPTER TWO

SELF-IMPROVEMENT OR SELF-REJECTION?

It is far more important that one's life should be perceived than it should be transformed; for no sooner has it been perceived, than it transforms itself of its own accord.

—Maurice Maeterlinck, dramatist

I'm having lunch with an old friend, a physican in his early fifties. After the usual impersonal chitchat about work, our marriages, and our families, I ask him how he's really feeling these days. His face lights up, as he proudly discloses he's "on chapter 4 of *The Course in Miracles*." "What?" I ask, knowing all too well this is going to be yet another episode in his lifelong quest for the truth—psychoanalysis, holistic medicine, EST, and the Guru Bwagwan. Now, it is another path; one evolved out of an alleged "automatic writing" experience whereby a psychologist became the channel for Jesus Christ himself, yielding revelations that have become the basis for a new movement.

As he talks, I have two reactions. First, I believe that any search for new wisdom is always interesting and, at least, thought provoking, and that's good. But second, I know that he feels lost and has always avoided grappling with some painful episodes in his past. After he explains how this is obviously better than his other experiences with the quest for happiness, he notes my lukewarm response. I apologize, look at him directly, and ask, "What would happen to you if you didn't pursue enlightenment so hungrily?" He merely shrugs, not really pondering my question. He can't, because to confront himself and who he is now, rather than what he hopes to become, is much too threatening. Trying to be supportive, I tell him, "As long you enjoy it, that's certainly okay."

And it is. I have no quarrel with the study of wisdom, and I admire my friend's intellectual thirst. Moreover, I respect his recognition that his malaise speaks to spiritual issues, rather than acquiring more things or pursuing some other equally empty path. But, once again, I recognize his eagerness for growth as a mask for unhappiness and, carried to extremes, a method of self-avoidance. My friend would like to believe he is growing. I believe he is unknowingly drifting farther away from himself.

I'm not writing from a position of self-righteousness. Psychotherapists, too—including myself—are not without grand illusions. When new patients come in to see me, they desperately want to believe that I have special powers. I wish I could have that kind of magic, but I don't. Therefore, I must repeatedly ask myself, "How much do I unwittingly feed into their expectations? How often do I go along with their fantasy of a total metamorphosis in their personality? How often do I throw my weight on the side of realizing their unrealistic expectations, rather than challenging them? Put more personally, how often do I promise more than I can really deliver?"

So many of us have become victims of grand illusions—wishes that only set us up for disappointment. We are ashamed to have modest dreams. Contentment has become a trivial goal, and acknowledging limitations or being reluctant to take certain risks has become the mark of mediocrity or, worse still, cowardice.

We assume we must constantly be growing to feel good about ourselves. We have neglected the possibility of self-acceptance and have substituted self-improvement as the key to happiness. As you will come to see, every treadmill starts out as a seemingly positive exercise in self-improvement. But something happens along the way that makes us go faster and blinds us to other options. What starts out as positive, becomes negative. We desperately try to be someone different from who we are. This wasn't always so. How did we end up with these guidelines?

THE PSYCHOLOGIZING OF EVERYDAY LIFE

It is faulty to believe that our contemporary values and beliefs have always been with us, that what is regarded as truth today has been around for ages. That's not so. All of us, psychologists included, need to have some sense of history if we are to put our present concerns into perspective. In my own lifetime there have been radical changes.

I remember the Eisenhower era as a time of backyard barbecues and big ugly cars, which seemed beautiful then, and as a time when the media happily focused on "togetherness." Stalin died in 1953 and the Korean War ended four months later. McCarthyism had abated. We were delighted just to be out of combat and immersed in our dreams of moving to the suburbs and achieving "the good life." Books like *Peace of Mind* and *The Power of Positive Thinking* were bestsellers.

The years from 1955 to 1963 were a time of consensus. We had a common set of beliefs and common values. Our only known enemies, the communists, needed to be contained, but we believed that we could make the world conform to our wishes. We believed in the perfectibility of American society.

After all, we had discovered that democratic capitalism worked: It created abundance, and we believed that with abundance would come social justice. We could solve social problems just as we solved other problems—with money and enlightened programs. The gospel of the new economic growth was the emergence of social programs.

President John F. Kennedy symbolized this confidence in the future, this fusing of social consciousness with sound conservative financial growth. Then from 1963 to 1965, the assassination of Kennedy, the escalation of the Vietnam War, and the breakdown of the civil rights movement came like earthquake shocks, making us doubt the very ground under our feet.

Our response was dramatic. Following was a time of polarization, fragmentation, and confusion. Leslie Fiedler called it the "great American cultural revolution." Young and old people alike questioned everything and introduced their own means of

social change. Rock and roll, drugs, love-ins, and protests became tools for changing our consciousness and discovering life
anew. Timothy Leary told us to "turn on, tune in, and drop
out."

Social upheaval led to new definitions of what was good,
what was right, and what was valuable. And we psychologists
got on the bandwagon, really fast! We not only observed what
was happening, we endorsed it and incorporated our views into
a new theory of human behavior. Instead of psychoanalysis,
with its emphasis on childhood experiences as the primary
determinants of one's personality, something new was brewing.
It was called the human potential movement, led by psychologists such as Carl Rogers and Abraham Maslow. They saw man
as continually evolving and capable of great change. *Potential*
was the key word, and *growth* was both the process and even-
tual goal. Men and women could actualize themselves and
realize their innate potential. We could transform ourselves.
The fifties belief in the power of economic growth now became
a belief in the power of personal growth.

Thinking itself was often seen as the culprit. Fritz Perls, the
founder of Gestalt therapy and advocate of living in the "now,"
derided the intellect, stating, "to understand is to stand under,"
to become a prisoner of one's thoughts and rationality. The path
toward freedom and growth was to "feel," and to be open to
one's emotions.

By 1972, the "revolution" had cooled. Enthusiasm waned as
we began doubting our power to change society, or perhaps we
drastically altered our expectations of political action to change
society. We turned back to ourselves and focused on our own
lives. Social awareness and concerns dimmed. This was the
beginning of what we now call the Era of Narcissism, or the Me
Generation.

What characterizes the Era of Narcissism is a marked lack of
belief in social change. We don't have common social goals that
unite us. We are skeptical about the efficiency of social action.
We focus on our own lives and how to succeed there.

We retained at least two convictions from the sixties. The
first was the tenant of feeling as truth. Focusing on sensations

and feelings created a new way of knowing whether we were on the right path toward happiness. Immediate gratification was no longer seen as vulgar or infantile, now it was a tangible sign that happiness was just around the corner. The second conviction was that personal growth is the one true path to happiness.

All in the name of growth, we strain ourselves to have it all or be the best or strive for excellence. These values are now components of the American dream. The result of the preceding psychologizing was that happiness became a feeling state, stimulated by a multitude of trendy goals, rather than a spiritual state, anchored in more basic long-lived truths.

As psychologists became more respected, in some cases even revered, they received intense media exposure. They became experts in telling people how to live. Patients who sought out psychotherapy were now viewed as having "problems in living" rather than deep-seated, childhood-based neuroses. The need for a better lifestyle became part of the expertise of psychologists— they became life management consultants.

One way people learned to realize themselves was by reading self-help and how-to books. Popular psychology was ushered in by publishers and the media. *Games People Play* and *I'm Okay, You're Okay* were two gigantic bestsellers that allowed laypeople to understand what had previously been viewed as the dark science of psychology.

The authors became priests, gurus of happiness, providers of the clues to life's eternal question: What is happiness? Or, more dramatically, What is the meaning of life? Still, psychotherapy was a long and costly process, available primarily to the more affluent. But where need and desire exist, the free enterprise system invariably builds a better mousetrap and, lo and behold, the growth seminar business emerged.

In the seventies, seminars such as EST and Lifespring offered a stab at self-transformation, and it cost only a few hundred dollars and took just one or two weekends! Other movements such as Scientology and various Eastern cults also promised psychological salvation and, implicitly, happiness. People flocked to these movements, genuinely expecting new answers to old problems.

One toxic legacy of all of these new "solutions" was their emphasis on transformation. Just as Americans are often accused of living in a disposable society where everything becomes obsolete and where everything old is denigrated or cast aside, such is the case with one's "old" self. Often, part of the sales pitch was a "new" you, a transformation or metamorphosis, implying there was nothing valuable about you until you took this seminar, and if you just keep repeating the new "truths" to yourself you will become a different person. In other words, they fostered our tendency to deny our "self."

In my experience, most of us may need a psychological tune-up, a few parts fixed, but not a major overhaul. It can't be done anyway. The only complete transformational experiences seem to be those that are overwhelmingly painful and catastrophic—concentration camps, war, or the death of someone you dearly love.

In the final analysis, what was seductive and illusory about so many of these new ways of thinking was the message that there was an easy or magical solution to life's mystery. Instead of recognizing the one valuable truth that we all need a personal philosophy to make sense of life, we were seduced into following fads. We were led away from our own core, from who we really are, from our own basic worth and humanness.

LOSING ONE'S SELF

"I don't feel anything," was the complaint I heard from a young executive who came to see me. "It seems everything I'm doing works out for me, I'm successful, making money, I've got all the women I want . . ." But he feels dead inside, numb. Externally his life seems to be in order, but internally he is without pleasure or satisfaction. It is as though an inner voice is trying to tell him something but its message is muffled and confused. He shakes his head, hoping something will click, maybe a light will come on, but he has lost touch with his inward reality.

This confusion is the primary symptom of the treadmill mentality and it often leads to emotional numbness. Going too fast in the search for self, we don't Stop and smell the flowers, because stopping is too frightening. Ironically, in a time when so much importance is placed on feelings, many people complain that they have lost the capacity to feel alive and vital.

Felicia, a thirty-year-old woman, comes in to see me. She's bright, attractive, and is a model. She's been married for eight years to a man she describes as warm, caring, supportive, and reasonably successful in his work as an executive recruiter. At first, she seems alive, passionate, animated, and highly motivated. Her problem? Her husband wants to start a family, but she feels she hasn't grown enough yet. To have a family feels like "settling." Her plan? She'd like to leave her husband, just temporarily perhaps, and "find herself." I ask how leaving him will enable her to find herself, and she responds, "If I leave, something will happen, I'll have to do something different." Like what? She doesn't know.

In our next session, again she is lively, animated, and eager to embark on life's adventures. I'm worried because she has all the right words, but something's missing. I ask whether she fantasizes about other men. "No." Does she visualize what this new life would be like? "No." Is there something she'd like to do that being married prevents her from doing? "No. I just need to grow, I need to live more dangerously, I need to take risks." Felicia fantasizes that creating a new psychological terrain will somehow enable her to feel more alive. Her wish isn't troubling, but the way in which she understands her dilemma is. Every time I hear her say she wants to grow, I really hear, "I feel dead inside, stagnant, bored." For her, as for so many people, *growth* is a code word for finding a solution to emptiness and meaninglessness.

I find myself getting restless in the next few sessions, an important signal for a therapist. It means the patient is really not speaking from inside. It means that the words are masking a problem, in this instance, a vacuum or a void. Felicia isn't struggling with who she truly is or is not. When she says having kids is settling, that may be true for her. She is obviously not ready to be a mother. But she's also unaware of what having children can mean. She uses the word *settling* because she has no experience with incorporating love and pleasure. Children are merely an abstraction that do not move her emotionally, and that's okay. But what does move her, I wonder? I share some of my thoughts with her, careful not to communicate criticism, but rather puzzlement.

Near the end of the fourth session, she appears sadder, less vivacious. She doesn't say it, but she's disappointed. She doesn't like the direction we're going in. Instead of looking outside for easy answers, we are moving inward toward her identity and her sense of self—the self she has now, not what it could be. She senses this could be a painful experience, rather than the exciting journey she had imagined psychotherapy to be. But, courageously, she doesn't run from her unease. I tell her it's okay to not be so vivacious; it's okay not to perform for me. Otherwise I'll merely be a mirror for all the ways in which she has performed thus far in her life. In time she stops performing and embraces the task of finding herself. It turns out that she has enormous talent and intelligence, but she was so consumed with succeeding in everything she did that she was only in touch with momentum, rather than the substance of her life. She had lost herself in a whirlwind of disconnected thoughts and actions. When she began to focus on "being" rather than "becoming," her therapy genuinely started.

SELF-REJECTION AND THE TREADMILL MENTALITY

It's common for us to deny our feelings of distress and emptiness, especially when, on the outside, we appear successful. But denying the gap between our internal "reality" and our external "image" is a curse and an invitation for us to follow

endless, dead-end quests. We all have the ability to rediscover ourselves. The question is whether we know how to
focus on what's already there, as opposed to hungrily and
desperately looking for what's not there. When you focus
on who you are and stop concentrating on improving yourself, then you can begin clearly interpreting yourself and the
world.

But most of us don't have such vision. We end up being
seduced by seemingly easy answers, and the first casualty
of such seductions is ourself. When your self-improvement
venture doesn't make you feel any better, you don't stop, in
fact you double your efforts. You get stuck even while going
faster. You never question the worth of self-improvement; it
is just a matter of finding the right path, coach, guru, or
motivational tape that will work for you. You never penetrate your illusions. You never see the self-rejection. If you
move fast enough, you end up losing yourself completely. It
is this emphasis on the relentless pursuit of something "out
there" as the key to fulfillment that defines the treadmill
mentality.

Each of us has our "window of vulnerability." Because growing up is often a less-than-perfect experience, we may have
come to feel unlovable or unattractive or unintelligent; we feel
insecure about something. But when we feel compelled to hide
or deny our insecurities, then they begin to loom larger and
larger in our lives. What we repress grows in the dark. The
skeleton in the closet rattles its bones even if we try to ignore
the racket. What we repress or deny will eventually come to
haunt us.

Carolyn, age forty-two, comes in for her first session, clearly
very nervous. A highly regarded film editor, she has never
been married and tells me straight out that she's always been
too picky about men. She also tells me she has had many
years of psychotherapy. She reveals that she is seeing a male
therapist for the first time because she'd like to get over
her fear of letting a man know her. I'm immediately heartened
by her insight into the roots of the problem, her awareness

that a fear of intimacy may have prevented her from being in love. I listen sympathetically, sensing how terrified she is. While talking about different relationships, she exhibits an enormous amount of anxiety. She is almost hyperventilating, not making any eye contact, shifting from one topic to another without transitions, not finishing her sentences. Even though I ask questions and make comments about these relationships, I know something else is going on that she's not talking about.

Near the end of the session, I ask her, "Are you sure there isn't something you want to tell me that you haven't thus far?"

She looks down, and takes a deep breath. "Well, about twenty years ago, when I was in college, I had ... I guess you would call it a nervous breakdown ... uh, I made a suicide attempt ... was hospitalized for a while ..." Then she looks me in the eye, almost defiantly, and adds, "But I don't want to deal with that. That's in the past. I came here just to be more comfortable with men. Why do I have to rehash that again?"

I tell her we don't have to open old wounds, but her past can't be kept a secret, because it influences why she feels so uncomfortable with others. She admits she feels as though she is defective, even crazy inside. It is her failure to accept that secret part of herself that prevents her from letting any man get close to her. And I tell her that she has good women friends and is accomplished in her work, which tells me the energy used up by hiding has caused her to lose sight of what is worthwhile. She nods, as though she understands, and sets up another appointment. There's no happy ending here. She canceled that second appointment and, unfortunately, I never heard from her again. Her failure to accept the past will make change impossible. She will continue to seek perfection in men as a way of denying her own imperfection.

A treadmill mentality determines how you process your inner experiences—what you acknowledge and what you ignore. When you deny something in your experience or in yourself that is too painful or embarrassing to face, you set internal processes into motion that become more dangerous to you than the original hurt or insecurity you were trying to fix. The first process you put into motion is selective inattention. If you ignore the pain, or deny it, maybe it will go away. The second process is secrecy, the conviction that "no one is going to know about this." And the final process is self-deception. Maybe, you think, if I muddy the waters sufficiently, I won't have to see what is going on.

Rejecting any part of our self, or part of our experiences leads, in time, to rejection of our whole self. The processes of secrecy and denial begin to cut us off from other parts of our self. Carolyn became so accustomed to hiding that she sealed off from her own awareness an acknowledgment of all her good attributes. When we turn off the light in one corner of our being, the darkness begins to spread. We lose the ability to read our feelings and understand what they are telling us. We distort our experience to conceal our fear. We lose the ability to put things in perspective. We rigidly focus only on our fantasies of an external solution and we pursue that solution desperately. We have developed a treadmill mentality.

SOCIETY'S BRAINWASHING

Under the best of circumstances, the task of building a secure self is tough enough. But our society not only presents questionable solutions to our feelings of dissatisfaction, it feeds the dissatisfaction itself. The media constantly hypes self-improvement.

Learning new things, developing skills, discovering new passions are all positive when accepted for what they are—affirmative steps, not a substitute for a real sense of self-worth and self-recognition. In fact, my concern is that recognizing one's self is more difficult than ever before! There are so many false gods out there that we are becoming overloaded.

The problems we encounter in life are challenging enough, when we add to that the "psychologizing of everyday life" and the insistent enticements of the human potential movement, the fantasies created by the advertising world, and film and television myths, we soon have so many new ways to get stuck that life's journey feels like a trip through a mine field. In many ways, the patients I see today are difficult to deal with, not because they are sicker but because they have accumulated so many new layers of self-deception in their quest to feel good about themselves that it takes longer to finally reach these patients.

Socially sanctioned treadmills attract us with all the neon beauty of a Las Vegas gambling strip—Money, *blink-blink*; Success, *blink-blink*; Self-Improvement, *blink-blink*. For the out-of-touch person, it is the perfect meeting of internal confusion and external glamour. Standing on the Strip, with money in your pocket, it is hard to remember that the odds are against you. You imagine that with just a little more money, you'll be content. Another rung up the ladder of success and fulfillment will arrive. One last attempt to change your mate and you'll feel loved and complete, and pushing those kids into the "right" school will make them better than they are now. Only a few more miles on the treadmill and happiness is yours . . . or is it?

TREADMILLS, TIME, AND ANXIETY

When you are on a treadmill, whether it is craving more money, working on the perfect body, or "improving" your loved ones, you have mislabeled the problem; therefore, the solution is useless. The truth is that all of us are enough just the way we are. But our anxiety about imperfection propels us unceasingly toward false goals.

Anxiety should be a signal to take stock, not a trigger for action. When we feel anxiety, we move as quickly as possible to get rid of the feeling because we naively think that anxiety is bad. Without understanding what you fear, you only accumulate more fear.

As we examine each of life's treadmills, you will come to see that they are especially dangerous because they initially reduce the anxiety you feel about imperfection. As you stay on the treadmill, however, your anxiety increases, because you are unknowingly confirming your sense of inadequacy. The greater the anxiety, the faster you go. And, you not only feel more anxiety, you no longer believe you have any alternatives.

Options and alternatives require that you slow down enough to reevaluate. Because we started our journey based on a sense of inadequacy, experiencing moments of anxiety is painfully intolerable. I find many people today renaming their anxiety "excitement." When these people do slow down, the first thing they experience is anxiety. All of us know people who find it difficult to really shift gears and enjoy a vacation. It's not that they are constitutionally incapable of relaxing, it's that they'd rather not let their fears surface.

For too many of us today, time is an enemy. As we get older and as society becomes more complex and if we think we have failed too often, there is an increasing sense of urgency to our search. The faster you go, the less time you have to think. When you do stop, the anxiety leaves you overwhelmed, confused, and unsure of what to do next. Still you feel you must act. However you realize that you are like someone being chased by a demon, and that there is no time to reflect on what has happened to your life.

LISTENING TO YOUR SELF

Because the search for something out there can never really solve our internal dilemmas, we inevitably feel sadness, emptiness, and, even more painful, a secret and growing sense of total worthlessness. I detect this in so many of my patients—in their eyes and behind their words. No matter how eloquently they may speak of their goals and aspirations, some have eyes that reflect their own disbelief, their own realization that they've conned themselves. Therapists, as the saying goes, must listen with their third ear. That is, they must listen with their intuition and with their own emotions delicately linked to their intellect. I often recognize the presence of the treadmill mentality by what I intuit, not because of what is said. And what I feel today, and this is shared by many therapists, is a hollowness in my patients, a sense that they are lost, and when they do feel safe enough to acknowledge what they feel and give expression to it, they are angry and resentful. They may not realize it, but they are angry because they have given up valued facets of themselves.

I vividly recall many patients and friends who got involved with those popular intense weekend growth seminars. What always struck me was how healthy those people were who resisted some of the processes that took place! Made to feel guilty and restricted during the seminar, more often than not, their resistance was based on an instinctive rebellion against a kind of brainwashing. Told to "ignore their mental tapes" by not paying attention to what was inside, they were unwittingly led astray in a miniversion of a treadmill! After the high of the seminar wore off, they were left only with rapidly evaporating traces of the external message, except by then they also distrusted their inner voices. I would always tell my patients to trust their discomfort and to remember they had a self before the seminar and the experience could now be used to get back in touch with that self.

We have lost the truth that human beings should not be improved but should be nurtured. Improving confirms our inadequacy, nurturing affirms who we are. Today's solution to the self-acceptance dilemma is too often self-improvement, which, as it gets out of control, inexorably leads to self-denial.

As you can see, I am issuing a clear warning here. Because goals can become treadmills, the search for self-realization often diminishes our self rather than nourishes it. Psychological growth can become a burden as well as an opportunity. There may be times when we should stop growing and simply be!

So, if your present prescriptions for happiness aren't working, consider setting them aside! As you will find, there is a compass inside of you, more trustworthy than you might have imagined, which will give you directions. Start becoming your own guide.

CHAPTER THREE

IS A "REAL ME" POSSIBLE?

To be nobody-but-myself in a world which is doing its best, night and day, to make you everybody else—means to fight the hardest battle which any human being can fight, and never stop fighting.

—e. e. cummings, poet

Melanie is a forty-four-year-old real estate broker who began therapy because she was developing a pattern of anxiety attacks while driving on the freeways in Los Angeles. It turned out that she was working so hard and had such a need to be in control that anything that made her feel out of control elicited an enormous amount of anxiety. In business with her husband, Al, also a broker, she insisted that she loved her work and their "dynamic" lifestyle—meeting new people, going out a lot, entertaining, and making a great deal of money in the hot southern California real estate market.

Intriguingly, Melanie wanted to stay in therapy even after her anxiety attacks disappeared, just to "explore things." I took this to mean she wanted to free herself and to speak those thoughts that never found expression in her daily life, not even with her husband. She admitted that she liked sharing feelings that she had not really thought about in years. She confessed that she used to love reading, yet recently she had been reading only one novel a year, if that. When I asked why she never allowed herself more of that pleasure, she said, "I'm embarrassed to admit this, but every time I read now, I feel guilty. I feel like I'm being lazy and should be out looking at properties and getting more listings."

One session she came in pleased with herself and eager to discuss something that happened the night before. She and Al were prepared to go out with a client/friend and his wife for dinner, but the other couple canceled at the last minute. Upon hearing this, Melanie turned to Al and said, "Thank God, I really didn't want to go out." Al laughed, indicating he felt the same way. They ended up renting a video of an old movie and had a wonderfully relaxing time, just lying in bed.

In the session, Melanie told me she couldn't sleep well that night. She got up so as not to disturb Al and just sat in the living room thinking. Then she described how she realized that aside from a few close friends, she really didn't enjoy all the socializing she was doing. "The talk is always the same, always about things we're buying, trips we're going to take, deals that are pending. For what, though, to what end? Al and I aren't any happier than we were when we started out in business and were struggling. Even when we're alone, we don't talk about and do what used to be enjoyable. We're both smart, and well educated, but we could be morons and still talk about the stuff we do. Last night, I realized that some of the happiest times I have are when I'm sick, lying in bed, and just reading."

Melanie was on the verge of discovering her "real self," which she had gradually lost, or forgotten, over the years. On one treadmill or another, she and her husband were moving so quickly through life that she no longer questioned anything fundamental. "The real issue isn't whether to buy a second home in the mountains or near the ocean, but what is going to happen in that home and inside me. How could I let myself get so far afield from what's really important?"

I believe that most of us forget more about ourselves than we remember. And above all, we lose sight of how to think about our existence even when we know that might be valuable. In my work, I have discovered that individuals who wish to get off life's treadmills need a set of conceptual tools to understand their plight. Such understandings or "labelings" are the essence of psychotherapy and prepare one to grapple with, and ultimately break, patterns that create unhappiness rather than peace of mind.

The treadmill mentality is a result of what we do, what we think, what we feel—in other words, it is inextricably linked to who we are—our identity. It arises out of problems in identity and at the same time it shapes, alters, and distorts our identity.

For our purposes, the concept of identity is best understood in what is called a phenomenological approach, which means understanding human behavior from the perspective of the individual's subjective experience of life. This is in contrast to a behavioral approach, which is objective and describes identity from the point of view of someone outside of the individual.

In exploring the treadmill mentality, I have discovered that most of us can recognize it in ourselves but rarely in others. People on treadmills typically look fine; they are often successful, highly motivated, goal oriented, and seemingly energetic and vital. But this objective view tells us little about the way they experience their lives from the inside.

When I encounter people with a treadmill mentality in my office, I perceive a very different picture than the image that those patients present to the world. They lack a sharply defined identity. Often they don't feel they possess a core. Like a sunless solar system they are but fragmented planets in orbit, empty and confused. Or, as I've indicated, their core is not one of substance but rather an idea; "I'm growing" or "I'm evolving" are correct-sounding euphemisms for "I'm in flux, but I suspect I'm not exactly sure where I'm going." The healthy individual has a core identity that may include evolving attitudes and beliefs, but also consists of stable and comfortable recognitions that declare, "This is who I am, how I feel about important issues, which beliefs I cherish."

When engaged in a battle for our goals, time is one of our biggest obstacles. But to have a firm sense of our identity, we must allow for a pause, or a respite, when we can reflect and contemplate not only what we want from life, but who we are. When we don't make reflection a priority, we won't have a well-defined identity. Instead of feeling whole, we are fragmented. In varying degrees, this is true for all of us. But we nevertheless do have facets of identity that

I wish to explore. I have chosen to focus on three selves because, in my view, they are the ones that map out our inner life.

THE PERFECT SELF

Everyone has an image or picture of who he would like to be, or who he needs to be to feel good about himself. This ideal is what I call the Perfect Self.

For many of us, the Perfect Self is the repository of all of our conscious goals, ones we believe are freely and willfully chosen. It tells you that if you achieve a certain goal, then you will feel good about yourself. If you don't, then you will feel dissatisfied, even deficient. For instance, the man who is desperately trying to mold his ideal body will incorporate this as part of his Perfect Self. If he doesn't get that ideal body, he is disappointed. For the person who wants a particular level of income or status, this goal is lodged in his subjective notion of a Perfect Self. For someone who needs to feel loved in a way that is much more consuming than he now feels, this fantasied love is craved because it may bring that person to his sense of a Perfect Self.

The problem with the Perfect Self is that it is fed by a number of streams, many of which are not conscious and freely chosen. Indeed, much of what drives or motivates us is unconscious—blindly and indiscriminately absorbed from our environment. As you will see with each of the treadmills, some of what we want is shaped by childhood influences, specifically our parents' values and goals. Some are influenced by feelings of inadequacy that evolved out of emotional wounds we experienced as we grew up. And perhaps more than both of those sources, our conception of what is good and what leads to well-being is, today, highly influenced by society's views of self-worth and self-esteem.

As I have discussed, I believe that in the last two decades or so the Perfect Self has emerged as much because of society's seductive influences and information overload as by internally generated ideals resulting from narcissistic concerns. Today, the drive toward the Perfect Self is no longer the sole proud possession of the narcissist. In varying degrees we are all geared toward this ideal.

Whenever I explain the Perfect Self to a patient, at first, he believes there is nothing wrong with having goals and aspirations. He uses the same logic and rationalizations as those obsessed with self-improvement. He fails to realize that there is a dark side to this quest. The Perfect Self is not only a goal, it not only says something about what you wish, it also determines how you feel about yourself right now.

THE IMPERFECT SELF

Coexisting with the Perfect Self is our experience of who we "really" are on a day-to-day basis, our sense of ourselves couched in what we believe to be realistic terms. This is "who I am right now, warts and all, my good points, my bad ones, my dissatisfactions, my insecurities, and my inadequacies."

This is the Imperfect Self that, for most of us, is a source of discomfort, always juxtaposed with the Perfect Self. The former is who we are, the latter is who we wish to be. For almost everyone, they are dramatically different. As we shall see, the gap between these two selves is what causes us the grief that eventually places us squarely on life's treadmills.

The Imperfect Self is a wellspring of anxiety. It is a source of constant and chronic apprehensions because we are pestered unceasingly with infinite scenarios that illustrate the tense discrepancy between our Perfect and Imperfect Selves. As soon as we say to ourselves, "Life's okay, I feel good about myself," the world tempts and taunts us, creating unrest where contentment and peace of mind could exist. Melanie, the real estate broker, discovered how her basic desires and pleasures had become obscured because minor insecurities had been fanned and fueled by societal dictates to be and have more.

Why can't we just have positive goals? Why do we focus so intently on negative imperfections? Unfortunately, the good always seems to be dwarfed by the bad—no matter how normal or healthy we are. In group therapy, for example, whenever I ask people to describe themselves, invariably they describe negative traits. This is not just because it is a therapy situation. When they're being honest in a safe and nonjudgmental environment, people are much more comfortable speaking about their deficits rather than their plusses, and there's a good reason for this.

Although it can make us miserable, it is adaptive to be vigilant about the negative things in our life. If we're on the lookout for danger, we won't be taken off guard by unpleasant surprises or unexpected threats. Moreover, we foolishly sense that by allowing the negative to take the foreground rather than background we will have an anchor to protect us from being too optimistic or grandiose in our expectations, even though these wishes reside in our Perfect Self. We believe that by hanging on to our fears, we won't lose control or become too euphoric or too happy, which might place us in a position to have our hopes dashed. Wishes are the mother of anxiety. To want something is, at the same time, to allow for the possibility of disappointment and hurt. That is why it is seemingly easier to fear love than to receive it; it can always be taken away.

The Imperfect Self is not merely a victim of the desire to be perfect, but it also plays an active role in creating the third self I will discuss. Because of the tension and preoccupation we experience while juggling our Imperfect Self with the omnipresent Perfect Self, we begin to ignore, neglect, and ultimately forget the attributes about ourselves we once valued. This selective inattention leads to the Forgotten Self.

THE FORGOTTEN SELF

Ironically, it is not only our initial vulnerabilities or insecurities that make us susceptible to getting on treadmills. By allowing our selective inattention to perform its self-protective role, we deny or forget what is good, ignoring the muted internal voices, and distrusting our capacity to cope. This is our Forgotten Self, the repository of valuable traits and accomplishments that are no longer part of our conscious identity.

Have you ever seen people with notes tacked all over their offices or homes—little sayings and reminders, all involving positive motivational thoughts, good things about themselves that somehow require constant reminding? The reason for such props, and mind you, I think they're a good idea, is that we forget good things. Maybe they are positive beliefs about ourselves that sink into the background, or maxims that we know to be true but keep forgetting. These reminders are necessary because we all have a Forgotten Self, a part of our identity that frustratingly gets sloughed off and no longer assumes an active part of our belief system.

Sometimes these positive beliefs are suppressed. A friend tells us how wonderful we are in some area, but we secretly believe we must have fooled him or he's being naive. We toss such valuable feedback away as though it's without any real value. We literally forget other facts about ourselves through years of neglect or lack of reminding, like Melanie, who "forgets" that she really enjoys a quiet read more than frenetic socializing. Or the person who is always surprised when he feels uplifted performing a charitable act—he "forgot" how it nourishes the soul.

Sometimes, the Forgotten Self becomes a repository for good things solely because these things are depreciated when measured against the Perfect Self. You may know you're good at something, but you have an underlying feeling that it's not really valuable in the grand scheme of things.

The Forgotten Self is one of the critical elements in psychotherapy. Therapeutic change is not merely the result of breaking patterns, or learning new behaviors. Actually, those are the final steps in the process. In my view, any therapy that is effective, regardless of the therapist's particular orientation, is therapy that helps reclaim the Forgotten Self. Before we can change, we must believe we are capable. And even though that belief is enhanced by taking risks out in the real world, the courage to take the risk must be firmly grounded in a belief in ourselves. We arrive by reclaiming aspects of our personality that have been denied, neglected, or forgotten. In other words, reclaiming the Forgotten Self provides a foundation for having the courage to risk.

But if the Forgotten Self is such a potential source of well-being and the fundamental building block of confidence and change, why is it so easily neglected? The answer is time, or precisely, the lack of time. In an era of timesaving devices such as car phones, computers, and fax machines, we are more driven and frantic than ever. Given our insatiable desires, modern technology may imprison us more than liberate us. We are all moving so quickly today, especially those of us on treadmills, and we're so overwhelmed by the overload of information we have to process, that what gets lost are those quieter, sometimes older truths about ourselves. Inattention and neglect are the precursors of the Forgotten Self.

THE MISERY GAP

The greater the gap between our Perfect and Imperfect Selves, the more miserable and anxious we become. We aren't comfortable allowing this gap to exist, we have been taught that we must always be moving toward closing it. It is this gap that leads us onto treadmills as solutions to this anxiety.

There is a difference between being neurotic or mentally ill and having a treadmill mentality. Mentally ill people are those whose Imperfect Self is so exaggerated, it stimulates a chronic and ongoing need to employ maladaptive defense mechanisms to restore a sense of self. This sounds similar to those on treadmills with one major exception. Treadmills are prompted by excessive attention not only to an Imperfect Self, but to a Perfect Self. People on treadmills believe there are particular paths to happiness and self-worth and these beliefs are endorsed and prescribed by societal values.

There is also an unfortunate footnote to this gap. The closer we get to our particular version of the Perfect Self, the more we up the ante! Monroe, an owner of a highly profitable laundry and dry cleaning business, epitomizes this process. Driven by a poor childhood to make it big, he worked hard and succeeded, but, as he put it, "Somewhere along the way, what I used to think was being on a roll, turned out to be an obsession. The more I made, the more I raised my sights, the more I wanted to fit into a higher status crowd, the harder I worked. There was finally no light at the end of the tunnel, no matter how much I succeeded."

The misery gap exists because most of us, even if we healthily accept our Imperfect Self, have no way of shutting out societal enticements that keep shoving images of a Perfect Self right in our face!

FROM TREADMILLS TO PLATEAUS

There is a solution to the trap of treadmills. The solution is reaching plateaus, foundations of self-acceptance. Acknowledging both the Imperfect Self and the Forgotten Self prepares us for this process. The Perfect Self fuels a sense of imperfection by extolling perfection as both a goal and a solution. But as soon as we slow down and reclaim the Forgotten Self, a new balance can be restored, the beginning of hope and optimism for living a different life.

Whenever we are conscious of both the Imperfect Self and the Forgotten Self, a different tension or dialectic emerges, allowing us to reach a plateau. At this point we can feel complete, and the possibility of self-acceptance occurs.

The final stage in maintaining a plateau happens when we can give up the idea of a Perfect Self. This is a kind of mourning period, which ends with self-acceptance. As you read about the various treadmills in the coming chapters, you will see that it is the mourning and giving up of the notion of a Perfect Self that enables us to extricate and finally free ourselves from life's treadmills.

LOOKING AT YOUR SELF

Many of you suspect that you are on a treadmill, and you want to get off. If this is true for you, you are in good company. Despite the pervasive power of treadmills in our society, more and more people suspect that they are being misled. Many of my patients and friends—myself included—have been trying to learn how to climb off the treadmills we unwittingly climbed aboard years ago.

As a result, at the end of each chapter I want to share with you some questions, observations, meditations, and activities that you can use to get in touch with yourself and get off your personal treadmill. Changing what we do requires both having insight and altering our behavior. If you don't act on what you learn, you stay stuck. Posing questions you normally wouldn't and stepping back and looking at yourself and your life in new ways represent a good beginning. But it doesn't end there.

Human beings are kaleidoscopic rather than simple. We're a collection of feelings, beliefs, attitudes, fears, hopes, and experiences. These are the stuff of identity. But some of these qualities are more essential than others. You must acknowledge and embrace your "basic" qualities before you can ever really change, transform, or even, if you still wish to do so, improve yourself.

The first step in identifying your self is honesty. By that I don't mean that old familiar self-loathing kind of honesty; I mean a simple and dispassionate taking stock of who you are. And to do that, you must allow yourself to be alone. The following are some strategies you may try and some questions you may ask yourself. You may not do this "well" or even come up with concrete answers. Don't worry, rather look at it as a way to begin slowing down and looking at yourself.

1. Allow yourself to be alone. Ask yourself, what am I aware of when I'm alone? Become aware of all the different ways you avoid solitude—talking on the phone, watching television, listening to music. Allow yourself to sit quietly for

an hour and see if you can get your thoughts off "worry," which is really not about who you are but about what you're afraid you'll be. Allow positive fantasies about the future to drift away also, for they are not about you, but who you want to be. Focus on yourself in the present.

2. Look at old pictures of yourself. They have the effect of bringing memories back to the surface. Study your eyes, they often reflect what you felt at the time the picture was taken. Allow that old you to become a companion just as he is, rather than what you had hoped that person would be. Who have you been over the years? Ponder the past, what made you happy, what made you sad, who did you think you were? This person is still inside you.

3. Look in the mirror. Who is that person? Notice how similar that face is to the one you saw when you were an adolescent. Become aware of how little has changed. Allow yourself to think about your life, year by year. Accept the continuity of who you are, and you won't need to frantically run after the future.

4. Confront sadness and emptiness. There is an old saying, that being alone is being in bad company. Experience this, accept your feelings of aloneness, littleness, or sadness. We all feel this and it's okay. In fact, allow yourself to remember old times in your childhood when you felt this way. Merely remembering will allow you to shed some of the negative sting attached to these memories.

5. Ask the questions "Suppose I never changed? Suppose this is who I am, what I have, who loves me, who doesn't love me, what I believe, what I do. Suppose this is it!" Try it out, see what happens. Tell yourself that it would be enough. It may sound silly, but it's something you have to do to reclaim your identity. I know you still have dreams, frustrations, and dissatisfactions, but let these be like a suit of clothes that you have chosen to wear. Know that you can take them off, and still find yourself underneath.

6. Assimilate the good and the bad: Allow both negative and positive feelings to coexist. Let the negative feelings come forward and recede and then let the positive feelings come forward. Only by becoming comfortable with this dynamic can you feel whole.

A BEGINNING: RECOGNIZING SELF-DECEPTION

Self-deception is always difficult to unravel, but the self-deception connected with treadmills is especially problematic because it's socially sanctioned and encouraged. To penetrate this mask of deception requires paying close attention both to yourself and to social trends. We are all too inclined to absorb, as if by osmosis, those trendy social notions and attitudes. In time, those beliefs are internalized and become self-deceptions.

Treadmills are built on self-deception. This is why so many people feel fraudulent, entwined in maintaining this vast network of self-deceptions in which so much has been invested.

Often self-deception is our way of denying feelings too painful to acknowledge: feelings of anger, hurt, unworthiness, emptiness, or shame. We deny them and build our camouflage over them. We keep our real feelings secrets, first from ourselves, and then from others.

In the process we conceal more than truths too painful, or overwhelming, for us to confront; we also conceal truths that are positive and life-giving. We conceal our core, our Forgotten Self. We conceal our strengths and our resources. As our deception protects us from our pain, it also leaves us empty. As we face the painful reality—truths we are sure will devastate us—we suddenly discover, within us, resources we didn't expect, strengths we didn't know existed.

There is nothing more difficult than being honest with yourself. By the time we become adults we are so filled with confusing beliefs and ideas about who we should be, that recognizing who we are feels like a complex archaeological task. Everyone has, in varying degrees, unconsciously incorporated ideas about happiness and fulfillment, many of which only make us feel inadequate. Most of us took these tantalizing notions from outside of ourselves and never really challenged them.

EXAMINING LIFE'S TREADMILLS

As you read on, I will give you examples from my own experience dealing with people caught on life's treadmills. I'm going to describe the feelings, ideas, and conflicts that characterize these treadmills, exploring their origins and present ways of overcoming them. In the process, I hope you see that some of the ideas and aspirations you may never have questioned aren't as trustworthy or seductive as they once seemed.

I need to warn you, if you choose to get off your treadmill you are going to have to give up something. You will have to give up some of the illusions that you now regard as leading to safety and comfort, and this is not easy. You will have to experience fear and even pain that you have kept at arm's length. You may even have to give up some grandiose notions about yourself. Some cherished illusions are going to go by the wayside. You certainly will have to give up your wish to be perfect.

What will you gain? Well, you may regain yourself. And you may gain energy for living that you've been using for protection. And you may be able to think and feel clearly again. You may come out of your isolation and establish real ties with those "intimate strangers" you've been living with. You may even gain peace of mind!

It isn't an easy commitment, but it is my hope that what I have to share will be helpful to those of you who have decided that the price you are paying for your treadmill ride is too high, and you want off.

As you read on, temporarily take as an act of faith that you can create your own philosophy of life, your own code of conduct. You already possess what you fundamentally need. It is never too late to undertake that challenge, never too late to stop being seduced by society's pressures and start living life on your own terms.

· II ·

OVERCOMING SOCIETY'S SEDUCTIONS

CHAPTER FOUR

REACHING EVER HIGHER: THE AMBITION TREADMILL

There is a mortal breed most full of futility. In contempt of what is at hand, they strain into the future, hunting impossibilities on the wings of ineffectual hopes.

—Pindar, Greek poet

Ambition is lauded as a virtue. To lack ambition in our society is to risk being called lazy, fearful, and even stupid. We are constantly reminded that people with drive, zeal, and enthusiasm made this country what it is. Dare to be great, or its equivalent, scream the subtitles of hundreds of books written for businesspeople and anyone who wants to stand out above the crowd. Is anything wrong with this? Is it possible that the desire to succeed can transform itself from a virtue into a curse? The answer, unfortunately, is a resounding yes!

Faye, age thirty, comes to see me about her marriage to Gary, who is thirty-one. They are both highly successful salespeople, MBAs from good business schools, and now in the same industry. Until recently, they epitomized the American success story. Both drove BMWs, they owned their own home, took a lot of ski vacations, and had a combined income of more than $200,000 a year. Their savings? None. They were two nice, stylish, attractive people, but now everything was falling apart. Faye left Gary six months ago and is now involved with a man two years younger than she and the exact opposite of Gary. Although intelligent and well educated, this new lover is not ambitious, his work is secondary to interests such as writing, hiking, and working with his hands in various crafts. Faye tells me she has never felt happier in her life and that she is finally taking a fresh look at the direction her life has taken.

Naturally, I tried to explore whether she and her husband could possibly salvage their marriage. "He wants to, and I don't," she responds tearfully. "I know Gary's basically a good person, but every time I tried to get him to work less . . . for us to work less, he just made me feel guilty, like I wasn't up to making it in the corporate world. And the fact was, I was making more than he was. Even when we tried to relax more, we just ended up going on vacations and spending a lot of money on restaurants, expensive wine, exorbitant hotels. I really felt disgusted at what we had become. But he couldn't see it . . . didn't want to."

Feeling lost and emotionally depleted, Faye was primed to meet someone else, and, of course, she did. I asked her to come in with her husband so I could at least make an objective assessment about what was possible in the relationship. When Gary came in with her, he was exactly as she described: caring, well-intentioned, and clearly upset at the possibility of losing his wife—it all resembled an article you might find in *SUCCESS* magazine. He was so immersed in a fast-track lifestyle that he couldn't really understand her doubts and disillusionment. And when I gently suggested he was blinded by his own driving vision of a good life, he couldn't shift his perspective, stating, "Look, I think she's just burned out, a nice two-week trip to Aspen, and she'll be fine." He never came in again. She only came in a few more times until it was clear to me that she didn't really want or need therapy, but only a kind of permission to entertain new values and discover who she really might be underneath what had been her runaway aspirations.

Looking at these two young, successful professionals, one could argue that the fear of success finally caught up with the young woman, explaining why she sabotaged a life that most people would envy. But I don't think so, I think her instincts are good.

For Faye, runaway ambition was not merely about making money, but creating a lifestyle of success and being perceived as a "somebody." The ambition treadmill is created by the illusion that reaching higher and accomplishing more will automatically make you happier. Faye understood the folly of such thinking. It used to be that some people lived to work, and others worked to live. Now millions of men and women are working to work!

THE EMOTIONAL TOLL

Success is a game with rules that lots of people talk about and penalties that few will acknowledge. Working with many people who have "won" the success game, I've become acutely aware of the price of ambition. Today, I find people on a treadmill that is grinding them up, and they are confused—confused that they feel so miserable when they are seemingly doing so well.

David is a fifty-three-year-old accountant who is expanding his firm and adding associates as fast as he can. He belongs to many charitable groups primarily as a resource for new clients. His wife feels estranged from him, his children no longer count on his being home for dinner, and he has drifted away from some of his oldest friends. He's been referred to therapy by his internist, who is worried about David's toxic levels of stress. Is David worried? "Not really," he tells me. He's willing to try therapy because he thinks he might be more effective in his work if he wasn't so stressed out. David wouldn't acknowledge it, but he is terrified to stop and reflect on his life—because he is really failing at the very time he thinks he's succeeding.

The ambition treadmill exemplifies the power of ambiguous life goals. The person on the ambition treadmill has two powerful goals: She wants to perceive herself as ambitious, and she wants to be a success. These goals seem to work together, but it is an uneasy alliance. There is no end to ambition because it is a drive. Once you reach a goal you have set for yourself—a job position, an income, public recognition, whatever the goal—you have to keep going, otherwise you lose your ambition. Success, the achievement or goal you were trying to reach, is only a momentary confirmation of your ambition, then you have to set new goals for yourself. It is only when you are successful that you find yourself in conflict with your ambition. You can't stop to savor any achievement for long before your ambition is again driving you up the ladder. Toward what? Well, toward success.

And what is success? We pursue myriad images, or mirages, of success, all of them externally defined. Each profession has its criteria for success, a collection of trophies, a list of rewards, that mark the path to making it. The most common metaphor we use is "climbing the ladder of success." Another metaphor we use is "playing the game," which may reflect some of our self-doubts about what we are doing.

The game of success we are playing has to be agreed on by the players, otherwise there are no rules and no way to tell who is winning. Such games are life consuming. They save us the need of finding out who we are, what will satisfy us, or what will meet our own uniqueness. We can, and often do, lose ourselves in the process.

Most psychologists find that behind a successful person is a lost person—a person who may even feel like a fraud. The split between her inner feelings and her outer reality has become a chasm. But when you look at the rules of the success game, this split becomes more understandable. When you're in the success game your attention is focused outward, and success demands an increase in vigilance, not a decrease. You must constantly be aware that you are on track and how you are perceived. Because it is a game of appearances as well as productivity, you measure yourself by the way others see you. You live on the edge, which is exciting but also nerve-racking.

The success game is a strange game. It takes place in a thrilling arena where you can win and other people know it. You make money, you get recognition, and, when the pressures aren't overwhelming, you have fun. The attraction and rewards of success aren't a mystery. But for the person who doesn't have a strong, clear, and established sense of self-worth, the success game invariably leads to the ambition treadmill. Well-being is measured by momentum and achievement, not inner peace.

Society defines success for us, using monetary rewards, recognition, or celebrity as a measure. Today especially, momentum alone is a gauge. Are you "on track," "moving in the fast lane," "climbing up the ladder," "ahead of the power curve," "on your game plan"? Society focuses on the visible rather than internal measures such as living life on your own terms or having the life you choose to have. We forget to question, we overlook the fact that most of these definitions are external, based on how we're perceived. This is why consumerism is so linked with success: Things are badges of success. If you don't feel successful, at least you can wear an expensive watch and look successful.

Your career identity eclipses your personal identity. The values and rules of the game become more important than your inherent values, your ambition becomes more important than your health. To play the game you begin to deceive yourself about the price you are paying, you begin to deceive yourself about the amount of control you have, and you begin to neglect your real worth.

On the ambition treadmill, we lose sight of the fears that may have motivated us in the first place. Such concealment builds its own pressure, as you work harder and go faster to keep fear away. The process controls you. Instead of simply being ambitious, you become driven. You ignore inner signals that tell you something is wrong; you deny feelings of powerlessness, because they don't fit your concept of a Perfect Self. You lose sight of attributes and accomplishments that should be remembered; instead, they become part of your Forgotten Self. You are confused, and confusion itself becomes a kind of protection. You can ignore what doesn't seem right. The external rewards and recognition quiet your inner voices. Giving up success to find yourself is unthinkable.

The ambition treadmill is all about reaching ever higher. It is a thief of time, a killer of contentment. Too often today, our affliction is nurtured and acclaimed rather than critically examined and moderated. We have been trained to believe we must realize our potential at all costs—it becomes mandatory rather than an option.

This ambition treadmill leads to exhaustion and an even more depleted sense of self. The cruel irony is that, as with all treadmills, those with the most insatiable appetites are the ones with the most fragile sense of self-worth! All too often, the conscious drive to be somebody is fueled and motivated by the fear of being a nobody, a failure!

LOSERS AND WINNERS

One of the most popular themes in American drama is the underdog striving to make it to the top. In the film *On the Waterfront*, Marlon Brando painfully confronts his brother declaring in anguish, "I coulda been a contender." Arthur Miller's *Death of a Salesman* portrays the demise of Willy Loman, a salesman who has failed himself and his family. Every man I've worked with in therapy, if he's familiar with the play, feels a tinge of fear that one day he could feel like Willy.

Just about everyone grows up wanting to be a winner in life, to feel special, to stand apart from others. Noted psychiatrist Alfred Adler spoke of a drive toward superiority that explained why people ambitiously strive to achieve a sense of mastery. Almost every study of children's personality development reveals a wish to win or excel, and this wish is part of the experience of growing up.

But positive desires and goals are not the entire story. There is an unspoken belief system operating as we grow up. While most of us may talk freely and openly about wanting to be a winner in life, more secret is our most terrible and chronic fear of being a loser. In this tough, achievement-oriented society, we have all felt the sting of shame whenever we failed at something. Early failure experiences become powerful images forever ingrained in our psyches, and they can live on as negative motivators for the rest of our lives.

For some of us, early experiences teach us how to feel like losers rather than winners. My male patients invariably tell stories of defeat or inadequacy in sports, where they were the last to be chosen for teams. Other male patients will often, in the course of their therapy, remember times when they chickened out in a fight, when they were too frightened to defend themselves and thereby retain their dignity. Female patients will remember being rejected by more popular girls. These memories never really go away, instead they become the images that drive some of us to succeed and/or to seek some revenge on others who made us feel shame. These early experiences can evoke intense pain, because we are forced into situations that cause us to feel bad about ourselves. We don't entertain the idea that being good at sports or being liked by the popular people may not really matter to us, but as adults, we must learn to question these scenarios.

Unfortunately, our educational system doesn't really deal with the concept of failure—instead it focuses on success, which is only half the story of any adolescent experience. We grow up with bromides like Try your best, but nobody wants to deal with the subtext of "If you don't you may well become a failure." We carry these rigid expectations with us, until we consciously explode them and define our own terms of success and failure.

Society teaches us that failure is a terrible thing. Young people mistakenly come to believe that success happens without failure, which is never true. Failure is integral to any learning experience, and success is about learning to deal with failure. Success is about tenacity. As Winston Churchill once said, "Success is going from one failure to the next without a loss of enthusiasm."

Most people are driven not by the wish to succeed but by the fear of failure. It is this fear that causes many people to run forever on the ambition treadmill; you fear that your Imperfect Self is all you really are. Even though most people say they want to succeed, they subconsciously fear any hint they might fail or be a nobody. That is really the stigma in our society.

We see the result of this faulty thinking among schoolchildren who begin to use the strategy of failure as a means of self-protection. Instead of attempting difficult tasks they make half-hearted attempts or don't try at all. So when they don't succeed the pain isn't great, after all they didn't really try and the task wasn't very important in the first place. That takes care of that. Adults, too, can learn to journey through stable, unchallenging lives and deny risky situations out of paralyzing fears.

Denying the presence of fear as a motivator is deadly for another reason. Those of us who are motivated solely by fear typically have unduly frail egos and fragile identities, and we can't deal with the pressures brought on by runaway ambition. If we lack a real foundation or plateau of self-esteem, failure is terrifying, it can paralyze us internally even though externally we go even faster on the treadmill. For us, failure is then a free-fall, a fatal drop in self-worth with no relief in sight. Even as we continue on the treadmill, we feel overwhelmed by unabating apprehension. As you read on, you will see there are ways to grapple with such fears and pressures.

Does it matter what drives us, if the final result is still success? Yes. Fear takes the joy out of our lives. It may be a powerful motivator but it burns up our energy and exhausts us. Unless we recognize the fear, and free ourselves from it, it eats us up. We will examine how such fear can be managed, but for now it is important to understand that while we may have outward success, we can still lack inner peace. Sadly, success will not get you off the ambition treadmill.

THE PITFALLS OF SUCCESS

Listening to those who have made it reveals one recurring observation: Success doesn't always bring the anticipated sense of fulfillment. For some, success evokes a vague sense of disillusionment. After attaining a goal, some people run out of steam and lose direction. They forgot, or more likely never knew, that the *process* of mastery or ambition should be rewarding on its own terms. They forgot success is a journey, not a destination. And like all processes that are worth something, it involves pain and sacrifice.

When Goals Become Dead Ends

Samuel, fifty-one years old, comes to see me because of a growing sense of depression. He's confused about why he feels so hopeless about life, because, on the surface, he appears successful at whatever he does. "So why am I unhappy?" he asks, after he tells me about his conquests. He is the major stockholder in a small bank. He was the CEO until a few years ago when he experienced a sense of aimlessness similar to what he feels now. He turned the reins over to someone else and chose to enter politics as a behind-the-scenes mover and shaker. He backed a candidate who then won an important city seat. The morning after the election, he woke up depressed. That's when he called me.

As I explored Samuel's motivations, it seemed he was focused on the target, or the goal, everything else was irrelevant. He even confessed that he didn't care that much about politics, it was just another game, another arena to test out his skills. He entered politics in the same way he entered banking: to make a score, to win at all costs. Samuel also told me that he thinks the answer to his confusion and depression might be in finding another challenge. I told him he was dead wrong. When I suggested that he would feel this same depression no matter what he did, he fought me for months, even insisting that perhaps I didn't have the killer instinct and maybe I couldn't really understand him.

After some time in therapy, Samuel began to see that only when you enjoy the process, will you ever enjoy anything that you do. Being goal oriented only leads to a momentary high, and then you're left feeling empty and sad. When you focus on and enjoy the process of life, success is incidental and only enhances the whole experience.

Becoming process oriented, however, is not the whole answer. Values are also important. Samuel saw that his seeming success was just one facet of life; therefore, it had to be incorporated into a larger belief system. Without this broader base, success left him adrift. Christopher Morley put it this way in *Where the Blue Begins*, "There is only one success—to be able to spend your life in your own way." This requires self-knowledge. Samuel embarked on the path of rediscovering himself, reclaiming a Forgotten Self that was long neglected. He had forgotten that much of what he really enjoyed was intellectual give and take with friends and associates, regardless of whether power or success came out of those dialogues. He came to this realization after I encouraged him to spend his time in therapy focusing on those moments, however insignificant, that were satisfying and pleasurable in themselves regardless of their consequences. (Interestingly, these are moments that are often discovered in therapy when the patient has nothing in particular she wants to discuss in that session.)

So few of us create our own definition of success. Instead, we allow society to do it for us. When success is defined in some way that is external, you are in touch only with the goal. But when it is intrinsic to the real you, you begin to enjoy the process or the experience of the quest without becoming obsessed with the outcome.

When I first met him, Samuel tried to convince me that power is an end in itself, and should, therefore, be satisfying. I disagreed. Even those who seek power as an end find themselves psychologically lost. There is a difference between achieving power, which is transitory, and feeling empowered, which is lasting. People feel empowered when they enjoy the process of gaining power, as opposed to the goal of power. That is why there are two kinds of competitiveness: One is based on a healthy sense of mastery, often found in competitive sports, and the other is based on superiority, not just being or doing one's best, but excelling others. When the emphasis is only on besting others, the victory is usually empty. Envy is a negative motivator that propells us to strive for success.

Jeremy, a successful screenwriter who once won an Oscar for his work, comes into my office grumbling after a recent Oscar telecast. He is furious that an acquaintance won for what he regards as mediocre work. When I suggested he was unable, in his heart, to let anyone else win, he vehemently objected. I reminded him of how critical he is of everyone in his business. When others win, he feels diminished. I suggested that if he could, in the spirit of generosity, allow others to succeed, he would feel a lot better about himself.

At first, Jeremy felt attacked, as though I was forcing some Judeo-Christian ethic on him in the guise of psychological insight. No, I insisted, my suggestion was solely to aid his own inner well-being. I told him if he truly relished the competition and truly enjoyed putting his colleagues down, I wouldn't be concerned—that would be his business. But I knew he was unnecessarily creating his own grief and he could get off his ambition treadmill. Envy is a reflex, as is the resentment that follows. When you catch yourself feeling envious, and you remind yourself that you are the same person that existed before that moment, you break the reflex chain. In time, when Jeremy was able to allow others to have their victories, he was shocked at how easy it was and how good it felt.

Neglecting Your Support System

One of the major pitfalls of the ambition treadmill is that along the way you may lose sight of cherished sources of fulfillment. The most obvious casualty is often family and friends. When you reach ever higher, and focus on success goals, you can miss out on the very aspects of life that are nourishing to the soul. Success is a demanding mistress.

Some on the ambition treadmill like to convince themselves they are doing it for their families, but we all know that's nonsense. Most spouses and children would like them to work less frenetically, even though it might mean that they have less materially.

The family life of those on the ambition treadmill invariably suffers. Superficially, there may be more things in the house, or the house is in the right neighborhood, and the children are aiming for the right schools, many of which cost a fortune. But things are much too hectic. There is no time to enjoy each other, no time for those admittedly old-fashioned family involvements, like calm and lazy Sundays when families do things together, or at least can hang out with each other. We miss out on those experiences that deliver more fulfillment than our narrow definitions of success bring to us.

Women and Ambition

A particularly thorny issue today confronts women on the ambition treadmill. Having it all has become a nightmare for many women. Pondering all those options can be a terrible burden, and there are no easy answers. Juggling career and home is difficult, but so is the so-called mommy track, where women compromise their dreams and aspirations to be a good parent at home.

Many women question their ambitions. For example, "Is it critical that I rise to the top?" "If I am process motivated rather than goal oriented, can I still enjoy the game?" And "Why not enjoy a number of games, including parenthood?" The question from other women is, "Why can't husbands and wives share equally in career and parenting?" The answer to the latter question is that it usually doesn't work out that way, although in theory it could. Invariably, men are more deeply invested in their careers than their mates. And women tend to want a more active role with their children. I'm not talking about right or wrong, I am merely looking at realities. Frankly, if men were as invested in family life as in their careers, it would probably make them a lot happier. Most men I talk to are not all that gratified in their work and when they turn to their families they rediscover simple and genuine pleasures.

No Time to Breathe

A number of decades ago, automation and technological advances were supposed to usher in a new era of leisure time, four-day workweeks, early retirement, and so on. But the exact opposite has happened. We are all working harder than ever. Time is a precious commodity, yet the more time we free up, the more we quickly consume it with more activities endemic to the ambition treadmill!

It is true that life is more competitive today, and those on the treadmill in some sense set the standard for others. If fax machines, computers, and the like make work easier or more efficient, they also give others the edge—and if we want, or need, to keep up, we have to follow suit. And that is exactly what is going on today, everyone is frantically working harder than ever with no time to breathe.

Driven, needing to do two things at once, impatient, and irritable, these are the symptoms of the treadmill. Sounds like everyone I know. Yes, I am fully aware that this is the era of information overload, that we have more and more ideas and facts to process, but something's wrong, too many people are out of control. And too many of these activities are not necessary, but are deadly symptoms of the ambition treadmill.

Rosalie, forty-one, a businesswoman with her own company, originally came to see me because she had anxiety attacks whenever she was alone with nothing to do. As a way of calming herself, she took tranquilizers and rather quickly became addicted to them. At first, I suggested she was terrified to experience who she was underneath all that success. She promised that she would try and find time to be alone and discover what was so frightening about being isolated. To assist her, as part of our therapeutic contract, she was instructed to cut down on business phone calls at home and in the evening.

Rosalie was making progress: She got in touch with some old insecurities about relationships, how much they scared her, yet how unhappy she was without a man. One day, she came in after a much-needed vacation. She proudly informed me that she brought along a portable fax machine and made a major deal while on vacation in the Bahamas! Sadly, she is typical of so many executives today who are finding ever-more sophisticated ways to stay caught on the treadmill even when they're supposed to be relaxing.

I congratulated her on the deal and then looked at her for a moment without saying any more. She laughed nervously, knowing exactly what I was thinking. "Okay," she said, "I get an A on the deal, and a *D* for homework." At that moment, she really began listening to herself. Sitting around, not thinking about work aroused in her a vague and diffuse anxiety, a general apprehension not tied to specific concerns. At first, she could not even concentrate on pleasurable diversions. But she found that merely focusing on this unease began to dispel it. In a relatively short period of time, she finally relaxed enough to reconnect with a Forgotten Self that, for Rosalie, encompassed friendships she had allowed to drift away.

FREEING YOURSELF FROM FEAR

Anxiety for those on the ambition treadmill is especially over-whelming. Often, it is secretly viewed as a confirmation of the Peter Principle—that perhaps we have reached the level of our own incompetence! Concealing your fears by running faster and faster never works—it only sets you up for more crippling anxiety, and when you encounter even more pressure, you're not at all pre-pared. Whenever you want something so much that your entire self-worth feels like it's on the line, there is the possibility you won't get it. It is that possibility that triggers even more anxiety.

But normal anxiety or fear is a constant companion for any-one who is ambitious. When we learn to reinterpret anxiety or fear, we can even make it a positive source of energy.

Anxiety as a Signal

Anxiety is a signal of fear or apprehension that something bad might happen. We feel its physical manifestations: sweating, heart palpitations, and shakiness. But anxiety is normal, and we all feel it at one time or another. Without it, we lose an impor-tant source of information needed to respond to our environ-ment. The phrase *fight or flight*, describes reactions animals have to fear or anxiety. So too with humans, fear is a signal for action. Denying normal fear doesn't make it disappear, it just makes you run faster on the ambition treadmill.

People who deny fear will take anxiety and turn it into a catalyst either for frenetic activity or paralysis, neither of which is effective. Those who are familiar with feeling anxious, those who consciously embrace the risk inherent in what they do, find ways to channel anxiety into something positive. In fact, studies have shown that anxiety is an emotion that is actually very similar to excitement and anxiety/excitement is understandable when going into important meetings, giving key talks, or any activity where success or failure hangs on the outcome. Performers know this and learn to reinterpret their anxious feelings as excitement. They use anxiety to fuel positive energy and empower and enliven their performance.

Learning from Failure

Those highly ambitious people who are not caught on treadmills know failure is a tool for progress. They don't hide their failures, they may even make them public to take the sting out of them. They know each setback is loaded with information as to how they got off track, and they can use those errors as a way to sharpen their focus and move more effectively toward their objective. In other words, they take conscious responsibility for the failures or errors that occur quite naturally along the way of any endeavor or adventure.

Positive Thinking as a Hypnotic

Denying fear leads many people to become consciously positive in their thinking, while underneath they are terrified. You've undoubtedly known people who read motivational books and listen to inspirational tapes for hours on end, but such methods never seem to work. That's because these people are totally unaware of the magnitude of their fear.

I remember a patient named Carlton, an exceptionally successful young man who by the age of thirty-three was already making close to a half million dollars in sales commissions. He was a model of positive thinking in his work. He had learned to convert any anxious thoughts into running faster and faster and, contrary to what I'm suggesting, it seemed to work. But, when his wife threatened divorce, he fell apart, and he couldn't cope at all. His work suffered to the point where he was thinking of quitting. And why? He couldn't handle personal anxiety or the fear of loss, rejection, and abandonment. All that positive thinking was based on strangling anxiety in its crib, killing it off before it had a chance to spread. He could have been fulfilled and allowed himself to know more about who he really was, but instead he tried to become an automaton.

Carlton's long-denied inner fears erupted. Like so many people, he had always channeled fear into action, which is certainly adaptive, except when it betrays a total fear of any setback. The road of life's journey is never completely smooth. Potholes and dead ends are commonplace, and Carlton discovered this—not at work, but in his personal life. When his wife felt his vulnerability, she became compassionate. She helped Carlton look at what motivated his thirst for success at any price. He did have a Forgotten Self: a desire for love, family, and values that would genuinely nourish him. All that had been neglected. He remembered a time when he did have a plateau of self-acceptance, when he took pride in his skills, when he and his wife planned on a life that was diverse rather than narrowly focused on the rewards of runaway ambition. "It's like it just got away from me, as though I left myself behind in the dust." Retrieving himself was not as hard as he thought, and the reemergence of genuine self-liking provided a new plateau inner peace.

Pressure and the "Real You"

The treadmill mentality is destructive because, as with Carlton, it prevents you from knowing yourself. When you are going nowhere fast, you lose sight of who you are, and that's deadly in your personal life and in your career.

The ambition treadmill fosters myopia. One reason why people are, for the most part, not outstanding leaders or executives is that they are performing in an ill-fitting suit of clothes—they are wearing costumes, and they are fakes more often than they realize. Furthermore, others sense this. They may not be able to put their finger on it, but they're nonetheless uncomfortable with their bosses or superiors. Real power and effectiveness comes from the real you, from dropping masks and eliminating self-deceptions. Women, for example, in the work world are coming to understand when they function as they really are, instead of "acting like a man," they are most effective. Their effectiveness comes not from being more feminine, but because they are being themselves.

The ambition treadmill almost demands a certain kind of fakery, because to slow down and discover yourself feels too scary. It seems easier to speed up, even though when you do that, you lose sight of yourself and eventually others fail to sense a real person underneath. People who may need to see only your strength can encourage this fakery as well. They mistakenly see your treadmill behavior as an asset!

LETTING UP WITHOUT LETTING DOWN

More and more people are trying to come to terms with the ambition treadmill because it, perhaps more than any other treadmill, is making them feel exhausted and unhappy. For those of you who do wish to get off, there are directions. You can begin to take stock; there are options people entertain today that are worth looking at.

Options or Fantasies?

There are two possible options, or alternatives, to runaway ambitions, but each carries with it some distinct limitations. And, for many people, these options can be illusory and the source of even further unhappiness, if they become objects of fantasy and obsession rather than real choices.

First, there is the Gauguin syndrome. As you may remember, Gauguin, the famous nineteenth-century impressionist, dropped out of the Paris art scene and moved to Tahiti, where he did his greatest work. His example has served to fuel the fantasies of many people for whom dropping out of society is not only an option, but a chance at really discovering their true inner self and shedding society's questionable values. While this option may be overly idealized or romanticized, it is nonetheless being revived by many individuals.

Today, there are scores of men and women who consider moving to less-frantic cities to find cleaner environments and a place where their children have a chance to experience a more traditional and emotionally nourishing way of life. And let me state there are people doing this and finding greater peace in their lives. But not everyone has the financial wherewithal to do this. Not everyone can afford to pick up and move. Not everyone can cash out and retire. And areas where life is serene and tranquil are typically areas where jobs are scarce or low paying.

This option/fantasy may be enjoyable to entertain, but it can also be a trap if dreaming about it prevents you from having a life now, exactly where you are. For every person I talk to that has a real chance of dramatically changing where they live and where they work, there are ten who won't be able to do it. But that needn't be discouraging, because contentment is ultimately about one's inner environment, not the external terrain.

The Entrepreneurial Dream

One solution to the frustration experienced by people on the ambition treadmill is the dream of having their own business, of being their own boss. This is a fine dream and it is made into reality by an increasing number of people today, but it, too, can become another disguised facet of the treadmill mentality. Entrepreneurs work just as hard as everyone else, and many of them are even more anxious than those who work for others. There are no easy outs, no easy ways to make a living. I hear many people who have gone out on their own express the wish to have that steady paycheck and the desire to come home and leave their work at work.

My concern is that these dreams can become avenues of escape and a source of dissatisfaction. Instead of learning how to live today, right where we are, we wait for an illusory tomorrow where everything will be all right. We don't have to do that. I believe there are ways to discover a new perspective and to strike a new balance right here, right now!

For those of you who know that you are on the ambition treadmill and want to get off, the following thoughts might be helpful. They are intended to provide a step-by-step analysis of what success means to you, what you'll pay for it, and how you can begin to regard it from a new perspective. As with all treadmills, getting off leads to a paradox: Only by getting off will you have the energy and drive to accomplish what you wanted to in the first place, except then you will be doing it from a plateau rather than from the bedrock of fear.

What Drives You?

Are you living to work or working to live? That's a question you've undoubtedly heard before and probably didn't pay too much attention to. Usually, we don't wish to ponder this, because we secretly know the answer. Too many of us are living to work, and we're not happy with our particular order of priorities. The first question to ask, therefore, is where did you begin this journey to reach ever higher?

When did you make your career choice? What were your goals in terms of prestige, earnings, and personal satisfaction? Where did you think you would be after five, ten, or twenty years? If you have exceeded those goals, when did you up the ante? When did you decide to escalate your wishes, and why?

And what drives you now? What is it that you still desire? Is it a bigger house, a better neighborhood, better and more expensive schools for your children? A second home? More expensive travel?

Are you driven by the obvious illusions of the ambition treadmill? Are you looking to get enough to cash out? Are you attempting to drop out or radically change your lifestyle? If so, that's okay, but are you really prepared to forego the present in favor of a possibly better and more enriching future? And how much time are you going to give yourself? How long will you defer present-day fulfillment for the future? More to the point, can you look in the mirror and ask whether you might be kidding yourself?

One way to take stock is by asking yourself how long you have been putting off the future and whether you always find yourself changing the time frame. Is your future happiness always being pushed further into the future so that you feel like a greyhound chasing a mechanical rabbit that will always be elusive and never attainable?

Your Energy: Positive or Negative?

As I have indicated, many people get caught on the ambition treadmill for no other reason than they are driven by the fear of not being successful. The dread of being seen as a loser, or a nobody, is sufficient to propel them into the frenetic, years-long quest for success. Indeed, for many this is a lifelong and very unhappy search. Therefore, it is essential that you ask yourself whether this applies to you.

Look back and be honest with yourself; how often do you feel anxious, frightened, or envious? If someone told you whoever you are now is going to be the best you'll be, is that okay? Or does that make you feel as though you're no good or not enough? If the latter is true, then your task is all about self-esteem and self-acceptance rather than pushing yourself up the ladder of success. Your task is identifying and consolidating your own plateau, your foundation.

Discovering Your Rhythm

Everyone has different life rhythms, just as we're reputed to have daily biorhythms. There are periods in our life when we want to aggressively move faster and conquer life's challenges and times when we want, or more precisely, need to slow down and relax, consolidate our evolving identity, and replenish our self. In some ways this view is similar to the Oriental notions of yin and yang, the masculine and feminine forces within us. There are times when we need to be masculine and forceful and times when we need to be feminine and passive and receptive. This is true for both men and women. To be a complete person, you need both.

Consider the Zen expression: When you sit, sit, and when you stand, stand. You must fully embrace whatever rhythm is predominant at a particular time to realize yourself. This is especially true of ambitions and psychological drives. Most people get in trouble emotionally because their lives are out of balance too much of the time.

The treadmill mentality is relentless and unending, and does not account for balance. Ambition in one's twenties and thirties may not be as destructive as when it extends into our forties, fifties, and beyond. Being aggressive in one's career is adaptive when we're young, it can accomplish a great deal and lead to significant achievements. The problem, however is that it becomes a habit—one that is very difficult to break. Working hard and chasing after goals is fine when you have the desire and energy to do so. But it is easy in the early stages of a career to fall prey to treadmill behavior that years later is much more difficult to undo.

What is your own natural rhythm? When is the last time you allowed yourself to relax, took time out to really enjoy yourself, had good times with your family and just hung out? When was the last time you didn't do anything and were lazy and delightfully nonproductive? I advise people to experiment with changing their daily and weekly rhythms.

For example, if you're the kind of person who rarely goes out in the evening because you're too tired, start making plans for at least three nights out, take classes, go to dinner with friends, see more movies. What happens is that you're forced to embrace another perspective, you force yourself to find out there are other things in life besides the pursuit of success.

Or maybe you're someone who goes out too much, always socializing, always hustling. Your task is to do the reverse; stay home, relax, become reacquainted with your spouse or children. Or just relax by yourself, watch television, read, and, most importantly, become reacquainted with yourself. If this creates a sense of loneliness, don't let it frighten you, listen to what the loneliness is saying; it may be telling you that you don't have an emotional support group and you need one. The only way to find your natural rhythm is to become comfortable spending time with yourself, shedding guilt about not always "doing something," and engaging in an inner dialogue with yourself that doesn't have to make sense or be explained.

Letting Up

More and more people today are declining promotions and turning down positions that require relocating. They're choosing to let up and gradually get off the ambition treadmill without allowing themselves to feel let down. They don't regard such choices as resignation, but rather life affirmations. Shifting down requires time, it's not something you can do overnight. It takes planning, it takes having the courage to turn down that new project, it takes consolidating your work to free up time.

A paradoxical effect sometimes happens here. Many people who let up find that they have even more energy available to do their work. The ambition treadmill drains energy, depletes one's reservoir of passion and enthusiasm. By down shifting, you replenish yourself and can then go on with even more vigor and vitality.

This may also be a time in your life when you can contemplate career changes or lateral moves that are more harmonious to the real you. Some women use the term *coasting* to describe a change in their momentum and zeal. It's a good concept and it applies to men as well as women.

If work is draining you, you have the chance to seek out work that is fulfilling. Some people truly love what they do, and this passion makes working, which takes up a great deal of our time, more than simply bearable. For others, a job is just a job, and that's okay. For many people work is really just a way to pay the bills. Acknowledging that doesn't take the edge off, it merely allows you to have a better and more focused perspective. Discover life. Find out what you can do with the other sixteen hours in the day.

The way to get the most out of career and life is by becoming process oriented rather than goal oriented. As I've indicated, focusing solely on attaining objectives keeps you constantly in the future and robs you of appreciating the present. Monitor your own behavior, ask yourself how often you are conscious of what you're experiencing at any given moment. If you are on the ambition treadmill, you'll find that most of your waking hours are spent planning, scheming, and worrying—all about goals in the future. By discovering your ambition plateau, you will find out how to rest and savor life. The ambition plateau is realized when you can say to yourself, "If this is how far I've come, it is fine. And if this is the pace or momentum of my aspirations, that too is fine." The ambition plateau does not imply a lack of progress or momentum, it merely says it is now defined personally and internally.

Plateaus Are Not Ceilings

Don't be afraid of letting up. It will not automatically lead to your becoming a failure or a nobody. If anything, the opposite is true. My patients who do get off the ambition treadmill typically feel more alive, more imaginative, more creative. In fact, they are more likely to create new dreams that fit them and lead to a sense of accomplishment. But let me warn you. You can't subtly creep back on the treadmill. You must really find your plateau of self-acceptance.

Slowing down or letting up is not a confirmation that you have peaked, but merely an acknowledgment that, right now, the treadmill is too exhausting. Career plateaus and ambitions are not mutually exclusive. A plateau is basically something you choose. Regard it as a new adventure.

CHAPTER FIVE

NEVER HAVING ENOUGH: THE MONEY TREADMILL

Money may be the husk of many things, but not the kernel. It brings you food, but not appetite; medicine, but not health; acquaintances, but not friends; servants, but not faithfulness; days of joy, but not peace or happiness.

—Henrik Ibsen, playwright

Derrick has been coming to therapy twice a week for two months. Forty-seven, divorced, and a marketing executive with a computer software company, something about him has puzzled me from the start. I have never seen him wear the same clothes twice. Each time he's clad in extravagant Italian suits, alligator shoes, expensive sweat outfits, and any one of at least five different $10,000 watches. I make a note to inquire about these accessories and what they mean to him. I also have to bring up his bill—which he hasn't paid. When I confront him, he confesses that he can't pay me and, tearfully, he tells me he's "caught in a vise"—the worse he feels about himself, the more he has to buy things that make him look richer—which makes him feel poorer, less worthy, and driven to buy even more!

Derrick's need to appear prosperous is bankrupting him! In the course of therapy, he admits that he's always needed to surround himself with wealthy people to feel like a somebody. In time, he realizes that pursuing money and spending it even faster was making him feel worse rather than better about himself!

The money treadmill can be torturous. A never-ending pursuit of more takes on a life of its own, accelerating in momentum. Reaching a place where our income begins to level off, rather than being a time to sit back and relax, is a signal for anxiety and apprehension. Not making more money, in the minds of many, is the beginning of a slide into fear and insecurity. The money treadmill often accompanies the ambition treadmill. Just as those caught on the ambition treadmill want to pile up success, those on the money treadmill believe that accumulating money and the things money brings will magically transform their lives. But it also differs in some respects. On a conscious level, the ambition treadmill is driven more by the Perfect Self whereas the money treadmill is driven by anxiety emanating more directly from the Imperfect Self.

The money treadmill is built on a misconception about what money is, what it does, and what it means. We have been brainwashed into thinking money itself, once we amass it sufficiently, will bring us happiness and an end to insecurity. And it can't and won't, but we may spend our whole life pursuing it for family love, or whatever, and find we have sacrificed our life to false goals and ideals. While money is often regarded as the source of our greatest security, it can also become the vehicle of our greatest insecurity.

A man comes into my office with his wife-to-be. He's forty-three, handsome, seemingly self-assured, and charming. His problem is that in the last six months he hasn't been sexually attracted to his fiancée. This loss of desire happened as soon as he committed to marriage. "Ah ha," I think to myself, "he's afraid of intimacy, the fear of losing himself in the sweet, but to him dangerous, bliss of sexual intimacy." Today this common fear masquerades behind the new diagnostic term *inhibited sexual desire*. He reveals this has happened with other women, and more critically, he pinpoints that it all started five years earlier. When I ask what was going on at that time, he shrugs it off; "Oh, I had some business troubles."

After some prodding, he reluctantly goes into some detail about how he made millions in a business venture that went bankrupt, something he assured me could have happened to anyone. He then tries to convince me, and himself, that it was a blessing in disguise because he didn't need that kind of lifestyle anymore. Now he had found a more peaceful existence working for someone else. In his present job he is even more successful in certain ways and receives more recognition than when he worked for himself; he just makes less money.

Yet, as he spoke, despite his articulate manner, and attempt at honesty, there was a deadness in his eyes, like a veil hiding an enormous amount of sadness. In spite of his good intentions and his wish to lead a different life, the sadness persisted. This man was doing the right thing for himself—scaling down and reassessing his values. But the pain of losing money and not having regained it was still there. And, with his pain came shame. Before any specific sexual therapy could begin, we had to explore something even more fundamental—the role money played in his life. Despite his protestations, he was still on the money treadmill and was still allowing money, and its loss, to shape his sense of himself. Getting close to the woman he loved could mean sharing that pain, and such closeness could work like a flame that would melt the icy barricade of his stifled emotions. But he kept her at a distance, terrified of all those suppressed feelings. Money and shame had become secret companions, trapping him, keeping him lonely and isolated.

OUR GREATEST SECRET

People mistakenly believe sex is the taboo subject in psychotherapy, because it is the most personal facet of human existence. But this is no longer true. Today, money is the taboo subject. Many therapists, including myself, will not ask a patient about their income level unless the subject is directly relevant to whatever is being discussed in a particular session. I have gone many months, even years, working with patients without ever knowing this most personal fact. Men and women, both in and out of therapy, regard this information as so private that they keep it among their deepest secrets. It's okay to ask almost any question in social contacts these days but it's regarded as tasteless and intrusive to inquire into another person's financial status.

When you keep the truth of what your earnings and extent of your net worth a secret it is an obvious reflection of what money means to you. Because money is accepted as a valid measure of who we are, to reveal our income is, we think, to share a great intimacy. No one wishes to expose himself so casually.

Even when men and women fall in love, the last secret they will reveal to each other is how much they earn. No matter how poignantly honest they might be in disclosing their most intimate feelings with each other money is left out of their revelations. Indeed, I have found that the moment when that disclosure is made is often the final stage in the process of commitment and bonding. Disclosing your income is tantamount to saying, "No matter what your impression of me, now you know something so telling, that I stand naked before you."

Why do we keep this a secret? Why are money and personal worth so directly connected? Even when we get over the possible shame and anxiety of not having enough money, this problem persists. Most of us are never secure when it comes to money. We always need more, and the illusive power of money is a constant goad in our side. Money has become our tyrant.

The primary goal of the money treadmill is to establish self-worth and security. But you can never make enough money, because your anxiety about imperfection and self-worth persist. Our wants have a nasty way of separating themselves from their origins thereby becoming unquestioned necessities.

AN AMERICAN DREAM OR NIGHTMARE?

The pursuit of wealth is part of the American dream—searching for streets paved with gold. That is one of the reasons why America is such a wealthy and powerful country—the American work ethic, and money as the measure of how well we play the game, is ingrained in most of us. Even though we supposedly know that money can't buy happiness, our response to this homily is aptly stated in a line uttered by John Huston in the film *Chinatown*, "Yes, but money can buy off unhappiness." Money has taken on mythical power. If it can't guarantee us the good, at least it can protect us from evil. We believe money will shield us against harsh reality.

We have been led to believe we should both hoard and spend money. Conspicuous consumption is a fact of American life. We are enticed from every direction to spend money. We should keep up with the latest styles in clothing, cars, dining out, and electronic gadgetry. Our possessions are signs of our worth and our status. The bumper sticker pronouncement He who dies with the most toys, wins is not merely vulgar it is a tragic social truth coated in humor. It also points to our uneasiness. If you don't spend money, no one will know that you have it, and if you do spend it, there goes your money, your security, and your thriftiness.

For most of us the problem is about having too little money, rather than too much. We watch "Lifestyles of the Rich and Famous" and read about the richest 400 in *Forbes* magazine, but we know that our personal drama is taking place on a lesser scale. We are trying to spend and have security at the same time, but having things and having security are at cross-purposes. We constantly struggle with and worry about our finances. A recent event has dramatically exacerbated such worries.

In 1980 we suffered a recession that forever damaged our sense of security. From that moment, we realized that the good old days were over. No longer could we count on any real job security or trust that inflation would keep rising our net worth. The early eighties saw the beginning of drastic corporate restructuring, mergers, and acquisitions, and the apparent corporate lack of interest in the individual. Becoming lean and mean was the order of the day. Since then, vast numbers of middle managers have lost their positions due to radical cost cutting. The implications of this dramatic restructuring is that employees in corporate America cannot rest easily, nor can they feel as secure as they could in the past. The effects of these changes seep into all levels of employment, spreading anxiety along the way.

While those on the money treadmill pick up steam, their anxiety about money zooms up as well. This treadmill has brutal speed, and the reality of its limitations often force people to think about getting off. One manifestation of this wish is the desire to own a home. As always, we see a home as an anchor of stability in an otherwise frenzied and insecure world. More and more people are now desperately trying to scrape together enough money for a down payment. As the members of the baby boom generation age, they are not going out as much and are trying to scale down, but nonetheless, they are having great difficulty letting go of needs that have become part of their life. They also find themselves struggling with their rarely questioned value systems. These are hopeful signs, but the tyranny of money has long teeth and won't be shaken easily.

Money has wormed its way into the center of our psyches. Over the years the value of everything in our lives has come to be measured by a single monetary standard. If we want to know the value of a car, a service, or a work of art, we ask the same question: How much did it cost? Finally we have come to value our own self-worth by the same standard, by our capacity to make and spend.

A young sales executive sits in my office, anxious because he is bored with the woman he lives with. After he describes his frenetic lifestyle and pervasive worries about not having enough, I comment, "How do you expect to have any genuine interest left over when your passion is spread so thin?" He only shrugs. So I ask, "Do you really know why you're doing all this?"

He straightens up, glad I've asked a question that will lift him for a moment. "Sure, it's all about money ... everything is about money, isn't it?"

Well there you are. Money for him is no longer a means of exchange, it has become an end in itself, even though the why of that end isn't clear. Money has always had its dark side, but now it has become synonymous with self-worth, and that equation isn't even questioned. When money becomes an end in itself, we have lost sight of its reality, of what it can do, and, more important, what it cannot do. Instead we have invested it with a dark power that it does not possess. Our projected god now becomes our curse and our tyrant, and we, its willing slaves.

WHAT MONEY MEANS

It's easy to stay stuck on the money treadmill. All you have to do is lose sight of what money is and focus on what you believe it means. It means success, it means power, it means sex appeal, it means security, it means happiness, it means, well, almost everything. Until we take back the power we have invested in money and divest it of its myriad meanings, we will unceasingly pursue it, for we will never have enough. Money is a fickle god—it seems to bring you closer to the rewards it promises, but never close enough for satisfaction, because the joy is fleeting, soon replaced by emptiness and the need for more.

Money and Self-Worth

Jason, age thirty-five, tells a story that is often heard in therapy. When he was young, his family lived in a rather modest home, had no conception of money and little idea of who had it and who didn't. His father seemed obsessed with work, never doing that well but still providing the necessities for his family. Some relatives on his father's side did have money. In therapy, he vividly recalled how every time he would visit these relatives, his father would become nervous, fearing they might disapprove of his children and how they behaved. Jason remembered getting in the car with the sense that he was visiting a different class of people, that these relatives were somehow better than his family. *Better* meant they had nicer homes and were more "Americanized" than his parents, who retained more characteristics of the old country. One of these relatives commented that Jason and his brother "ate like animals." He found that amusing, but his father was ashamed. He would forever hold up these relatives as models Jason should emulate. So Jason's first lesson in self-worth, as is true for so many of us, was subtly tied to money and the status associated with it.

Parents, of course, reinforce the link between money and personal worth when they pay their children for doing well, such as receiving good grades in school. Early on, we link our identities with financial reward. Reward means money. Child-hood rites of passage are tied to money; we get money from the tooth fairy when our baby teeth come out, and we get money on our birthdays, reinforcing the notion that as the years progress there should be some corresponding increase in our financial value.

Money and Love

Those who have difficulty giving praise or expressing love, often give presents. Again, money becomes a medium that has both real and symbolic value. Parents who have difficulty giv-ing to their children in meaningful emotional ways can always evoke appreciation and love from them by giving them money or material things. We sometimes believe that the more our parents care, the more they give. We may know deep inside that they just find it easier to give financially than emotionally, but we accept what we get and value it.

As we learn to connect love and money, we also come to believe that money will bring us love. Even though we'd like to think that we are loved for who we are, we soon learn that money makes us more attractive. We are all familiar with the remarkable desirability of people with money. After all, there is more to love than simple chemistry. Love and money help us overlook many flaws that would otherwise annoy us.

Money and Security

Anyone who grew up with parents who went through the De-pression knows that money and security are inextricably linked. Children overhear their parents talking about money, worrying about it, and fighting about it. They learn it is critical to a sense of well-being and security. Advertising is constantly warning us to Save for a rainy day. Indeed, one can hardly argue that money doesn't afford security, but how much money do we need to have that security? That's the issue. Just when you think you have enough, hardships can take it away or you can unexpectedly lose it in a financial crash. Security is an elusive goal.

The stock market crash of October 1987 created a sense of insecurity in millions of Americans that still exists. I remember patients coming to my office that day, shaken, frightened. Even those people whose basic needs and security were untouched by the crash felt deeply affected because of the money they lost. I reassured them that their real basic security was still intact, but at that moment they couldn't believe me. If you are motivated only by a Perfect Self, you will always believe that having more will make you feel secure.

Money and Power

Having money enables you to exert control over those who are dependent on you, just as a boss has control over his employees. Those are obvious forms of control. But less obvious are the ways in which people cater to those with money. People will defer to you, you get to call the shots: where to meet for lunch or dinner, whose house to go to when you socialize, and which table you are seated at in a restaurant. Having money gives you the edge over others. These, and many other privileges, come with money.

Another power connected with money is the power of vengeance. When the less affluent finally accumulate money, it is an especially charged turnaround. I had a patient named Barry, a man in his late thirties who had already made millions in real estate, who still wanted more. When I asked him why he so desperately craved wealth, he recounted an incident from his past. His family had just moved to a new town, but in contrast to everyone else who lived in nice houses, they moved into an apartment. He remembered his first open house at school. His parents kept to themselves and even looked different from the other parents because of their modest dress. As he described that evening, from at least twenty years ago, Barry was overcome with emotion, clenching his teeth. When I pointed this out, he replied, "I hated all those people, and I still do—every time I meet one of them today I feel like rubbing his nose in my money." It was clear that this whole drama had taken place primarily in his own head—there was little evidence that his schoolmates had ever put him down or treated him as an inferior. Yet his obsessive response to his imagined slight was to make a lot of money. He never questioned that his money would bring his schoolmates to their knees, groveling and apologizing. The money treadmill offered a guaranteed solution for him: power, superiority, and vengeance.

We attach self-worth, love, security, and power to money. The associations we make between money and what it can bring are somewhat accurate. Our problem starts when these associations become equivalents. In other words, money can bring you recognition and this recognition can feel like love, but in the final analysis, it isn't. Having money can make you feel more secure than not having money, but ultimately security is an inner state of mind. Money can always be lost. When we create, in our mind, an equivalency between having money and having love, security, and power, then the pursuit of money becomes an illusion. The pursuit becomes a treadmill because we never get what we really want; with these misdirected efforts for well-being, all we get are deceptive imitations.

MONEY AND EMOTIONAL PAIN

By focusing so intently on the wishes and fantasies surrounding money, we blind ourselves to the negative results that come from its pursuit. We do this partly because the rewards seem so enticing and promising that it all seems worth the effort. But beneath the zeal and excitement, there are other feelings building up, emotions that gradually take on a toxic quality. This is inevitable, because ultimately we have been pursuing an illusion.

Most people think greed fuels the money treadmill, but I believe that is psychologically naive. To a psychologist, the real culprit that leads people onto the money treadmill is a fear and dread of never having enough. We begin to focus too much on an Imperfect Self that is acutely aware of not having enough. This fear is evidenced by a visceral anxiety about not being enough, of feeling as though our sense of self-worth is eroding and crumbling, and there is no way to stop it.

Anxiety is the most basic and primitive catalyst for getting on the money treadmill and staying on it. Money is not the root of all evil, nor is the love of money the root. Greed is a powerful motivator but it doesn't touch the power of raw, unacknowledged fear. The pursuit of money is aided by our greed but not necessarily driven by it. Money is the great impostor, behind it we find the face of fear.

Shame, envy, competitiveness, and greed lead people onto the money treadmill each individual singularly fueled by anxiety. For each person, money is the fantasized solution. It is important to understand each emotion's connection with money, for by identifying your path onto the money treadmill, it will be easier to find your way off of it.

Shame

The American dream is predicated on the notion that we all have equal opportunity; therefore, not making the best use of that opportunity is to fail, to somehow not accomplish what we are supposed to accomplish. One facet of that dream is to make money and to grow rich. Falling short of that goal makes many of us feel ashamed, even humiliated.

Young children and teenagers often know all too well the stinging sense of shame that comes from not being as well off as their peers. When Jason was in junior high school, his father drove an old, beat-up Chevrolet, and whenever he had to pick up Jason and his brother from school they would tell him to park a block away because they were so mortified by his car. To Jason that car signified some kind of failure. He had the hypersensitivity of youth, completely attuned to the outer signs of success. Children who are obsessed with designer labels are not merely victims of materialism, they are already conditioned to the very specific signs and symbols of success. There is very little nobility in being poor; there is even less nobility in being out of fashion.

But today, the possibility of feeling shame exists at all levels. It's not just a matter of how much you have, it's a matter of who you compare yourself to. If you drive a Volkswagon, you will feel shame if you think you should have a Mercedes. Shame is a widely shared feeling among the upwardly mobile. And most of us are upwardly mobile, regardless of where we started on the social ladder.

Patricia, age twenty-nine, comes in with her husband for counseling. She is bright, a former teacher, and now home-maker. Her husband is relatively successful in his new medical supply business. They live in a closely knit community bound together by its religious commitments. Their place of worship is the center and crucible for their social activities. Most of their friends are already well off, partly due to their well-paying professions, but also due to the good fortune of having wealthy parents who bought them homes and gave them a strong start.

In tears, Patricia describes how terrible she feels because they don't have more money. According to her, money dictates the order of everything in their community—who socializes to-gether and which private school you send your kids to. Even in the school, family money, not ability, determines which classes your children attend. Luncheons are segregated by wealth, and social alliances are formed purely on the basis of wealth. Her husband doesn't disagree with her assessment of this miniculture, but he seems sufficiently secure to overlook the slights that come their way. He is confident that as time goes by he will succeed. Shrouded in pessimism, his wife couldn't wait, badgering him on a daily basis. Finally I asked, "Why don't you move?" But moving was out of the question, because their families where there and his business couldn't be relocated. Patricia means well, she loves her husband and family, but she lives in a seething hell of discontent. How much of her hell is in her head, and how much is in the community?

What do I say to her that she doesn't already know? She's sophisticated enough to know that there are values more important than those she is imprisoned by. But she is caught on the money treadmill so deeply and feels so ashamed and humiliated, that she can't let go of these obsessions. Whenever she hears a neighbor mention a new addition to his house or that he's building a swimming pool, it's like a knife in her.

As we explore her past, which was financially modest, and we unravel her evolving identity, it becomes obvious that Patricia has never really felt good about herself. I suggest that there are other ways to feel important besides having money, that there are other ways to have self-esteem. Patricia looks at me, agrees, but is notably unimpressed with my admittedly routine advice. I know the battle has been joined and I had better come up with more than banalities and platitudes. So I tell her that our first task is to see if we can convert her shame into more commonplace envy. I tell her envy would be a step up for her. She laughs nervously and agrees.

Patricia knows her values are distorted, but this doesn't change her reality. For her these values are no different than those of her community. I warned her, "If you continue like this, you are doomed to a miserable existence, and you will make the rest of your family very unhappy . . . there is no way out for you unless you make a real choice to let go of these values. As badly as I feel for you, I will not continue to see you in therapy unless you are firmly committed to change even though at this moment you have no real faith in the possibility of that change." I wanted to shock her, frighten her about the future, otherwise there would be no genuine motivation, only superficial attempts. She got the message and, grudgingly at first, began to rediscover and accept who she was before these beliefs so infected her.

Patricia feared that if she changed she would no longer belong. I helped her see that she was focused on a Perfect Self as defined by this community. As a result, she was only aware of her Imperfect Self. Forgotten was her deep love for husband and family, a nourishing bond, which she unwittingly relegated to a Forgotten Self. Finding a new perspective gave her the courage and insight to stand on her own feet and reexamine her priorities. Slowly, she reached a plateau of well-being and inner calm based on the emotional gratification she received from her family. She now found herself focusing on her family as an anchor, and her need to fearfully look beyond that core of support gradually subsided.

Envy

There is a saying The poor spend their time counting the rich person's money. If we examine the media's fascination with the wealthy, this seems all too true. Cynics might say the American free-enterprise system is geared toward stimulating envy and therefore pushing people to consume more goods. If that is their intent, it has certainly worked. Feeling painful resentment for those who have more is a key emotion for those on the money treadmill.

Feeling envy is a natural, but invariably corrosive, emotional state. It can lead to obsessional periods when the desire to possess what others have dominates your waking hours. Envy requires keeping your eyes off yourself and focused on others.

Richard is a forty-year-old physician who is consumed by envy. He practices a speciality that he enjoys, but it is fairly low on the hierarchy of physicians' earnings. Happily married, with two children, he is in a state of crisis as he struggles to make more. "Do you need more?" I ask. He nods in the affirmative. I ask him again, this time with a preface, "Do you really need more, or do you just want more?"

He's silent for a moment, knowing full well where I'm going with these questions. "Look," he finally says, "when I went into medicine, I wanted to make a good living and enjoy my work. . . . I'm doing that, but it still galls me when I look around and see friends of ours making so much more, and I know they're not smarter than I am, they just chose to go into a business or into law—careers where there's no limit to the amount of money you can make. And yeah, I feel like I need more—we want to remodel our house, and someday I want to afford a second home, and I want more recognition I guess." Later he admits that he gets plenty of recognition, and he acknowledges that he doesn't really need a second home. He is obsessed with money because he is the victim of envy and doesn't know how to stop his cravings. He has lost sight of any day-to-day conception of happiness. The thought that someone else might have something that he doesn't drives him crazy and keeps him going.

In the course of therapy, Richard had to deal with letting go of a Perfect Self composed of matching the income level of his friends. He had to "allow" them to have their rewards without letting that diminish his sense of worth. This was difficult for him at first and involved a genuine period of mourning. Fortunately, he trusted that after this period, he could find some inner contentment that would make it worth the struggle. Richard found that he enjoyed his work and his life outside of work. He also found that living in the present was more rewarding than fantasizing about the future.

The obsessions of envy can be a way to camouflage the fact that we have lost a sense of direction and purpose. We are often motivated by discontent and limited goals. When we reach those goals there is nothing to drive us. Envy moves in to replace motivation; envy is discontent without limit. The fear that fuels envy is the fear of having no direction.

Finding that you have peaked financially in your profession is inevitable for most of us. But instead of experiencing this as an achievement, we experience it as a dead end. The money treadmill dictates that we should make more money, but we've reached our limit. So envy fills the gap, and keeps us on the treadmill.

I believe that these dead-end peaks can be reinterpreted as plateaus. They can be new beginnings for us, a time to reevaluate what is truly important to us, and a time to set new goals and directions for ourselves. It's only when you're on the money treadmill that you can't consider any other goal than making money, or envying someone else's money. The treadmill has a momentum that prevents any new assessments from being made.

Competitiveness

Marilyn, age forty-two, comes in for marriage counseling. She is fed up with her husband's abrasive and obnoxious behavior when they're out with friends. Charlie owns a small retail business that is doing relatively well. "But apparently not well enough," he says sarcastically, nodding in his wife's direction. She ignores this and tells me she's happy with their lot in life, but he's not. "That's a lot of crap," he retorts. This time she speaks directly to him. "All of our friends are richer than we are and you want what they have. Sure, I'd like to fix our house and get some new furniture, but I can live with it, it's you that's unhappy." I wonder who is the discontented partner here?

It turns out that Marilyn is from a wealthy family, whereas Charlie's family was poor. Most of their friends are hers from her high-school days; they are from wealthy families and have been set up in business by their parents. It is that latter fact that galls her husband. Charlie still feels "less fortunate," as he did when he was in school. He envies their having rich parents. He feels disdain emanating from them, although Marilyn insists it's only his paranoia, as is his belief that she is disappointed in his ability to provide. In time, and as he lets his guard down, he acknowledges the depths of his envy and his almost obsessive need to compete with their friends. Charlie's need to focus on what they have and ignore who he is, has made him lose sight of his own value. He has lost himself, and, at the same time, lost sight of Marilyn—a woman who really loves him.

I suggested something I've done with many men and women on the money treadmill, that he seek out a variety of friends, both rich and poor, to keep some perspective on what is real. I don't mean that he should feel superior to those with less, but merely that he should begin to focus on what is real and begin to distinguish reality from what is fleeting, illusory, and out of reach. As I said to him, "You'll never be the son of wealthy parents, you'll never have that sense of ease—most of us don't, and in the great scheme of things, you'll find that's okay."

For Charlie, envy always led to competitiveness. Every encounter became a contest, which accounted for his abrasive, argumentative style. He always locked horns, because he had something to prove. He had to prove, despite his grievous disadvantages, that he was as good as anyone else. This compulsive competitiveness was driven by the fear that he really wasn't worth very much, that his disadvantages were permanent and couldn't be overcome. While Charlie was energized by these contests, they never settled larger questions.

When these contests are financial, as they often are, they keep us on the money treadmill. When worth is determined by money alone, we gain worth by counting dollars. The problem is that our worth keeps going up and down with our bank account, and other people, especially those with advantages, start out with a bigger account than ours. When we enter the money race, there is no finish line.

Greed

The drive most commonly associated with the money treadmill is greed, the insatiable hunger for more. As the old stock market saying goes, There are bulls, bears, and pigs and the latter always lose. Everyone is familiar with this concept, but less well known is how often the passion for easy money afflicts people as they pursue their careers. This hunger for money distorts thinking and inevitably impairs good judgment. Let me cite an example.

Donald is a thirty-eight-year-old stockbroker who has recently become rather depressed. He is not making the money he feels he needs or that his skills indicate he should be making. He is bright and aggressive. But in reviewing his history, a familiar pattern emerged. Since graduating from college he has had at least five different careers, none of them successful enough to hold him. He'd like to think he is suffering from that familiar, and somewhat romantic, ailment the fear of success, but in reality, he doesn't seem to have the patience or the willingness to work hard enough and long enough for his effort to pay off. Instead he thinks there is a fast and easy buck to be made and that he deserves a break. He thinks smart people take shortcuts. He doesn't acknowledge that patience and persistence, not greed, lie behind most success stories.

During therapy, Donald was able to slow down enough to experience those frightening moments when he could finally confront the anxiety that relentlessly propelled him into desperation over money. Whenever he thought about his career, he felt a vague apprehension that he might be destined to be a loser, a fear from his college days. In college, he had been told by friends, teachers, and his parents that he was gifted and had a great career ahead of him. Instead of patiently trusting himself, he was driven by the wish for a Perfect Self and would blindly plunge ahead into yet another venture, yet another quick-buck activity, and each time he would invariably lose!

Donald's impulsiveness removed any semblance of good judgment. I thought his ideas sounded brilliant at times, but he had to go slow enough to correct the inevitable errors that would crop up, and more to the point, he had to learn from failure rather than just trying to avoid it. Only when he could reclaim a Forgotten Self, aspects of his personality that he liked and valued, could he have the presence of mind to learn from failure.

Greed, like shame, envy, and competitiveness, is fueled by fear. Sometimes our fear, when we run from it, becomes vague and unspecific. Donald was fleeing a sense of failure, certainly an ethereal demon. As we lose touch with the reality of ourselves, our solutions also become magical and grandiose. We will be the lucky one, the one in a million who hits the jackpot or wins the lottery. Because we are special, we can avoid the hard road of work and patience, and take the easy road. Lady Luck is fickle, but she won't resist our magnetism. Greed is like that; it is rooted in the magical efficacy of more. More will solve everything. As we attain more our own spirit becomes less and less and we take on the pinched meanness of the greedy. The money treadmill is a tailored ride for those of us who believe in the magic of more. Charlie found that trying to refrain from arguing and from being competitive was difficult at first. But he learned to take pride in controlling his emotions and began to enjoy relationships with other people more than he had in the past. "It's actually kind of nice to come home from an evening without being filled with a bitter aftertaste. I like people more, but more importantly, I am starting to like myself."

ACKNOWLEDGING THE MONEY TREADMILL

If everyone is concerned about money, does that mean we are all on this treadmill? Well, a lot of people are on it, but concern over money does not in itself define this treadmill. It is our illusory and inescapable obsession that defines being on the treadmill. A number of indicators can help you make your own diagnosis.

Something Feels Wrong

Whenever men, and lately, women, get together, invariably two kinds of discourse arise. First there is talk about making money, making deals, finding "angles," self-promotion, and boasting. The more honest they are, the more likely we will hear hints of anxiety, concerns about what it's all about, and, occasionally even straightforward admissions of feeling adrift. The common thread is a sense that something is wrong, somehow they have gotten off track. This is one of the most basic and subtle symptoms of any treadmill.

"I know I'm not living the way I wanted to, even though I can't quite put my finger on it." Eric continues his probing: "If I try to talk to my wife about it, she's sympathetic and well meaning. Usually she suggests we take more trips and do things that are fun and relaxing. I know she's right, but these solutions seem to miss the point. It's more basic than that." Eric is forty-eight, and reasonably successful as a painting contractor. He's in pain, but it's a pain that can be the catalyst for a new way of life, if he chooses to view it as such and not run from the truth he's trying to reach. Most of his life energy has been invested in making more money. Like most of us, his feelings are multilayered. He's not depressed, he has times when he enjoys his work, his family, and his friends—but these times are becoming less frequent, even though he is doing well in his business and doesn't have any unusual pressures. Sadly, he has lost sight of what life can provide and he rarely feels contented. He is on the treadmill.

Thinking About Money Gets You Depressed

Most of you are probably living beyond your means; therefore, some of the anxiety of depression you feel is probably appropriate. But that doesn't mean you merely have realistic concerns. What it does mean is that you have found a way to disguise the treadmill by looking at one symptomatic expression of it, namely excessive consumption. The depression you feel should become a signal not that you need more, but that you need to take a good look at how you are participating in your own entrapment.

Feeling sad, remorseful, or depressed is not always a bad thing. Negative feelings are signals for taking stock, and reevaluating choices and lifestyles. If depression is about psychological emptiness or fatigue, then its antidote is nourishment and replenishment. And the solution is not more money, just as the solution to other kinds of depression is not food or drugs. Solutions that do not ultimately include getting unstuck or getting off the treadmill are merely illusory self-deceptions.

Putting Life on Hold

The life you are living right now is not a rehearsal, it's the real thing. Whenever I work with a patient who doesn't fully accept this, I tell him, "The way it is right now, is the way it's always going to be—unless you do something different." The patient will retort, "Come on, I know that, but as soon as I get this work done . . . things will change." Or ". . .I'll take more time off." Or ". . .I'll take that vacation." People turn their lives over to self-imposed necessity, to a schedule that can't be broken, and their choices disappear. Too many people live to work rather than work to live; or more to the point, the pursuit of money has become an end in itself rather than a means to a more fulfilling life. I hear the refrain "I know that's true, but . . ."

It's understandable to be preoccupied with money in your late twenties or early thirties, the time to aggressively establish or consolidate a career. Unfortunately, most people don't know when to shift gears and enjoy the fruits of their labors. Gradually the reasons for work and money become obscured, the pursuit is an end in itself, the game becomes everything. When you feel that you must do what you are doing and everything else must wait, including life, then you are on a treadmill.

Joshua, age fifty, owns a small, well-run insurance agency. But his wife tells me the way he acts on vacation would suggest that the business needs his constant attention. He is unable to relax, feels vaguely anxious most of the time, and is forever calling into the office to check up on things. His wife, Eleanor, said, "He thinks he's fooling me, pretending he's having a good time, but I know better. Most couples I know go away, and at least while they're gone, they make love more often and get close. We go away and have less sex, and I think the reason is that he can't relax, he's too uptight. My God, you'd think the office was going to fall apart, but they do better when he's gone. And when I confront him about this, he tells me he's worried about cash flow, or about new business, and I know that's a lot of crap."

After hearing this, I turned to Joshua, expecting a heated denial but all I saw was a tired man, looking sheepishly at me, shrugging his shoulders. He knows she's right, and he knows he's sailing without a rudder. Joshua is unwittingly allowing life to pass him by. Time is slipping away, he knows it, but he doesn't know how to stop. Thankfully for him, he has a wife who not only wants a more enlivened marriage, but who cares about his happiness too.

People on a treadmill foster something akin to a slave mentality—except that they are both the slave and the taskmaster. They dash about trying to hold up a house that is on the verge of collapse. They have schedules, beepers, and a sense of importance. They have given up choice and time, the very stuff life is made of. If you see yourself in this picture you are on a treadmill. Necessity is your master, and you created him!

Relationships Tarnished by Money

I have already described the envy that money stirs up in those who feel they don't have enough. Money stirs up a lot of things in us and our relationships. It stirs up envy, greed, competitiveness, and anxiety. Such feelings color, distort, and diminish our relationships with everyone, with our spouses, with our children, with our colleagues, and with our friends.

Rhonda, thirty-nine, married for sixteen years, has fought at least once a week for each of those years with her husband, Phil. They fight about friends and the quality of their social life. She believes he doesn't aspire to sufficiently lofty heights, and he feels she's a snob. "Whenever we meet a new couple, she's always hypersensitive about the car they drive and where they live. If they're too modest in what they have, she always manages to find something wrong with them. We met a very nice couple in a night class we took, we hit it off real well, and then she found out where they live. When we were driving home, out of the blue, she starts criticizing them."

Rhonda is on the money treadmill in a way that is as destructive as it is for the person desperately chasing after money. She ascribes an unreasonable worth to money. She looks down on those with modest incomes as though they were tainted, as though associating with them will somehow infect her and make her a lesser person. When I asked what made her uncomfortable, she said, "Oh, I think it would be hard for them to fit into our lifestyle." I pointed out that she was projecting onto them the same questionable values that were driving her. I also suggested that not all friends have to be alike, or even have to meet each other, and that she was cheating herself of new experiences. At this point, Phil chimed in, "Rhonda, you know damn well we had more fun with them than we do with couples we see all the time." Ultimately, of course, the challenge for Rhonda was not whether she could accept this new couple, but whether she could accept herself. When she developed some self-acceptance and confidence, she wouldn't have to be a chameleon, fearful of taking on the color of those around her.

Taking Foolish Chances

If you find yourself repeatedly engaging in risky ventures, you may be in more trouble than you imagine. It's one thing to open the paper every morning to see whether you've won the lottery; it's another thing to risk hard-earned dollars in the foolish hope you can make a killing. Those on the money treadmill are intrigued by the great leverage one can gain in stock options, commodities, or any highly speculative game. This is all part of the obsessiveness that hooks us into the treadmill. It blinds those involved to the sound maxim Rewards require risk, and people obsessed with money are typically the very ones who cannot handle the emotional swings and frightening downside of financial risks. Whenever I have patients who become overly entranced by risky financial adventures, I find that they are the very ones who are least able to handle the inevitable anxiety that accompanies such risks. If this applies to you, take a good, hard, honest look at yourself and start getting off this treadmill.

WHEN ENOUGH IS ENOUGH

There are very few people who ever feel they have enough money. You can never be too rich or too thin is more than a saying, it is part of our collective belief system. But as a starting point, should you wish to get off the money treadmill, you must believe that needs, unlike wants, are finite. This means there is a point where enough is enough, and the problem for so many of us is having the courage to clearly define that point.

Needs or Wants?

When I ask people if they have enough money, they usually say no, because they feel some discrepancy between their desires and their financial means. In their minds, they need more money, unable to distinguish *wants* from *needs*. When wants become

long-standing and intractable desires, they are felt as needs—
they are no longer options but necessities.

Needs are normally finite and definable, but our wants are
potentially infinite. This means that we must constantly choose
among our wants and balance them against each other. When
we are unclear about what we want, or disguise our wants as
needs, we can mess up our lives terribly. We are prone to
mushrooming our material wants and neglecting our psychological, emotional, and spiritual needs. Then we replace our neglected spiritual needs with material wants, and never feel
satisfied or fulfilled. If you are unclear about what you need and
want, or you can't tell a need from a want, then you may be on a
treadmill. You can, however, learn to distinguish between needs
and wants. For now, it's worthwhile to take time to think about
these issues, and remember money can't ever buy everything
you need, or want.

What about "F——— You" Money?

Yet another delusion. The fantasy that there's an amount of
money that will give you total freedom and enable you to say
"F——— you" to those people and situations that you believe
keep you dependent and imprisoned. This cherished notion that
there is a magical amount of money that will free us from any
further responsibility or obligation to others is nonsense. I have
seen scores of friends and patients get caught up in this variation of the treadmill. They believed that a particular dollar
figure or a certain net worth would allow them to retire, or do
whatever it is they wish to do. Unfortunately, the magical
number keeps changing as our life changes. It keeps slowly
creeping upward and is always just slightly out of reach. Individuals who pursue this disguised treadmill are forever preparing for the good life they're going to have while they put up with
the unsatisfactory life they now have. They live for the future
and do what they can to ignore the present. Little wonder they
believe in magic.

Once a Worrier, Always a Worrier?

Is it true that we are born worriers? Not necessarily. I have found that men and women who have been chronically plagued by money anxieties can be helped to find peace of mind. Sometimes, the first step is simply recognizing that their insecurity is totally irrational and extremely primitive. There is a concept known as "ontological insecurity," which refers to a state of apprehension about our very existence. One fantasized solution to such basic insecurity is, of course, wealth. But it is only a fantasy. When we come to terms with our primitive insecurities, we won't be thrown off track by illusions, or by external solutions to internal problems.

Oddly enough, you don't really have to solve this basic insecurity, you just have to know it exists. You may have been born with it, and you may struggle with it the rest of your life, but it won't turn you into a chronic worrier and it won't ruin your life. Just defining it, or identifying it, by itself leads to a sense of relief. Understanding your basic insecurity allows you to put it into proper perspective. It is primitive and irrational, but it is not "neurotic" or crazy. When you put this insecurity into perspective and stop trying to fix what isn't broken you will find that you have renewed psychological energy to begin living your life.

Can I Accept Limits?

You had better learn how to accept limits, because they exist, no matter how much money you make. Acknowledging limits may create a momentary sense of anxiety and sobriety, but when you accept them and learn to live within them, limits actually foster a newfound sense of security. Anxiety thrives on the unknown and the unexpected. Becoming realistic about what you have doesn't have to be depressing. It can be liberating.

Another need for the acceptance of limits occurs as you get older. Eventually your earnings will level off. That is not to say that you cannot continue to have dreams and actively pursue them, but it does mean that you must begin to come to terms with what you have accomplished. It is very possible to accept how far you have come and what you have. As a matter of fact, a realistic assessment of what you have accomplished allows you to have realistic dreams. I cannot overemphasize the point that having a plateau does not mean giving up on dreams, but it does mean liking and appreciating yourself now.

FINDING A PLATEAU: WHAT YOU WANT AND WHAT YOU REALLY NEED FROM MONEY

The following are a series of questions and personal inquiries to ponder. They are designed to help you get off the money treadmill and start living your life.

1. What does money mean to me? How much of it has to do with things I can buy and how much involves status, i.e., what it says about me and how I will appear to others? Try making a distinction between what is intrinsic and feels good for itself and what is extrinsic—meaning that which sounds good because of what it means or signifies.
2. Will the things I want to buy truly make my life better? What are my needs as contrasted with my wants? Try imagining having these things. Obviously they sound great at first, but carry out the fantasy in your mind and see if they will make as great a difference in your life as you now believe.
3. What are reasonable financial goals? Begin to realistically assess how much you can make and the lifestyle you can afford. More specifically, ask yourself, what am I willing to do for money? What sacrifices will I make in other sectors of my life if I totally devote myself to making money? Remember, family and friends definitely get neglected if you become a workaholic.
4. Can I scale down? If this becomes part of who I really want to be, can I do it? Visualize what it would be like, how you would live, what your friends would say. Embrace what

you visualize as a choice, not a necessity. Be clear about your emotions—resignation and a sense of remorse is not what I am talking about here. Scaling down is, for an increasing number of people today, a blessing, a welcome relief from life on the treadmill. If you can explore this honestly, you will find yourself feeling better and perhaps even being courageous!

David, a fifty-one-year-old financial services sales executive, got off the money treadmill the hard way. He was referred to therapy by his cardiologist. He had triple by-pass surgery three years earlier and recovered nicely, but he continued a hectic and driven work and personal lifestyle. Both his doctor and his wife, Allison, also a stockbroker, worried. After a month or so in therapy, David told me, "I know what you mean by plateaus. I felt I had reached one when I turned forty. But every day I was reading stories about young investment bankers making midsix-figure incomes, wheeling and dealing, and I guess I got caught up in the whole thing again. That's when Allison became a broker. Not that I'm blaming her, she knows how to leave work back at the office. She jogs in the morning and I'm sitting next to the window waiting for the delivery guy to drop off the *Wall Street Journal!*"

David had allowed himself to be seduced by societal images that created a Perfect Self he was driven to achieve. Rather than resting on his laurels, he was driven by a vague sense of not having accomplished enough, the "me" he was at forty became his Forgotten Self. Relieved that he might get off this treadmill, he asked that Allison come in with him. Together, we explored what money and status meant to both of them. At one point they turned to each other laughing about how happy they had been in their previous neighborhood, which was far less affluent than the one they lived in now. They noted how their family loved camping just as much, if not more, than the upscale resorts they now chose as vacation spots.

David and Allison had the courage to liberate themselves from false goals and reclaim beliefs and experiences that were truly satisfying. David regained the emotional plateau he needed.

They both realized the security and freedom they wanted was already at hand, waiting to be embraced.

As a final thought for those on the money treadmill, consider the old Oriental saying A man can measure his wealth by what he can do without.

CHAPTER SIX

LOOKING JUST RIGHT: THE APPEARANCE TREADMILL

> *Whatever is in any way beautiful hath its source of beauty in itself and is complete in itself; praise forms no part of it. So it is none the worse or none the better for being praised.*
> —Marcus Aurelius, Roman philosopher

There is a health club in Los Angeles that is elegant, large, and busy. It is the "in" place to go, not only for working your body but also for meeting upscale single men and women. Inside lurks everything that is wrong with our present thinking about appearance and looks. Men and women arrive dressed to kill in surprisingly stylish work-out clothes. Even when exercising, the women wear makeup. Expensive, sexy leotards are a must. As a meeting place, it fulfills a legitimate need, but it nonetheless exemplifies how obsessed we've become. Whatever happened to sweaty health clubs, where people didn't care how they looked while exercising? We're so preoccupied with appearances that we've lost sight of our original objectives of good health and physical well-being.

Even so, I suggested this club to Maxine, a thirty-three-year-old patient who bemoaned her fate as a single person and was increasingly overwhelmed with difficulty in meeting men. She looked at me in horror. "I don't have the body to go there. I'll have to go somewhere else first, and then when my body looks terrific I'll be ready to take that place on." She couldn't face comparison with other women who might have a competitive edge on her. This frustrated me because she was quite attractive and had an engaging and vivacious way that most men would find charming. I understood her concerns, but was sad because she reminded me of how twisted and confused our values have become.

We are so used to competitively comparing ourselves with others, that we don't know how to stop. Instead of focusing on our unique and valuable strengths, we contrast ourselves with others and keep coming up short. Why? Because we contrast our imagined failings with their imagined successes. There's always somebody for us to feel inferior to. We believe that if she looks better, she must be better, and in contrast we feel diminished.

We are told "if you look better, you feel better," and "attractiveness follows confidence." To a point, that's true. It is easier to walk down the street when you feel attractive. But the drive to work on one's appearance is, for many, a negative experience rather than a positive one. They may think of it and describe it as positive, but its wellsprings are a secret sense of feeling physically defective, and, therefore, unattractive and less likely to find love. Changing our external appearance doesn't automatically change our inner sense of ourselves. And although people mistakenly assume this, being beautiful or physically fit doesn't mean we're automatically and incontestably good people.

Any of us can get hooked on the appearance treadmill for a simple reason. When we focus too intently on our appearance, we deny our real self inside until it becomes part of a Forgotten Self. We grow increasingly anxious and depressed because improving our appearance alone doesn't lead to what we hoped it would. Feeling betrayed, we hate our body because it fails to deliver fulfillment. And as we hate it and as we strive for a Perfect Self exemplified by looking just right, we work that much harder to fix or improve our body! We have entered the vicious circle of one of life's treadmills.

The appearance treadmill exemplifies our split between our inner and outer selves. If we lack confidence, we assume that the answer is to create an appearance that will inspire confidence within us. We deflect our attention exclusively to the outside, eschewing our inward need. Our positive goal of looking good becomes a disguise for neglecting ourselves and our inner needs.

Neglect leads to increased pain. As this process becomes chronic our frustration grows and we turn against ourselves. We believe there must be something desperately wrong with us, nothing we do works, or at least we can't seem to carry through. The seeds of our self-loathing hide in our frustration and failure. Because we strongly believe in our recourse of self-improvement, the only way out of the trap is to blame ourselves.

Our compulsive drive to look better means we must change fundamentally, accelerating a sense of self-loathing. Any activity that is fueled by negative origins will invariably have negative outcomes.

A principle called the law of diminishing returns says the more energy you expend, the less the expected results. In *The Myth of Sisyphus*, Albert Camus likens life to rolling a stone uphill, only to have it roll back down at the moment you thought you had reached the top. The appearance treadmill is like that. We start out feeling sad and depressed about our physical well-being, but hopeful enough to engage in activities that seem like antidotes. They distract us for a while, but our life doesn't really change, we feel disheartened again, and then we have to start all over, trying even harder. And the harder we try, the fewer the returns.

Life on the appearance treadmill has no respite. Instead of confidence, we experience disappointment; instead of joyful sweat, we experience the sweat of the addict, feeling high and chasing the next high all in the same moment. Instead of pride, we feel shame. We slowly lose control of what started out as a positive drive for physical self-improvement.

Other people are obsessed with aspects of their appearance that cannot be changed. They are convinced their body has simply failed them. They are in touch with an embarrassing and shameful sense of deficiency.

Terry, age thirty-two, is tall, reasonably attractive, quite intelligent, enormously successful in his executive recruiting business, and already wealthy. He shares anxieties about dating after recently breaking up with his girlfriend. "I'm uptight about my physical being," he discloses.

"What do you mean by 'physical being'?" I ask, sensing what's coming.

"Well, I'm too short, I'm not muscular enough, I've got small hands . . ." he trails off.

"What? You've got small hands? Are you planning to date a woman or strangle her?" I ask, attempting humor to help relax him.

He doesn't laugh, because this is serious confession time. "Seriously, Dr. Kinder, I just don't feel very masculine," he says.

"I assume you think your penis is too small also," I suggest, knowing this matters a lot for most perfectionistic men.

He laughs nervously, relieved I brought it up. "I'm pretty sure I'm a good lover . . . at least I'm told that, but yeah, I wish it was bigger."

While he couldn't do anything about the size of his penis, he was considering working out at a gym so he would appear more masculine. As the session progressed, I attempted to discover not why he felt bad about his penis size, but why he lacked a sense of his good or outstanding qualities. It's as though his assets didn't count, even though everyone, women included, found him attractive, and as I found out later, many women thought he was a real catch. But in his mind he would only be judged by his physical appearance.

I didn't reassure Terry about his appearance, knowing it wouldn't do any good. He needed to be the best at everything, and he just couldn't tolerate anything less than perfection. I believe he is the modern rule, rather than the exception. Perfectionism may be a positive motivator for some; but for most people it is a disease that causes them to focus on the negative in their pursuit of the positive. Only when Terry recognized how much he relegated what was good about himself to a Forgotten Self could he gain a new perspective. Gradually, he discovered how he got on the path he was on. For him, the combination of perfectionistic parents and living a fast-track life, which emphasized being and having it all, made him susceptible to the appearance treadmill.

The appearance treadmill is based on both self-denial and self-deception. We deny our self when our exterior is the sole indicator of who we are. When we allow that—assume our value is measured by our form—our shell becomes our totality when in reality it is only one facet of our personality, only one reflection of our identity.

We deceive ourselves when we narrow our focus to the shell, improving it feverishly in the vain hope that we will feel better about what's inside. It is true that bettering appearance can enhance self-esteem, but the more we deny our inner being, the more effort we must invest in our exterior until we lose sight of our essence. Ironically, when we embrace our essence we are most attractive. We see this in others, in a sense of inner fire and self-possession that touches us more than any one of their physical parts.

THE ROOTS OF PHYSICAL OBSESSION

From the time our mothers tucked in our shirts and made us comb our hair before visiting relatives, we learned that it was important to look just right. We inferred that if it's important to look your best, then the better we look, the greater the social value. Sure, we also learned that wonderful maxim "beauty" is in the eyes of the beholder, but we came to suspect that the "beholder" still expected us to look our best.

An obsession with appearance doesn't usually begin with adulthood, but rather the roots of this treadmill start in adolescence when our perspective is filtered through the prism of desperate approval seeking. Most of us remember times when as teenagers we were ashamed of some aspect of our appearance: Maybe we had acne, thought we were too fat or too thin, thought we were too tall or too short, or worried about the size of our breasts, thighs, or nose. Our parents told us we'd grow out of it. We tried to believe them and harbored secret hopes that as we got older our infirmities would no longer matter. But such positive thinking seems of absolutely no use to teenagers.

The adolescent years forever shape the psyches of millions of men and women. A teenager barely has an identity—who they are is simply how they are perceived. For teenagers, feeling unattractive is a curse. There is a weird confluence of forces during this time. Adolescence is a time of defining your identity, typically in terms of peer relations and groupings. It is crucial to believe you belong. It is also a time when boys and girls go through a very awkward change in their physical beings and appearance. Teenagers typically have the fantasy that if they looked better, they'd be more popular, and by and large that's true, especially for girls. Boys can rely somewhat on being an athlete or on being the life of the party to make up for a marginal appearance.

Cute boys and girls survive, and their self-doubts take their own unique course. Almost everyone else harbors painful memories of secret shynesses and insecurities. As we grow up, we usually don't confront and handle our adolescent pains very well, and we carry them with us. The often stated law of history that Those who forget the past are doomed to repeat it has its personal application; those who repress their past must carry all of its burdens. And today, large numbers of men and women are reliving their teenage years, still caught on the treadmill of appearance and its promised reward of social approval—popularity.

As adults we don't go around saying we want to be popular, but we act as though we do. Perhaps it wouldn't be so bad if we simply wished to look our best. Instead the ghost of high school still haunts us—the specter of rejection, of not belonging, of just not being good enough.

A phenomenon occurs for many adults whenever their tenth, fifteenth, or twentieth high-school reunion rolls around. Many women, and some men, spend up to a year preparing themselves for the occasion. Sometimes it is a happy kind of preparation in the way that a wedding might be. More often it is a dark ritual, a prelude to an act of vengeance, a way to get even, a way of showing them that you are now important, in spite of the fact that they made you feel horrible and insignificant.

Adulthood often provides some relief from these concerns. But omnipresent and insistant social forces still conspire and seduce us to step blindly and willingly on this appearance treadmill.

THE ADORATION OF THE PHYSICAL

In ancient Egypt, eye makeup was thought to simulate the look of sexual arousal and thereby attract men. The front lines of attraction have unfortunately been the physical, what is visible to the eye. And, of course, styles of beauty have changed over the centuries. We all know the Rubenesque beauty of hundreds of years ago is now viewed as overweight. Regardless of changes in style or physical dimensions, we have always been overly focused on physical attraction as our one standard of beauty and well-being.

The power of the media to shape our lives is one of the most striking changes to take place in our lifetimes. Public opinion polls taken in 1961 showed, for the first time, that the majority of Americans got their information about the world primarily from television, the ultimate medium of appearance.

The interest in inward journeys, especially those stimulated by drugs, faded, but the focus on appearances grew. We could, at least, look good. Fitness, dieting, exercise, the creation of a beautiful body moved to the forefront of our consciousness. Now we could turn on our television sets and in the privacy of our own homes do aerobics with the beautiful people, and thank God, there was no one to laugh at our bulges or our erratic gracefulness.

We all know exercise is good for us and that it's healthier not to be fat. But as we embraced healthier ways of living, we ignored our inner needs. A beautiful body alone does not make us beautiful. Beauty has an inward dimension as does fitness. The neglect of this inward dimension, the inattention to our inward needs, put us on the appearance treadmill. Again, the narrowness of our focus led us to the rejection of ourselves.

Businesses sprang up to cash in on and perpetuate the fitness craze, and quickly fitness became an industry and part of our culture. For example, in the fifties it was sufficient to wear sneakers, now there are dozens of exercise shoes to choose from, and we need a pair for every type of exercise.

Along with the fitness craze came an emphasis on physical appearance that persists today, unchecked. In some ways it has been stimulated by television. We are continuously exposed to a barrage of visual images, role models, examples of beauty, taste, and style. Everyone should be slim and attractive and if someone is overweight, they must be humorous. In the recent past, movie idols dictated our standards of beauty. Today television not only dictates standards but also distorts reality. This is a new phenomenon, but it is part of our view of reality. Three thousand years ago, Cleopatra was an idol, not a role model to teenage girls. The ideal cannot be the reality for most people!

YOUTH AND APPEARANCE

The baby boom generation ushered in a new order focused on youth. Young people dominated the news and dominated our images of what was valuable and what was in. What was not in was getting older. A popular cosmetic in the 1970s was Eterna 27. Aging was something to dread. Because youth was in, people felt compelled to deny the inevitability of aging and all the concerns that came with it.

Luckily baby boomers are getting older, and jeans are being made with more room in the seat, and no one thinks of thirty-five as middle-aged anymore. We may be entertaining a grudging respect for getting older, but it is still difficult to acknowledge what it does to our bodies and looks, because looking young and being slim have been all-important for so long.

Overall, the outcome of these historical influences is not encouraging; indeed, our obsessive concern with appearance fuels envy, vanity, and, for all too many, a sense of not being good enough. In a society where everything moves too quickly anyhow, our worth is too often measured by looks alone, and somehow we never meet the standard.

People still get on the appearance treadmill vainly attempting to control what is increasingly out of our control, if for no other reason than the fact we are getting older. Advertising still exhorts men and women to fight the aging process, but it's obviously a no-win struggle. Dissenters from this position would argue that the fitness and appearance craze is all about enhancing confidence and building a sense of well-being, but the realities suggest something far different.

MIRROR, MIRROR, ON THE WALL

Getting on the appearance treadmill always starts out with good intentions, but these concerns have a nasty habit of spiraling out of control. What seems like a reasonable goal becomes excessive and before long we are in search of a Perfect Self reflected in the mirror. We are driven by a fear of imperfection. We work on our appearance, we work on our bodies to a point beyond what they can be, and toward an ever-fleeting goal of what we think they should be. A compulsive and driving frenzy for physical enhancement is now a commonly accepted part of our culture.

It is essential to confront our beliefs in each facet of the appearance treadmill to take stock and to break patterns that make us miserable.

Pretty Feathers Make Pretty Birds

If we are born with less than spectacular looks, maybe dressing well will keep us in the running. Clothes make the man, the saying goes. We can select apparel that brings out the best in us and conceals what we secretly and shamefully feel is unsightly. Unfortunately this is not easy and elicits further pressures.

Today styles change faster than our wardrobes can. Looking our best this week may not work for next week. Not only do you have to keep up, you have to be able to pay for it.

The impression we make on others is partly dictated by what we wear. Today, these concerns start out early in life. In fact, what used to be an adolescent concern with clothing, and what your clothes say about you, is now a preteen concern. Mothers select designer clothing even for toddlers so they don't seem out of place, or God forbid, so they don't develop what used to be called an inferiority complex. Sadly, our preoccupation with how we appear is being passed on to our children before they can question it.

In this era we dress for success and wear power ties. The symbolic nature of what we wear may be the critical issue in our drive toward success. This seems as true in our private lives as in our careers. In the singles world, women have turned the tables on men, regarding them as sex objects and expecting them to dress the part. That may be a well-deserved reversal, but many women now sound as shallow as those men who only see women as sex objects.

Recently, a single woman patient expressed disappointment in the previous night's date. "As soon as he walked in, I knew he wasn't for me. His shoes just looked awful."

I nod in understanding, shooting a quick glance at my own scuffed shoes, and then uncross my legs to put my foot down. "What does that tell you about him?" I inquire.

She then goes on to say something about his not being dynamic enough, not enough charisma, not enough chemistry. For want of shoe polish, a potential relationship has been lost. To say that's shallow on her part is to miss the point. Men have been describing women's physical features for years with the same kind of picky and dehumanizing fascination with the parts, rather than making any attempt to see the whole person.

We will always be concerned with first impressions. Today, I sense there is an important change in our calculations when it comes to how people appear. Looks, clothing, and hairstyles may have some importance and aesthetic value, but they say precious little about what is underneath. That's not news, of course, but what is news is that we are more preoccupied than ever with those impressions. In the past we were willing to look beyond first impressions. Today we say What you see is what you get, and we don't look for anything else.

Eating Your Heart Out

Food tempts us everywhere. Next to the Bible, the longest running, bestselling, nonfiction books include *The Joy of Cooking*, *Betty Crocker's Cookbook*, and *Better Homes and Gardens Cookbook*. In addition to cookbooks with their mouthwatering pictures, consider all the interest in new and trendy cuisines, the just-around-the-corner junk food stand, and television ads tempting us with delicious-looking morsels. And what is the result? A lot of overweight people. We all want to have our cake, eat it, and still stay slim and, of course, it doesn't work, pounds keep appearing where they shouldn't. So we look to dieting.

It's a truism in the publishing world that if you come out with a new diet book with a hook—a strange euphemism for something new, simple, and relatively painless—it will sell a lot of books. People are desperate for new solutions, especially easy ones. The sad fact is that for most people sensible eating requires too much willpower. The clash between the hunger to fill ourselves up and to still look good is one that arouses a great deal of unhappiness.

Today many young girls are put on diets, frequently by their mothers. Teenagers go off to "fat camps" in the summer, desperately hoping that the first day of school in the fall will bring them the attention they crave. They are literally starving for attention.

Eating disorders are epidemic today, not only because of deep-seated conflicts between girls and their mothers, but for a much simpler reason. Often eating disorders arise from our attempts to have a socially acceptable body. The superthin body of the anorexic has the sought-after look of a fashion model. When we lose control of our inner conflicts and feel that our inner world is chaotic we try to regain control by manipulating our bodies.

This illusion of control, of course, doesn't work, and the look of a model soon gives way to the look of a death camp survivor. But the original intention was to look beautiful.

Bulimia, a common eating disorder, afflicts scores of women and, incidentally, men as well. It starts out harmlessly: first you glut yourself with forbidden foods to fill a huge inner emptiness; then you vomit and purge to avoid the inevitable weight gain. It is the ideal neurosis in this age of wanting to have it all.

While eating disorders like bulimia afflict a relatively small part of the population, dieting afflicts almost everyone. The cruel truth about dieting is that only positive motivation ensures lasting change. Many of us are running nowhere so fast on our appearance treadmill that we don't realize we hate ourselves and how we look. Our wish to lose weight comes not from some positive source of energy, but rather from our self-loathing. And self-hatred is a very poor motivator. Self-hatred feeds on itself and stirs up more tension, and we try to relieve this extra tension by eating more. This is the vicious circle of the compulsive dieter or the compulsive eater.

A patient told me, "I keep thinking I'll really decide to work on a diet when I hit bottom like an alcoholic, when it gets so bad that I just can't get into any of my clothes, and I'm totally disgusted." What he didn't realize is that hitting bottom is something a lot of alcoholics do, but the few who use that as the catapult to a long recovery back are those who choose or decide that they can no longer destroy themselves. It is this decision that is the turning point, the act of will—not the self-loathing. Yet, I see many people driven only by this inner hatred, this disgust with an Imperfect Self, hoping it will become the catalyst for change, but it never does. That's the curse of the appearance treadmill; you keep running in the same place, driven by negative energy.

Just as dieting doesn't work when motivated by self-hatred, it also fails when it is inspired by unrealistic fantasized rewards. Some people think their lives will magically change for the better, all their early childhood dilemmas will be resolved and this will bring them peace. But you still have to go on with your life, go to work, pay the bills, face other commonplace conflicts that still require a struggle to resolve—no matter how you look. As any dieter knows, the-solution-to-everything fantasy never comes true. You're still left with the need to affirm the real you inside! Why not turn around and meet the person who has always been there?

I believe the great paradox of dieting is that you must come to accept your self and your body before you can change. That doesn't mean you have to like everything you find, but you can't hate it. The hidden trap is the belief that you can only like and affirm yourself after you've made everything okay. In fact, you have to start with liking yourself just as you are. It's surprising how this simple idea runs against the grain of those who are into self-improvement, yet is the only one that leads to genuine change.

Exercise Junkies

The new rage, especially for younger fast-track people is exercising, which is certainly a welcome alternative to compulsive eating. But in our quest for better and harder bodies and the longed-for, admiring glances they will inspire, we have lost sight of our original intentions.

Initially, exercise was meant to be health facilitating. And, as a special bonus it felt good! The endorphin-producing effects of exercise can also be the stimulus for relentless exercising. If we lack other ways of feeling high, then this seems like a nice alternative to harmful addictions. Yet, when our time is overly consumed by exercising, it becomes another treadmill.

For Karen, a patient of mine, who is twenty-nine, her exercise regime is out of control, but she won't acknowledge it. She is attractive and already much too thin. Nevertheless, she starts out every day by waking up at 5:30 A.M. so she can ride her exercise bicycle for one hour. She then spends another hour putting on her makeup before she goes off to work as a management consultant. By nighttime she is so exhausted she can barely think about going out; instead she is in bed by 9:30 P.M. after eating a small salad for dinner. She's moving so quickly that she barely has time to notice how mechanical and unfulfilling her life is.

Karen chases fantasized rewards that never seem to arrive. None of her friends and associates will ever be able to tell her often enough, how great she looks. Karen will, of course, burn out, and at her pace, probably sooner rather than later. The question is what will stop her and force her to step back and reassess her life?

Karen was actually quite motivated to talk about those issues. But talk is not enough, neither are insights. What she needed was the courage to try to break patterns. I told her how therapy itself can be like a treadmill, when people vainly hope that insights magically lead to transformations. Finally I suggested, even demanded, as part of her treatment that she stop all these activities for a few weeks. I likened this suggestion to what physicians call a "drug holiday" where a patient may be on so many medications, it's difficult to tell what's beneficial and what's not.

With some initial resentment and trepidation, Karen took my advice. At first, she became alternately anxious and depressed. I reassured her these feelings had always been there, driving the treadmill. Anxiety over some ill-fated relationships had left her vulnerable and insecure. Time alone would have healed those wounds, but in her emotionally weakened state, she became infected with perfection seeking. She gradually became acquainted with a Karen lost in her Forgotten Self. She began to sleep later and listen to music in the morning rather than exercising. Oddly enough, while relaxing, she still thought about work, but her anxiety was replaced with a clear, thoughtful, and productive manner of thinking that made her feel that she was on top of things. This refound self-assuredness was part of her Forgotten Self. She also gained some weight, which because of her new perspective, didn't bother her in the least. She regained her sense of humor, became calmer, more self-accepting, and more contented than she had felt in years. Not surprisingly, she was even more effective in her work and more confident with men.

Scores of men, as well as women, are caught on the same treadmill; running every morning, stopping off at the health club for some racquetball, and then working late into the night. They will justify such frenetic activity as necessary to keep their edge in business, but I suspect they're ultimately going to blunt that edge. When these types of men and women decide to marry each other, their sex lives often suffer. They have expended their libido on the treadmill, pursuing images of what they should be, rather than stopping and replenishing themselves so they can feel passion and desire.

The Cosmetic Scalpel

When nothing else works, you can always have your appearance shaped by the wonders of surgical technology. More and more people are discovering that for a reasonable investment they can finally look like the person they so desperately long to be. You can fix your face, your eyes, your nose, your chin, your hair, your hips, your breasts, your thighs, or your buttocks—you name it, you can get it done. When successful, these alterations do bring some happiness and, for a time, build confidence.

One of my patients was flat chested and chose to have breast augmentation. I'll never forget when she came back into therapy, proudly wearing a rather low-cut blouse and beaming from ear to ear. She had suffered for years because of her sense of inferiority. Never mind that there are plenty of flat-chested women who feel sexy and desirable. For this woman, a relatively simple operation did, in fact, have a powerful effect on how she viewed herself.

Another patient had such enormous breasts that men leered at her; yet these same men would typically choose not to go out with her for obvious reasons—they didn't want to be with a woman that a lot of other men were staring at. Over the years, she became tired of hunching over, wearing large clothes to hide her figure, and never going to the beach in a bathing suit. She decided to undergo breast reduction. After a successful operation she finally could stand tall and feel attractive, without feeling that men were snickering at her. For her, cosmetic surgery was also a major boost to her self-esteem.

There's no question that for some people changing a body part about which they feel extremely self-conscious can have positive effects. The problem for most people who choose such surgery is that they tend to focus on their externals exclusively. So, when they finally have the surgery, they are disappointed to find they don't feel the way they thought they would and the things that were supposed to change in their lives, haven't changed. As time goes on, they realize the person they thought they were going to be hasn't yet materialized, and that secret person inside is still there.

But I also know scores of men and women who can't accept the fact that certain kinds of plastic surgery are only temporary solutions. They forget the aging process can't be halted by a Blue Cross card. They keep getting their eyes done, another chin job, more silicon injected into those facial wrinkles. They desperately want to move back the hands of time, unable to acknowledge their wishes are futile.

A plastic surgeon refers a woman to me for a consultation. Greta is forty-five years old, married, formerly a legal secretary and now seemingly devoted full-time to enhancing her physical appearance. Although looking younger than her years, she has obviously had some cosmetic surgery on her face, which is a bit too taut and unnatural looking. She is not happy to see me. "Look, I don't need therapy and to be honest with you I don't want to be here." I nod, shrug my shoulders as if to say, "Well, you're here you might as well talk." It turns out that she's had a face-lift, liposuction on her thighs, and two breast surgeries— one was augmentation and one was, as she casually noted, "just a lift." Her surgeon refuses to do any more work on her. "All I wanted was some silicon injections in my lips, you know that's in now."

I respond, "Apparently your doctor thinks you've had enough. Maybe you need to look at why you're so insistent on all this work."

Greta tearfully went on to tell me that her husband works in the film business, surrounded by beautiful women, and, according to her, "he likes it when I look my best."

"So you're afraid you could lose him?" I ask.

As the session progresses, she acknowledges that she's terrified of growing older, and maintains that nothing is wrong with her solutions, as she helps herself to her third tissue.

I suggested she bring her husband in for our next meeting, so I could get a sense of their relationship. He came in, annoyed at my request and irritated with her. As it turned out, he clearly loved her, but was becoming increasingly detached the more insecure she became. "If I wanted a starlet, I could have any one I want. We've been married for twenty-five years, and I have no intention of leaving. But I've got to tell you this, I'm sick and tired of my wife and her friends spending all their time and money on doctors, spas, the whole bit."

She could barely hear him. She was so obsessed with achieving a Perfect Self that she was totally immune to any reassurance from him. On top of that, every woman in her social world felt as she did and only reinforced her anxieties about getting older.

At one point in the session she angrily accused him of always looking at younger women. His response was, "That's my business. You don't see me running off with them, do you?"

She couldn't believe he was sincere and, more important, she could not see that her obsession with her looks was making her less desirable in his eyes rather than more. He was not exactly the warmest and most reassuring of husbands, but her way of looking for security was totally self-defeating.

Greta was caught, indeed impaled, on the appearance treadmill. She began a period of psychotherapy, which was focused, first on her finding the courage to stop searching for a Perfect Self, and then on mourning the loss of her youth. She had to discover her Forgotten Self for that would be her only anchor for self-liking. It turned out that she wanted to go back to work. She was very bright and well read, especially in the area of classical art, an interest that she kept hidden from her peers. Slowly, and gradually, she began to discover someone inside she liked. We even reached the turning point I told her might happen—she began coming into our sessions without any makeup—a small but significant step suggesting that her inner self was becoming more important than her exterior self.

ACKNOWLEDGING YOUR
BODY AND RECLAIMING YOUR SOUL

The most neglected concept in everyday life is the inner person and the possibility of inner beauty. I know this may sound corny, but consider this fact: Most of what men and women regard as attractive, dynamic, charismatic, appealing, or engaging has very little to do with appearances themselves. It is the person behind the makeup, behind the surgery, and behind the clothes that ultimately matters. I'm not saying this because I simply wish it to be true or because I'm sitting in judgment of all those people caught on the appearance treadmill. It happens to be a fact that you can check against your own experience. Ask yourself to whom you are attracted, beyond first impressions. A pleasant/striking appearance may let you in the door. But the reality that finally attracts people to each other, that really makes for chemistry, is a complex combination of many factors, most of them subsumed under the catchall word *personality.*

Remember when you were young, the most left-handed compliment was that a potential date had a good personality. That was tantamount to saying the person wasn't much to look at. When you grow up, however, that rather tepid compliment is the one that means the most.

We really can't afford to be taken in by the beauty contest the media foists on us, whether a favorite politician, star, or anchorperson. These images of success and beauty are not the standards we experience in everyday life. In real life, people are drawn to each other for a variety of reasons—an engaging mind, a sense of humor, a smile, a charming voice, a sense of presence and self-confidence—these are but a few. Our everyday ways of accepting and judging each other are much broader, and more generous, than the narrow image-conscious standards of the media. We take in so much more than what our eyes alone apprehend—feelings, intellect, energy, and confidence.

GETTING OFF THE APPEARANCE TREADMILL

Now that I've presented you with the negative trappings of the appearance treadmill, I'd like to offer a way of reclaiming your physical self and learning to live comfortably with what you have. Or, if you insist on making improvements, do so from a plateau of acceptance rather than dislike and shame.

Acknowledgment

Try this with and without your clothes on. Stand in front of a mirror and take a good look. What do you see? Using a hand mirror look at your back as well. This is you, look at the totality. What looks bad and what looks good? Turn around, walk back and forth in front of the mirror, stand up straight, don't allow your sagging thoughts make your body sag. Are there things about yourself you like or think others would like? They need not be the obvious. Sometimes it's just a curve, a softness that is actually enticing rather than distracting.

Try to tell yourself: "This is me, this is how I really am, and it's okay." Remember, acceptance is the key. Even if you don't like parts of yourself, own them.

Dissatisfying aspects can always be worked on, and maybe you need to. Exercise done from a plateau of acceptance is not only good for your health, but it helps you accept your body rather than hide it. But remember, the greater your negative body image, the less likely you are to take care of your body. You only take care of things you like. We've criticized the exercise frenzy, but reasonable exercise does help people accept their body and their appearance.

Try to remember what other people have said about you and your appearance. Remember the positive things. See if you can incorporate them; maybe it's your eyes, your smile, your walk, the way you laugh. This sounds easy, but it's not. Typically, we discount the positive because we're focused on the negative. See if you can believe the positive things that have been said about you; see if you can take them in.

Letting Go of Perfectionism

Life is too short to envy others and strive for physical perfection. Perfectionism isn't a virtue, it is usually a neurotic trait designed to bring you a level of love and approval and a sense of completion that you'll never really achieve.

For each of us, there needs to come a point when we say, "I've done the best I can do with myself." Having modest goals is a virtue when it comes to our looks. Often, there's just not enough reward to do more. Ultimately, we must all develop a workable/livable sense of what is reasonable for us.

To better learn to cope with perfectionism in the realm of appearances go out purposely not looking your best, even looking a bit sloppy. You'll find that no one reacts negatively and you may loosen up. I occasionally ask my female patients to come in without any makeup on, as a way to experience themselves unadorned. At first slightly anxious, most end up feeling relieved. Most women realize that if I don't have an adverse reaction to their bare faces, other people won't either. And for those women who wear makeup out of a need to cover up, rather than enhance, the exercise is a step toward loosening their burden.

Make Appropriate Comparisons

Start comparing yourself with people who look similar to you, but appear content with their appearance. For example, there are many shorter men who are successful leaders, actors, or bus drivers; so if you're short, don't choose a tall man as a role model. Don't compare yourself to people who are obviously different. If you're overweight, think of someone you know who fits your notion of happiness despite their extra poundage.

If you feel homely or unattractive, look at homely or unattractive people who are successful, even in the glamorous professions. It didn't stop them from developing confidence and moving ahead. Stop assuming you won't find the love of your life, it only seems as though physical attractiveness is the key issue. It's not. I've lectured and spoken to single men and women all around this country and found one glaring truth, whether you're attractive or not, that's not the key ingredient in finding love! Only when you think it is, are you in real trouble!

Aging with Grace

Central to the appearance treadmill is our denial of ourselves and of the aging process and our pessimism about any possible rewards for getting older. First, you'd better accept that, no matter what you do, you'll still get older. You can't stem the tide, and there are rewards waiting for you. When it comes to your appearance, you can try to age gracefully. Barbara Bush is a positive new role model. Our looks will evolve, but that doesn't mean they get worse. They're just different. It's only when we compare ourselves to youth that wrinkles seem out of place.

We must stop comparing ourselves to younger people. A patient of mine, a man in his late forties, feared aging because he had no sense of his life or what his journey had been, and was in the habit of going to dance clubs populated by younger people. No amount of exercise, hair darkening, or trendy clothes could erase the sense of despair he felt at these clubs. When I suggested he socialize with people his own age, he seemed shocked. "I just don't identify with them," he explained.

"Yeah, that's your problem," I said. "They're you, and you just don't get it yet." My remarks provoked him to stand back and look at whether he was really living his life or just trying to prolong his youth.

Risking Exposure

A number of years ago, I worked with a woman who hated her body so much that she was on the verge of suicide. Her breasts were too small, her thighs too big, her hair too wispy, her chin too small, and on, and on. Finally, exasperated with her fixation, I suggested she go to a nudist camp and see what people really look like. She actually took me up on my suggestion, and went about two hundred miles out of town and spent a day at a camp. Naturally, she found out something quite interesting:

Most of us don't look all that terrific nude. We are so conditioned by television and films, magazines and fantasy to adore the ideal body, that we have forgotten what the majority of us really look like. It was a remarkable experience for her and the beginning of a new level of self-acceptance.

There's something about going public that's curative for many people. Allowing yourself to be exposed usually results in the realization that nobody really cares all that much about your appearance. If they care, they care about you. If they don't care, they probably didn't see you in the first place. Remember, most people are thinking more about how *they* look, than about how *you* look.

Go out and let people see you. Wear an outfit that exposes parts of your anatomy that you're embarrassed by. Declare who you are. Go to the beach even though you may not feel ready to do that. Go on that resort vacation, even though you think you look awful in a swimsuit. You won't die. I'm not suggesting it will make you feel terrific, but I am suggesting it's the beginning of self-acceptance, which is fundamental to feeling better.

Take Some Chances

I've been speaking of self-acceptance, but I would be remiss if I did not address one often-overlooked issue. Sometimes, we are so ashamed of how we appear and fearful of rejection or scorn that we don't even try to do our best. We don't fear success, we fear trying and the subsequent possibility of failure, so we don't try at all. We may feign lack of interest, or claim that new possibilities just don't fit who we are, or we put down what really appeals to us. Some men and women get caught up in the "not-me" syndrome. They won't try out new styles of clothing, or new hairstyles for fear of being laughed at. Such individuals often miss out on what's possible. They hide behind a mask of self-acceptance. Real self-acceptance allows us some room to try things, but these individuals fear any attention they, or others, might pay to their appearance. Their wish to hide dominates their lives, and in particular, their appearance.

If this fits you, take some chances, take a few risks. It doesn't matter what happens, because, at the very least, you will own, or reclaim, another part of your being. See what happens if you try on clothing that is more stylish than you now wear. Change the way you comb your hair, wear different colors, see what happens. Whether others like it or not, you will have a more enhanced sense of possibilities and the diverse ways you can express yourself.

Your Physical Plateau

It is possible to discover a plateau of acceptance when it comes to our appearance. After taking reasonable measures, without making ourselves miserable with self-hatred, we can discover a resting place. The motivation for doing so is the paradoxical effect of mourning the quest for a Perfect Self as reflected in your appearance. Once that is done, you can find inner peace.

I remember Jerry, a patient of mine who at the age of thirty-eight had been terribly unhappy most of his life because he was always significantly overweight. Both of his parents were vain and constantly critical of him. He had been on and off diets his entire life, usually with little or no success. His self-loathing made him shy around women, although he was a highly aggressive and skilled commodities broker. Jerry had been to see many therapists, always intending to be more "disciplined" and hoping to lose weight. When he first came in, I told him that I would probably be as unsuccessful as his other therapists had been in helping him to lose weight. I did say, however, that I could help him find a person inside whom he might come to like enough to develop some confidence that would help him with the opposite sex.

Over the course of many months, I struggled with Jerry to flush out his concept of the Perfect Self that had made his Imperfect Self so painfully present in his nonwork encounters. "Look, if I help people make money trading corn and soybeans, they don't give a damn whether I weigh one hundred seventy-five pounds or three hundred pounds" (the latter is what he weighed at the time). I told him this was his way of telling me he had no worth in the realm of romance and love, this was how his real value became part of his Forgotten Self. I told him to start talking to women as though they were clients in his office. He laughed at this but knew instantly what I meant. I wanted him to use all his resources when he presented himself to women. In time, his aggressiveness and his sense of humor had the impact on women I expected it would. They were impressed. In fact, people began to see him as larger than before, not in the negative sense of "fat" but in the sense of "presence." The postscript is that he never really lost much weight, but he feels better about himself than ever before and he's been happily married for a number of years.

When all is said and done, it's what is inside you that counts. Who you are inside creates the most powerful and impactive impressions. There is a very simple equation I've been trying to communicate: Self-acceptance leads to confidence, and confidence is what's truly attractive in people. Confidence is what is engaging, stimulating, and, yes, even sexy. Life is filled with paradox and what seems like the right path is often the wrong one. Self-acceptance will bring you all the hoped-for rewards that you thought you'd get when you got caught on the appearance treadmill, the very treadmill you climbed aboard to avoid self-acceptance.

CHAPTER SEVEN

HAVING TO PERFORM: THE SEXUALITY TREADMILL

Sex is the great amateur art. The professional, male or female, is frowned on; he or she misses the whole point and spoils the show.
—David Cort, American writer

Today, men and women feel more pressure than ever before to be "good" at sex. We have been seduced into believing that if we are healthy, growing individuals, we will do it more, be better at it, and derive more pleasure from it. And if we don't, we're not just missing out, we're seen as cold, uptight, repressed, and inadequate. We have a lot to live up to. Believing in these "shoulds" places us squarely on a sexuality treadmill. We are victims of a sexual misinformation overload. Millions of Americans are secretly on a sexuality treadmill, believing that sexual behavior is a measure of self-esteem rather than a source of pleasure and/or an expression of loving feelings.

The more importance we place on sexuality, the worse we feel. The most deadly aspect of being on this treadmill is that it prevents us from achieving anything even close to sexual freedom or contentment because the prerequisite for any sexual ease or sexual pleasure is being relaxed. If we aren't relaxed our bodies won't respond in a way that allows us to feel tactile and sexual pleasure. The irony then is this: Trapped in the treadmill mentality—desperately wanting to feel more, last longer, and above all, do it right—no one can be relaxed and no one can experience pleasure. Instead of nights filled with erotica, the treadmill only brings secret anxieties and lingering displeasures.

Even in this period of so-called sexual enlightenment, more anxiety, confusion, distortion, and outright ignorance surrounds the subject of sex than almost any other dimension of the human experience. It is no accident that "inhibited sexual desire" is the most frequent sexual complaint heard by psychologists today. It seems people just don't seem as interested in sex the way they used to be. I believe diminished desire is the primary symptom of the sexuality treadmill—an overemphasis on sexual performance and a neglect of genuine sexual fulfillment.

Because the subject is so loaded, any therapist can tell you that urging couples to communicate more about their sexual likes and dislikes as a way of drawing them closer, can just as likely pull them apart. Talking about sex to a loved one has a high probability of stirring up feelings of anxiety, inadequacy, resentment, and confusion. Indeed, there have been times, when I have worked with couples, that avoiding the topic altogether was the best prescription for their ailing relationships, at least until they had worked through other issues.

Dan and Susie came in for marriage counseling. Together for just two years, they were already having difficulties. He was in his early thirties, she was in her late twenties. He was very sexually experienced, or so he claimed, whereas she only had one prior sexual experience. So naturally, he felt very confident in his assessment of what was wrong with the two of them in the bedroom. For Dan, sex was a "dramatic event" that he felt compelled to choreograph. However, inexperienced as she was, his wife intuitively felt that sex was something that should evolve out of closeness, caring, and mutual desire. But as she tearfully acknowledged, she had always felt shy and inhibited and, therefore, concluded that maybe he was right, perhaps the fault was hers. Their disputes centered around his need for her to dress up in sexy lingerie, high heels, and garter belts. Early on, she went along with his wishes, without feeling too uncomfortable about it. But because of his nightly insistence on such "costumes" as she called them, she was increasingly alienated from him.

I immediately wondered if he had some need for a sexually inexperienced mate so he could be the expert, the one in control. In fact, I tried to get him to examine this hypothesis as a way for him to back off, stop pressuring her, and look at his own sexual limitations. He saw my logic, but nonetheless was compelled to seek the kind of lovemaking (his term) he most desired. As it turned out, their sexual differences were ultimately a symptomatic expression of deeper issues of trust and intimacy. He was as fearful of genuine intimacy as she was of letting go. Like so many therapists, when sex is miserable or nonexistent for my patients, I routinely attempt to teach them standard sex therapy techniques involving relaxation and facilitating some dialogue as to what feels good for each party, and so on. But, whenever I tried that with this couple they would become so nervous and alienated from each other that they would drift closer to the brink of divorce.

Over a period of time, a rather odd thing happened. They had sex less, but became closer to each other! In fact, because we were focusing on other issues I almost forgot to ask them about their sexual relations after I had been seeing them for more than six months. When I finally inquired, they both looked at me, laughed nervously, with Dan saying, "You know, we feel more loving than ever, we finally feel like we can trust each other, and we're starting to believe it's really going to last." But they were still having sex infrequently. I told them I sensed their relief from pressure. And then, a few minutes later, I said, "Maybe we should take the remaining time in this session and take a fresh look at sex and the two of you. Maybe we should just start from ground zero, as though you were two virgins, and start from there." They did, and this time they were able to talk without arousing all the old feelings of distress and anxiety.

The point of this story is not that stopping sex altogether is the road to marital bliss, but that setting aside the burden of sexual performance—which they both felt—allowed them to rediscover a sense of trust and liking that had been choked off by sexual demands and sexual refusals. Each had become caught on the sexuality treadmill. And each desperately needed a plateau where he or she could rest, take stock, and then move on.

All the "shoulds," "musts," and "supposed to's" connected with sexuality and lovemaking can become sources of anxiety and confusion rather than guidelines for clarity, understanding, and personal comfort. I am convinced that many of our present beliefs and expectations have become traps. Rather than being sexually liberated, millions of men and women are secretly imprisoned. The irony is that we find this imprisonment only twenty years after the great sexual revolution! The fact is, this revolution was the first stage in linking a treadmill mentality with sexuality.

SEXUAL REVOLUTION: STARTING WITH A BANG, ENDING WITH A WHIMPER

Some say the sexual revolution began with the Pill, others say it began with college students rebelling against authority and parading around half-nude at rock concerts. Some cite the publication of *The Joy of Sex* as the starting point, and many think it happened with the dissemination to the masses of the sex research findings of Masters and Johnson. Granted this disagreement about its exact cause, the sexual revolution was underway by 1965, and for many it was an exciting and tradition-breaking epoch in the history of the sexes.

Decades earlier, Freud had talked of the pleasure principle and the reality principle. The former indicated the uncensored and uncritical expression of primitive impulses. The latter was the instrument of society's restraints, the notion that the delay of gratification was central to rational conduct, an ethical life, and a viable civilization. It was the revolt against the reality principle that fueled the sexual revolution. Millions of Americans believed the time had come to throw off the shackles of conventional thinking and to indulge themselves in activities that yielded immediate gratification.

Let me state at the outset, that many of the notions that prevailed at the time seem terribly naive today. But at the time, these beliefs were buttressed by psychologists, psychiatrists, and social scientists who saw liberated sexuality as a vehicle for personal growth and self-realization. Liberated sexuality was seen as an antidote to all those repressive and constricting beliefs that led to neurosis and atrophied passion.

Scenes come to mind that appear quaint and nostalgic at best, championed by "experts" many of whom are now embarrassed by their past zealous and naive pronouncements. I remember a psychiatrist in Los Angeles who proudly spoke about wife swapping—or, as it was called then, "swinging"—as a tonic for the tired marriage and a boon to self-realization. And a psychologist husband and wife team, with similar confidence, wrote a how-to book spelling out ways to negotiate extramarital affairs while keeping the sanctity of the marriage alive and well. Indeed, the publication in 1972 of *Open Marriage* and its subsequent bestselling status lent a kind of respectability to all this.

As I've noted, one of the unquestioned tenets of the self-actualization movement was that the purest way to achieve greater self-awareness and to transcend social brainwashing was to get in touch with your feelings. And because that was the case, what feelings were more powerful or more basic than sexual ones? For single people especially, getting to know someone meant getting to know them sexually. Terms such as *casual sex* and *recreational sex* came into use. Think of that now: *recreational sex*, as though sexual union was no more mysterious or meaningful than a game of Ping-Pong!

These new attitudes wouldn't have been so destructive if sexual activity was, or could be, just fun, delightful, and playful. The more serious problems began when individuals were regarded as neurotic or uptight if they were unable to engage in such "fun." In other words, men and women were told there was something wrong with them if they believed otherwise. Social pressure held this revolution together, and ultimately it was an unconscious psychological rebellion against this pressure that destroyed it.

The sexual revolution was founded on a denial as to why sex through the centuries has always been taken so seriously. The sexual revolution often moved sex from the realm of the profound into the realm of the trivial. This was the time of the swinging singles.

I remember, at the time, a session with a woman in her mid-twenties who was somewhat shy and inhibited. She was describing a sexual encounter with a man—someone she liked—that she had dated three or four times. As she related her anxiety over not being a good enough lover, she laughed and said, "You know, I wish I was living in the fifties when you weren't supposed to enjoy sex so much." We both laughed, realizing that sex, which is supposed to be so natural and pleasurable, had, in fact, become a source of pressure and apprehension. The sexual revolution was a time when sensual pleasure was not only available, but obligatory as well and that is how so many people experienced it.

I remember many sessions during which men and women described sexual encounters with seeming delight but behind their words I could sense a confusion. They knew something was wrong. When a man and woman had to face each other the next morning, it was not a close and intimate time, instead there was an awkwardness and a lingering sadness, because each person knew they were not really close, not really lovers. Each knew he was not on a path toward greater enlightenment, but rather he was moving inexorably toward a spiritual deadening.

While the sexual revolution is over, some of its negative effects still linger, and it is this residue that drives today's sexuality treadmill.

THE DESEXUALIZING OF AMERICA

When the media-generated information eventually reached a critical mass, people became satiated and fatigued by sexual performance pressures. Psychotherapists sensed this. Instead of feeling adventuresome as the sex manuals suggested, men and women became turned-off. Instead of being relaxed, they compared their behavior to the hypothetical couples in the manuals and they felt threatened. Sex manuals presumed that the reader felt relaxed and open to casual or erotic sexuality, but they were not. The sexual advice offered was too simplistic for one of life's most complex experiences. You cannot just say to people, "Hey, relax, lighten up, and give this a try," as if you were talking about a new flavor of ice cream.

Concepts such as free love and recreational sex ignored the multidetermined nature of sexuality, the fact that lovemaking presupposes caring, tenderness, and trust, which take time to create, certainly more than one evening. So when the media unwittingly coerced men and women to be as uninhibited and expressive as possible, they were inadvertently setting up an inevitable backlash. The conflict was between pure hedonism and a deeper need for meaningful intimacy.

Men and women were instinctively looking for a plateau where sexual feelings and pleasures rest and are consolidated and integrated into a larger body of feelings. When eroticism is separated from love, enormous emotional and spiritual consequences result. After the sexual revolution, a kind of desexualization occurred. People became fed up with various pressures to be more sexual and to reach peak experiences. They were smarter than the experts; they knew something was missing.

Oddly enough, at the same time the sexual revolution was dying, men and women were listening to another message about learning to become friends with the opposite sex. This was a good message, but one that inadvertently fed into the move toward desexualization. Prohibitions grew against regarding the opposite sex as a mere object to be exploited for one's selfish sexual appetites. In addition, traditional sex roles were also becoming blurred at work and in the home. In a strange, unexpected way this positive view of androgyny contributed to the sexual malaise that was already in progress. Androgyny dissolves the mysterious differences between men and women. So now, not only were people getting tired of being on the sexuality treadmill, they were even losing sight of the accepted ways in which men and women are attracted to each other!

The dissolution of the sexual revolution was complete with the onset of the AIDS crisis. This was the final nail in the coffin of the sexual revolution. People now have a concrete reason to slow down and get off the treadmill; sex can kill you! Men and women have been forced to not only consider safe sex, but to reevaluate sex in general and what it means in their lives.

Whenever I am interviewed about relations between the sexes, invariably the topic of AIDS comes up as a reason why men and women are taking new paths to get to know each other. My response, however, is that AIDS is only a convenient excuse for the sexes to do what they have been wanting to do anyway, and that is to find new plateaus regarding sexual behavior, to find new ways of understanding what sex means. And this desire for a new approach, or perspective, evolved directly out of the backlash against the sexual revolution and the growing wish to deemphasize meaningless sexual encounters as the road to self-esteem.

But the pressures remain. The externally arrived at prescriptions and beliefs about sexual behavior are still with us. There is still a pressure to perform, there is still a secret sexuality treadmill.

PRESSURES: "WAS IT GOOD FOR YOU"?

We are inundated with information on how we're doing sexually and how to do it better. The first Kinsey report came out more than forty years ago, and since then we are yearly presented with one kind of survey or another letting us know just where we stand. Even the most conservative women's magazines seem to have their annual sex survey. We anxiously read each survey hoping to find that we're at least sexually average and maybe even better than average.

When it comes to sex, however, average is never good enough. In no other area of life is the notion of average so terrifying, so clearly synonymous with mediocre. Can you imagine your beloved telling you, "Oh, you're fine, honey, there were only ten or so other lovers that I thought were better!" Not on your life.

Sex is measured on a scale with the most exaggerated of expectations. Books about sex scream out superlatives as the goals to aspire to: *Super Sex* and *One Hour Orgasm*. While we may laugh at that old line The earth felt like it moved, we still secretly wish that our experiences were occasionally of such seismic proportions.

The Quantification of Sexuality

Sex, for too many of us, is a numbers game. How often? How big? How small? How long did it last? How many did you have? The questions are endless. The important questions—Are we feeling close? Was it mutually enjoyable? Are we really intimate, both physically and emotionally?—are not asked. The fear of being average is what catapults men and women onto the sexuality treadmill. Instead of being as loving and intimate as possible while making love, we are still burdened by sexuality as sport, as a kind of competition with others measured by numbers. Average is important only when we measure ourselves by external standards. Love is internal and personal, and not reducible to numbers.

Sex as a numbers game is not dissimilar from the numbers game of the money treadmill. How we measure up sexually has become a major index of our self-worth and self-esteem. Being "manly" or "womanly" connotes sexual charm and charisma. Unfortunately, these qualities are too often reduced to numbers, which don't tell much of a story at all.

Eric, forty-three, smiles ruefully at the way women characterize his sexual prowess. They tell him he's "a fantastic lover" and that he's "the greatest I've ever had." And technically, he may be. A handsome and quite charming man, for years he has struggled with the problem of retarded ejaculation—it takes a long time for him to achieve an orgasm. There were complex roots to this dilemma, which finally brought him into therapy. He came in for therapy because he wanted to get married and find a level of intimacy he had never experienced. Deeply distrusting of women because of painful rejections he had with women early in his life, sex for him was about dominance, power, and refusing to surrender emotionally. As a result, he couldn't let go, and he couldn't allow himself to feel helpless and defenseless as he might during the orgasmic moment. Because of this he lasted a long time; indeed, he frequently never had an orgasm with women. At first women thought he had wonderful control. After a while, they would become fatigued and suspicious of him, and then, of course, he moved on. In sessions with me, with tears in his eyes, he said he yearned to know what it would really be like to make love, and to authentically be a good lover. His external "success" was in remarkable contrast to his inner frustration.

Men's Sexual Anxieties

Because men have to "get it up," the result of their anxieties, concerns, and worries is all too obvious when they fail. Even in these days of supposed sexual enlightenment, too many men are plagued by those nagging questions—Was I good? Did I "come" too soon? Is my penis big enough? Did she "come"? From adolescence to the grave, sexual prowess is still one of the critical definers of manliness.

Things got tougher for men after the rise of feminism and the sexual revolution. Sexual conquest was no longer a clear male prerogative. In the old days, men could easily cover up performance fears because they initiated sex. So when men felt up to it, they made overtures, and when they didn't, they didn't. But when women were given societal license to allow their sexual interests and appetites to be known, a lot of men began having headaches!

Men can't fake it. That's just a physiological fact. When a man is nervous, it affects his autonomic nervous system, which leads to a constriction of blood vessels and—Voilà!— an embarrassingly flaccid penis. Interestingly enough, many women still fail to understand men's performance fears. For example, they think men are selfish when they neglect foreplay and just "hop on" too early in the lovemaking process. Women don't realize that a lot of this apparent eagerness is fueled by the fear that waiting will cause a man to lose his erection. That's also why some men don't like it when a woman stops to put in a diaphragm, or when they have to stop and put on a condom. Interruptions break the "mood" and therefore create "failure."

The most recent pressure area for men came when they suddenly learned they were at least partly responsible for women's orgasms. In the past, a man could accuse a woman of being frigid and not have to really expend a whole lot of effort and sensitivity in helping her. This is one reason we now are seeing more and more cases of inhibited sexual desire in therapists' offices. A large number of these cases are men who thought they wanted sexually liberated women, and, lo and behold, they got them!

As Vince, a tired young married man confessed to me, "I gotta get it up at work everyday. . . . And when I come home at night, I just can't get it up for my wife, even though I'd like to." Thus the essence of inhibited sexual desire for men. When everything is a performance arena, the body rebels.

Women: Entitlements and Anxieties

Unlike men, many women today are dramatically liberated sexually. The physiology and psychology of the female orgasm is now well documented, as is the overall entitlement of women to sexual pleasure. But there has been a dark side to all this liberation. Women now have their own performance concerns— Can I have an orgasm and how do I achieve it? Is there a so-called G spot and just where is it? If I can only achieve an orgasm through manual manipulation, is there something wrong with me? And, if she is in analysis with a classical Freudian who is still living in the dark ages, she may be wondering if she can have a "real"—vaginal—orgasm and thereby affirm her womanhood? Research indicates that almost 40 percent of all women do not have orgasms solely from sexual intercourse. Whether this is a result of physiology or psychology is beside the point. When this statistic is presented by the media as a failure, thousands of women feel inadequate and unhappy.

Women are equally vulnerable to their own external versions of being good or doing better. They, too, are waking up, only to find themselves on the sexuality treadmill.

Sexual Communication or Criticism?

Another pressure for many men and women is the current prescription of so many psychotherapists and other experts today: "You need to communicate more and let your partner know what you like and need." Now that's not a bad idea, but it's more difficult than it sounds. Most men and women fear appearing naive, awkward, or inexperienced. So, talking to your mate may be an invitation to a whole range of potentially shameful or embarrassing moments.

For men on the sexuality treadmill, there is the possible shame of looking unmanly. While women are reputed to like sensitive men, they don't like sexually sensitive men. As one man patient said to me when I suggested he tell the woman he was dating that he felt nervous about his relative lack of experience, "I'll turn her off, I just know it. In fact, she always tells me that she likes it when a man is in charge and experienced about everything."

For women, communication presents the possibility of looking unsexy or naive. Women still face an age-old double standard. If a woman is sexually experienced and lovingly, but precisely, communicates what turns her on, she takes the chance of incurring her loved one's suspicion that maybe she is too knowledgeable about sex. Even in these liberated times, men are still inclined to wish their lovers to be hot and sexy, but, paradoxically virginal in their pasts!

Communication can be dangerous for both men and women on the sexuality treadmill. We are all incredibly sensitive in this area, and any talk of change in routine or technique can be immediately perceived as a criticism. Most people are still unable to engage in a conversation about sex without fearing reprisals, misunderstandings, or a condemnation of their sexual persona. Most of this fear exists because we are on the treadmill and are terrified of being regarded as average. And in spite of all the available information, most people are still in the dark regarding sexual realities. Confusion leads to insecurity, which, in turn, leads to hypersensitivity, and the protective cloak of silence keeps us firmly in place on the treadmill.

LETTING GO OF MYTHS

The sexuality treadmill is sustained by sexual myths that linger on and reinforce our mistaken belief that sexual performance is a direct measure of our self-worth. The following are misconceptions that keep people on the sexuality treadmill.

Ignoring Differences

Men are biologically capable of impregnating hundreds of women per year, whereas women are able to bear children only once per year. Some sociobiologists and evolutionists believe women, by nature, are more discriminating than men and sexual union is a far more profound act for women than it is for men. This hypothesis seems to fit the data, but it also keeps women on that very special pedestal, which they find at least annoying and at most a disguised form of repression. Nonetheless, it is one way of understanding why the sexes may differ in their sexual disposition.

One thing is clear when we consider differences: Men differ from women when it comes to romance, courtship, foreplay, and affection. In another book, *Women Men Love—Women Men Leave,* I theorized that men seem to operate according to what I have called the Polarity Theory. This concept helps explain some previously inexplicable male behavior. It is also a theory that arises from early childhood experiences that a number of people, including feminist psychologists, are embracing today. The theory is as follows.

Men are born united to their mother in the same way as women are. However, unlike women, to form a gender identity, men must psychologically separate from their mother and form an identity with their father. When they do this, they set in motion a tendency that is with them forever, a kind of polarity, or oscillation, between feelings of attachment (feeling connected to their mother) and yearnings for independence and autonomy (identifying with their father). It is this going back and forth, wanting to be close and then wanting to feel strong and independent, that characterizes a great deal of male behavior in relationships. Men are much more torn between the two poles than are women, who are much more comfortable with closeness, affiliation, and attachment.

This explains why women seem more comfortable with affection and intimacy. It explains why men, even when they feel loving and emotionally close, may still bound out of bed after making love, whereas women will typically want more cuddling and affection after sex.

In the Mood or out of Sync?

Remember during the sexual revolution how men and women desperately strove to achieve another one of our sex myths, that of simultaneous orgasms? That was certainly a nice idea, but now we realize it rarely happens. Men and women don't necessarily desire sex at the same time, nor do they achieve a sexual climax at the same time. Such oneness happens more often in romance novels.

Most couples are more out of sync than in sync when it comes to the timing of and desire for sexual contact. This fact should not be disheartening, instead it should relieve those men and women who feel vaguely inadequate because they can't seem to get together at the right times. Typically, most couples don't want sex at the same time; one likes it in the morning, one at night; one routinely, one only during more romantic times or only on vacations. These are issues that, by trial and error, get worked out in good relationships. They need not be the cause of dissension or indicators that the right chemistry is not there. They are just part and parcel of the facts of life.

The person who wants to make love unfortunately tends to become irritated with the one who doesn't. If people accepted that both optimal windows of opportunity and temporary emotional impasses are part of living, there wouldn't be so many accusations and hurt feelings. It seems true that men are more likely to be ready for sex more quickly than women. Men can feel "horny" late at night, just after the news has tuned out, while a woman wonders why her mate doesn't understand that she doesn't feel turned on just because it's 11:30 P.M.

Men, too, feel the consequences of being out of sync with the women they love. How often have you seen a woman approach a man with love and affection, only to see him pull away, as though it's his mother combing back his hair? Men, just as women, have to be in the mood to feel receptive to sexual overtures. And men have an additional burden. If they are not in the mood, besides feeling put upon, they have the additional anxiety of perhaps not being able to get it up, even if they choose to go along.

Sometimes it's surprising, considering all the recent information about human sexuality, that both men and women still are unaware of their differences and that sexual harmony emerges, not by eliminating these differences, but by becoming sensitive to them.

Does Love Keep Sex Alive?

Love and sexual desire are related, but there is no one-to-one correlation. People who love each other deeply may not place their sexual relationship very high on their priority list. Love is necessary for a good sexual relationship, but insufficient sex doesn't mean you are not loved. If your sexual relationship is not what you would like it to be, and if you think that is an indication of a lack of love, then you will probably end up on the sexuality treadmill trying to make it better. If you want to make it better, do it for the right reasons, namely that you would like more pleasure out of life or you want to increase your feelings of closeness with your mate. But the sexuality treadmill is exacerbated by self-deception and illusion, in this case, the illusion that sex is a measure of your self-esteem and how much you are loved. Sex is not a validation or measure of love. They may be related, but are not necessarily highly correlated. It is more important to focus on the love you have, than the sex you don't have.

THE FORGOTTEN SELF AND SEXUAL PLATEAUS

Clearly, sexuality is one area where pressure and the need to excel is likely to backfire on you. If you need to have a Perfect Self sexually, if you need to perform to bolster your self-esteem, the sexuality treadmill will make you miserable, producing results diametrically opposed to what you wanted to happen. If you turn sex into work, it will exhaust rather than please you and its fruits will be an Imperfect Self that you hate.

Sexual comfort zones require inner ease and relaxation, even while you are filled with sexual desire! For men, anxiety prevents the ability to perform. And for women, anxiety prevents the ability to achieve an orgasm.

So how do you come to accept who you really are sexually? The first step is accepting your sexual behavior as it exists now, not how you'd like it to be. This means mourning the loss of a Perfect Self, letting go of the anxious need to excel sexually. And ultimately, this means reclaiming a Forgotten Self, which means dealing with shyness, normal timidity, and the inhibitions that we all grow up with. Most of us have denied our bodies and what they feel because such feelings are either taboo or not intense enough. As a result, it's as though we forgot our bodies or we were ashamed of what we felt.

A fear of criticism and ridicule prevents most men and women from learning to discover their sexual plateau. Facing your fear and timidity may at first seem intolerable, yet that is the only way you can feel comfortable. And then, if you so desire, you can become freer and more experimental in your behavior—but only if you choose to do so, and some of you may not! And that's okay too!

I once gave a lecture titled "How to Be an Average Lover Without Getting Depressed," and everyone in the audience laughed with a sense of relief. They laughed because being average, as in every other area of our lives, is synonymous with mediocrity and, ultimately, with failure. Yet accepting your sexual plateau may, for many of you, mean that you are perhaps nervous or awkward. You may not always wish to be that way, but nonetheless that's where you're starting out.

Only after you have allowed yourself to mourn the loss of a Perfect (sexual) Self and have accepted the person you have denied can you then go on. Accepting yourself is the only prerequisite to getting over sexual shyness, what I call the "not-me" phenomenon. Shyness is part of the Forgotten Self, or denied self, but so are your natural feelings and your receptivity to pleasure.

The Forgotten Self is the wellspring of sexual enjoyment. Some of what people need to do is to just act on the wish to be more sexual. Yet people are afraid to try, they say, "That's not me," or "My mate will think I'm just faking it." You won't be faking it. Breaking old patterns requires willful and conscious attempts at new patterns. People who become freer sexually must go through a period where they take steps that feel very unspontaneous. This is okay. One doesn't instantaneously become loose and lively, unless you are one of the few who were born that way.

Dina, age thirty-six, married five years, always suffered from a fear of looking foolish, or being humiliated, a fear that began because she was an unusually skinny child. Her marriage to Jason was fine, except she was still quite shy in the bedroom. She acknowledged to me that she envied "sexy" women and wished she could be that way. She tried to read books to loosen herself up, but her shyness enveloped her. I told her that feeling sexy would happen after she acted sexy. "That's not who I am. Jason will laugh at me." After weeks of helping her defuse her fantasized humiliation by urging her to visualize what she could be like as a more confident sexual person, she began to role-play with him. He did laugh but good-naturedly and with clear delight at her attempts. She took the step of overcoming the "not-me" phenomenon.

So, if you want to be more sexually fulfilled, accept the present you. There's no other way to do it. And, if you want to enjoy sex more, start by thinking about pleasure rather than about getting better. You can find loads of books on sexual technique, but none of them will help you unless you can begin accepting yourself as you are now. The absence of this self-acceptance ensures that you will remain on the sexuality treadmill. And there you will find a complex and false measure of your self-worth.

So many books on sexual technique fail to help people because they don't address self-acceptance. They assume that we're free enough to utilize the advice, and that's not the case for most of us. Reducing anxiety and learning to relax come from an inner attitude toward yourself rather than from external techniques. You need to remove sexual expertise as a criterion for your manliness or womanliness. Nothing is as powerful as accepting who you really are.

When you mourn the loss of being the perfect lover, the paradox of self-acceptance comes into play; accepting yourself is what frees you to be relaxed enough to find more fulfillment in this area.

When I work with couples I often strip away layers of self-deception by suggesting we start at ground zero, which means the couple should act as though they know nothing about sex and are going to learn about something that could be fun and interesting. I suggest they should pretend they're children again and they're going to "play doctor." Even sex therapy terms such as *sensate focus* or *pleasuring* can be inhibiting. I prefer words that are commonplace and not so threatening, such as *cuddling* and *stroking*. This doesn't trivialize the sexual experience, with its many dimensions, it simply moves it into a realm that isn't filled with danger and performance demands.

After self-acceptance, you are then free to make sexual activity a new source of tactile and sensual pleasure. Men can become comfortable with not getting an erection or with losing one while they are engaged in sexual activity. Women who are self-accepting will not regard orgasm as the sole criterion of their femininity.

When I work with men who are concerned with sexual performance, one of the first things I attempt is getting them to accept a flaccid penis. The fear of losing an erection is behind so many male sexual problems that it is important to remind them that it is more common for them to have a flaccid than an erect penis. Men are just not comfortable enough with the waxing and waning of their arousal, which is always reflected in the strength of the erection. They need to match their expectations with their physiology.

Both men and women can benefit by allowing themselves to experience those sexual behaviors that previously might have been terrifying. By accepting your feelings, and using them as your foundation, you don't accept sexual mediocrity; instead, you merely become sexually self-accepting, which is the only real and reassuring prerequisite for further experimentation—if you wish!

What I have been describing is the treadmill paradox; the only way to experience what you think the treadmill will bring is by getting off! There is no way around it.

Ellen, thirty-seven, and Mike, forty, exemplify exactly what I'm talking about. Both were driven, high achievers, and caught on the sexuality treadmill. When I first saw them in treatment, they told me straightaway that they felt successful in everything but their sexual relationship. He was secretly anxious about losing erections, and she was so nervous about orgasms that she never had them. When they came to see me, they had read every book imaginable, and had all the right phrases. They were deeply in love and were quick to inform me they were highly motivated to remedy their problem. My first response was, "You're too motivated," adding, "You're treating sex as though it's like learning a new word-processing program." They appreciated this because both were executives in the software business. Disappointed at my initial response, they nonetheless plunged ahead.

I agreed to see them only if they did exactly what I suggested. They did, and I told them to do the following. Ellen was to have at least five lovemaking sessions where she only focused on pleasure without orgasm. Mike had to have at least five lovemaking sessions where he did not maintain an erection. Of course, you know what happened. He kept getting an erection, and she started having orgasms. But the answer is not merely about relaxation, it is about acceptance.

When they came back after this, they believed they were "cured." I told them they would be cured if they were off the treadmill, which meant he had to spend the rest of his life accepting his Forgotten Self, which included the shame of not getting erections. And Ellen had to accept the inevitability of sometimes not having orgasms. I warned them if they did not accept this part of themselves, they would be back at another therapist's office still on a treadmill, still questing after an illusory Perfect Self.

Feeling freer with sensory and sexual feelings is something that can only be done at your own pace and with an acceptance of your own imperfection. Don't allow yourself to be seduced by societal pressures. Allow sex to be an expression of pleasure and love, rather than burden it with false meanings about who you are and what your value is.

CHAPTER EIGHT

WAITING FOR LOVE:
THE SINGLES TREADMILL

Love kindled by virtue always kindles another, provided that its flame appear outwardly.
                    —Dante Alighieri, poet

Marty, a thirty-nine-year-old physician, is bright, warm, humorous, and reasonably attractive. Approaching forty, he is determined, like his bachelor buddies, to get married. He entered therapy to explore any blocks that may have prevented him from "connecting" and falling in love. One day he comes in, totally exasperated. The night before, he attended a singles function hoping to meet someone. "There was a talk by a psychologist discussing techniques to 'find the love you want.' One thing this psychologist suggested was that people smile and create eye contact. So afterward that's exactly what I did. I was friendly, tried to talk to a few different women, and nothing. Everyone applauds the lecturer, but afterward they walk around like they're trying to avoid each other. No one seemed friendly or receptive, yet meeting other people was their sole reason for going. What the hell is going on?"

As a psychologist who wrote a bestselling book on single life in the mid-eighties, I frequently lecture on dating behavior and the psychology of attraction. I have worked with hundreds of single men and women in psychotherapy and workshops, and I've talked with thousands more. One question keeps insinuating itself into our dialogues: "Why is it so difficult to find a mate now?"

It was easier. Years ago, both single and divorced people were markedly less cynical and frustrated than they are now. And their uncensored enthusiasm created stimulating encounters and allowed people to connect with an ease that seems to have vanished. Because a sexual revolution was taking place, one could argue these male-female connections were primarily fueled by libido, by hormonal forces. Regardless, as any psychologist will acknowledge, men and women were more trusting, less restrained, and wore less psychological armor than they do today. Being single also, for a time, carried a certain cachet.

Today, however, in this era of searching for life-affirming values and attempting to restore traditional, time-tested beliefs, remaining single isn't a choice but a reluctant and temporary state for most people. Living alone, or being in an uncommitted relationship, is eventually dissatisfying for most of us. Only a small number of men and women freely choose to stay unmarried. Some singles are confronting the possibility that they will remain single and are making the best of it and that's psychologically smart. After all, it's damaging for singles to regard life without a companion as a cursed sentence of loneliness and emotional isolation.

The urgent wish to marry is precisely one of the reasons it seems more difficult today. Combined with rigid, perfectionistic and idealistic dating criteria, singles face a real dilemma: the singles treadmill.

Most single men and women today are consumed by a desperate pursuit for the right mate, a quest fueled as much by anxiety and self-deception as anything else. The singles treadmill is not merely about searching, but doing so with an intensity that breeds self-deception and inevitable unhappiness—the bitter fruits of any treadmill.

The singles treadmill, like all other treadmills, is fueled by misperceptions and erroneous beliefs. Those caught on the singles treadmill believe that a "perfect mate" will solve their problems of self-worth. We all begin with a composite picture of who we would like to marry. But as we continue to look, constantly more convinced that our elusive future mate will rescue us from diminished self-worth, we create more anxiety for ourselves, and consequently become even more selective. At this point, we are driven by the quest for a Perfect Self and our search becomes a self-defeating singles treadmill. The more rigid our standards, the more likely we are to create an atmosphere where the opposite sex feels guarded, wary, and resentful. We come up empty not just because we are too perfectionistic, but because that very perfectionism creates a negative experience with the person on the other end of our microscope! Frustrated and fueled now by our acute awareness of an Imperfect Self, we are irretrievably caught on the treadmill.

What happened to our simple wish for a loving spouse? How have we developed such increasingly sophisticated and complex criteria for identifying the right person?

Eleanor, a thirty-four-year-old account executive with her own ad agency, is caught in this dilemma. "Look, I've dated so many guys, I'll be damned if I'm going to settle now for the kind of man I've rejected so many times over the years." She then goes on to acknowledge, "I know this sounds kind of shallow, but I couldn't face my friends if I ended up marrying someone like the guy I'm dating now."

Eleanor is neither stupid nor superficial in her values and attitudes, but she is desperate and increasingly saddened by her diminishing marriage prospects. Eleanor is on the singles treadmill. She fears "settling," although she is hard pressed to explain what that means. Her ideal man is difficult to find. He's financially successful, reasonably attractive, and definitely stylish. He's "evolved," which means he's not a macho throwback to the old days before women's liberation. And he is sensitive, meaning he is at least aware of the psychological context of a relationship—in other words, he can talk about his feelings and he's aware that she has feelings, too. Eleanor is aware that few men fit this description, but she plaintively insists her goal is not to find Prince Charming. Her hypothetical mate is out there, she's seen and heard about him. Unfortunately, Eleanor is unaware of the impact of her behavior on men.

Edward is a successful thirty-eight-year-old physician who immodestly regards himself as quite enlightened. So how come he hasn't found Ms. Right? Let's examine his shopping list. The ideal woman is attractive, slim, bright, educated, and a lively enough dancer on the floor of contemporary psychology that she wants children and family and yet is willing to go back to work as quickly as the pocketbook demands. Like Eleanor, he knows he's selective, but insists, "They exist, I've seen plenty of them out there."

"They look as though they're out there," I answer, "but they've got other qualities, some of which seem to turn you off."

Edward and Eleanor have the same problem. On the singles treadmill, they are not just overly selective, but so desperately searching for someone that they are less likely to find the mate they want. Why? Because the treadmill itself drives them to succeed at making a successful catch, and fast, so that what is important and what they need, as opposed to what they think they want, is obscured. The more they search, the more self-deception colors what they see—both in the opposite sex and in their own behavior.

Those on the singles treadmill don't allow themselves to naturally fall in love, in the inexplicable ways we often will. Instead, they view each potential encounter as an interview with what would be their perfect or ideal love. Engaged in a search that has little to do with genuine, spontaneous human contact, the already-desperate single grows more confused and less able to interpret these unexpected feelings.

THE QUEST FOR PERFECTION

The cruel irony of the singles treadmill is that it keeps us away from the very experiences and people we need, while we desperately pursue what we think we want. As a result we don't really search for a person, we search for experiential states, qualities, or moments that make us feel complete, or at least elevate our mundane lives. Instead of thinking sensibly, we search for sensations. Our pursuit of love is more about self-enhancement than about finding someone to love, who in turn will love us for who we really are.

Single men and women often insist that their standards are reflections of what they hunger for in a spouse. Their prefabricated ideal mate is composed of mandatory traits, attributes, and personality characteristics that are prerequisites for everlasting love. Love isn't this calculable. When we look for a mate with this type of agenda, we become less focused on others and more on ourselves. There are reasons why we demand certain things of others, and these reasons have to do with our own self-loathing. We want out mate to embody the things we fear we're not.

Our Three Secret Wishes

As we grow up we carry with us three secret wishes that eventually coalesce into romantic yearnings. First, we wish for a sense of union not unlike the primitive bonded state we experienced in the womb. This sense of oneness, poignantly expressed by our great poets, is something we all hope will transpire from finding our loved one. We believe that we will never be alone again.

Second, we wish for validation. We all hope for unconditional love and want our parents to make us feel special and worthy. Most of us were validated in varying degrees, but many were not. And our yearning for the perfect mate is partly driven by the fantasy that they will finally validate us with the stamp of worthiness.

The third wish is to feel alive. As infants, we all experienced a soothing bliss, an overpowering sense of security. Even if we didn't get enough attention, we remember the rush of having our parents pay attention to us. It made us feel alive with excitement, love, and safety. And later on we try to resuscitate those vital feelings.

But we are all separate beings, no matter how married or bonded. At times we will feel alone, sad, and estranged. In a good relationship, these feelings do not last long. But men and women who insist on large doses of feeling stimulated and alive cannot tolerate their absence for too long. Because we lack the patience to endure the less-spectacular moments of our lives, we blame the person closest to us and often allow important relationships to go awry, for all the wrong reasons.

Powerful primitive wishes can push us onto the singles treadmill. And the more we insist on the rightness of these wishes and the condition that another person should fulfill them, the faster our desperate search becomes. When well-meaning friends suggest our judgment or perspective is off, we retort, "I'll know the 'right one' when she comes along."

A Mate as a Symbol

Today, more than ever, a mate is a measure of our value. Feelings of excitement that occur with the opposite sex are signals of what we're about to attain. An exciting man makes his woman feel excited. A sexy woman makes her man feel sexy too. The external partner becomes a sign, a confirmation of heretofore questionable worth. If I attract a wonderful partner, then I must be wonderful. Far more people regard a mate as an accessory than will admit it. They may not consciously see it that way, but too often the person they choose to love is also a symbol of success. A mate becomes more than a companion; she becomes a statement of who we are! Our great internal need for confirmation distorts both our expectations and the other person's actual qualities.

The more frail our ego, the more tenuous our grip on self-esteem and the more likely we are to look outside for a solution to painful inner feelings. For too many people today, the right mate is an external solution to lingering, lifelong, inner dilemmas. The cruel paradox, of course, is that the worse we feel about ourselves, the more likely we are to be caught on the singles treadmill. When we feel inferior to others, we try all the harder to make up for it. We never dare to broaden our standards, fearing accommodation will indict us.

Like all the treadmills, the faster we go, the worse we feel; the less we cherish our real selves, the more vicious the circle becomes. Single men and women make increasingly foolish choices as they become more desperate. The treadmill increases our misperceptions and confusions about the opposite sex, and it blocks our ability to create and foster real connections. The longer we're on the treadmill, the more we lose sight of who we are, and so we become false; and then ironically, the less attractive we are to the opposite sex.

The quest for perfection is a curse. The treadmill is caused by and exacerbates the fundamental and problematic denial of our real selves. Being overly selective isn't something to brag about. Yearning for feelings that you mistakenly believe are signs of love is ultimately foolish, because we are drawn to one another for complex nonsensical reasons. And we end up loving people for reasons that don't always fit. We can teach ourselves to react excitedly when someone meets our predetermined criteria, but we can't teach ourselves to be open to the unexpected, which may be what we need.

"I guess I'm like a junky," exclaims a female producer. "Everytime I meet a guy, who I secretly know is probably rotten in some way or another, I still get hooked on him. I still want to see if I can get him. I know he's the wrong kind of man for me, but I keep hoping this time it'll turn out differently."

The self-deception in this statement is evident. Initially she doesn't know that he is rotten or the wrong kind of man. That is in hindsight, when she is looking for someone to blame. All she knows is that she doesn't have a good track record, but she doesn't change her expectations or take responsibility for her failed relationships. She comes away from one failure having learned nothing and just takes another shot at the unattainable, elusive, and perhaps even the nonexistent she yearns for.

Today, a mate is not just a lifelong companion, but is a willing or sometimes unwitting accomplice to our quest for an enhanced lifestyle, one that will prove our worth and value, especially in the eyes of others.

For example, the appearance treadmill and singles treadmill sometimes merge. Women speak coldly and dispassionately about men as if they're evaluating a job offer. They discuss his lifestyle—his income level, his business prospects, how well he dresses, what kind of car he drives. It doesn't matter that these criteria don't necessarily add up to anything. We invest them with great significance. Men, who have always been picky about women's physical attributes, are more critical than ever. I've heard men dissect a woman's looks with the precision and lack of feeling of a coroner performing an autopsy. Like women, they are shopping for a commodity—although they think they are looking for a relationship.

Don't forget that it's the least confident and least self-assured among us who demand so much from our mates. Instead of being more tolerant of the opposite sex, the insecure person is a harsher critic. It's another signal of the self-defeating treadmill mentality.

Patricia is a successful thirty-eight-year-old woman in the fashion business. Although she dates a great deal, she keeps picking the "wrong" men and this frustration has brought her into therapy. She's puzzled because she doesn't see herself as someone who is drawn to slick guys or "rats." She is solidly rooted in most areas of her life and she wants a man with a background similar to hers. She comes from a close, moral family that is prominent in the community. She wants a man who can fit into her world. But her relationships never work out.

Patricia is on the singles treadmill. She dates men from affluent families who are seemingly drawn to traditional values and who appear to reflect her tastes—stylish, cultured, drawn to the arts and community activities. But she never looks deep enough to see what they are really like. At first she hated to admit her mistakes, but her emphasis on surface indicators such as lifestyle, rather than substance, was leading her astray. "You're too enamored of their seeming promise rather than what's actually delivered," I told her. Time and again, she describes men who are aloof and ungiving, but she keeps thinking there's something wonderful beneath the facade. She confuses their inability to make commitments or their lack of soul with their highly esteemed status. "You think if someone's really worthwhile, you have to work harder at winning them," I suggested, knowing that she took the concept of no pain, no gain to heart. One of the illusions behind the foolish choices of single men and women is this belief that if something is too easy, it can't be worth that much. Why not give ourselves a break? Life is hard enough ... so why deny the ease of a relationship when it comes?

"Style" is so emphasized today that it's easy to confuse it with substance. Patricia spent one year with a well-known attorney who was so cold, detached, and caught up in the appearance of things that he had nothing to give her. In her heart she knew he was emotionally impoverished, but she kept waiting and hoping that any man who was so charitable and philanthropic toward others, must have a heart for her, which would awaken someday. But it never happened.

Patricia finally got tired of waiting. She came to understand the tension between the Perfect Self she sought and a growing, semiconscious sense of her Imperfect Self. Grudgingly at first, she allowed herself to entertain the notion of letting go of her lofty criteria. At the same time she mourned the loss of this Perfect Self, she embraced the notion of broadening the range of attributes in a man that she could learn to value. This was not easy for her because her family had always supported her selectivity. She turned to friends for support and got it. It was almost as though she had to ask for permission to "settle," although in her heart she knew she was going in the right direction. Stopping the search for perfection opened her eyes to qualities in men that she had overlooked—a sense of humor, a desire for family orientation, and genuine day-to-day companionship.

Malcolm is a businessman who has reached the age of forty without getting married and he's scared to death. This fear has brought him into therapy. He knows something is wrong; he knows he is getting nowhere as a single man. He has dated hundreds of women without really connecting for too long. He represents the "homely-but-highly-successful-man syndrome." Perhaps this sounds harsh but it is a real phenomenon, leaving these men on the singles treadmill. Feeling unattractive as teenagers, or when they were in college, they became doctors, lawyers, and successful businessmen. When they look for a mate, they desperately look for a beautiful woman who they fantasize will make them feel attractive. The woman must be perfect, as one man described, "slim, willowy, chiseled features, maybe a Grace Kelly type, though not as heavy." I duly noted these requirements, gently offering that a life mate and a piece of Baccarat crystal are two entirely different things.

Over the course of a year of therapy, I listened to scores of dissections of the anatomical deficits of various dates. I suggested to Malcolm that his wish for perfection was an attempt to mask or eliminate what he saw as his own imperfections. And if he chose to deal with himself first, with his Imperfect Self, he might discover enough latitude in his choice of women to allow him to find someone to love. Thankfully, he broadened his attitudes enough to shed the Hollywood syndrome of dating beautiful would-be starlets that make wonderful arm pieces, but for whom he ultimately had intellectual disdain.

As Malcolm came to accept himself, he began to see women as people, companions, friends, and not as physical objects to bolster his sagging self-esteem. As with any treadmill, getting off is difficult at first. Malcolm had to confront secret anxieties such as worrying about the way he would be perceived when he walked into parties or restaurants with women that were not especially beautiful. He discovered the more he reclaimed a Forgotten Self and embraced the fact that he was an accomplished and respected businessman, the less he needed to accessorize himself with beautiful women. In time, he admitted the task was easier because he felt more relaxed and less anxious. "I never realized how much I worked at getting social approval."

Both Malcolm and Patricia got off the singles treadmill tentatively at first and then eventually wholeheartedly by entertaining new criteria in their search for a mate. They found themselves wanting to know more about people that didn't fit into their preconceived categories. They began using all of their senses, rather than just their eyes; and they began to use their hearts, putting away their cold ledgers. They began to ask themselves, "Do I have a good time with this person? Do they care about me? Can I share my deeper fears and anxieties as well as my triumphs with them? Can I trust them? Can we be gentle and tender lovers as well as pals? Do I really know them, and do they really know me?" They each lost their self-conscious preoccupation with the status of relationships. In other words, they began looking for a mate as a companion rather than a solution to problems of self-worth.

THE PSYCHOLOGY OF ATTRACTION

Something is troubling singles, although they can barely put their finger on it. I hear it every day, from single patients who come in and relate the week's activities—too often a litany of missed opportunities or frustrating encounters. Their constant complaint is that they fail to find "chemistry" anymore—that excitement and recognition that awakens the hope they've finally found the person they've been looking for.

When I ask people to describe chemistry, they typically say, "You know it when you feel it." My response is, "Well that's not very helpful. I wonder if you can elaborate or describe the last time that happened?"

Sometimes a patient can tell me the clues that point to chemistry. "We both had a great time. We even talked about how easy it was to be with each other, as though we had known each other for ages." When I hear that, I know there was indeed some chemistry, for by definition, *chemistry* is a mutual uncensored expressiveness—a reciprocal receiving and sending of messages that create positive feelings and begin stimulating fantasies and hopes of possibility.

But as I indicated, most people don't experience much chemistry anymore. Rarely do I hear, "It's like we've known each other forever" or "We kept talking and before we knew it, hours had gone by" or "Every time she calls we're on the phone for hours." Each of these responses is an indicator of chemistry, the rather immediate and spontaneous blending of hopes, desires, values, and interests. The experience not only feels wonderful, but is an indicator of real compatibility, and it is the single best predictor of successful male-female bonding.

Now for the bad news. The more men and women get caught on the singles treadmill and desperately pursue the love they are yearning for, the less likely they will experience chemistry!

First of all, we talk a lot about chemistry, but don't understand it. Most people think chemistry is like falling in love, that it's something that happens to you. If chemistry is inexplicable and magical, we have no control over creating it, right? Wrong. This perception is patently false! Chemistry is not beyond our control. Nor is it about mere looks or personality. Nor is it about acting in a calculated way to impress someone. Chemistry is something you create by allowing it to happen. It will either happen or it won't. If you are desperate in your search for chemistry, you will be less likely to experience it! This cruel paradox has many specific explanations.

In its most abstract sense, chemistry is the result of the amount of personal information you share with someone. It's about psychic energy at the most basic level, and energy communicates information. Those who frequently experience chemistry have a simple secret. Chemistry doesn't ignite because someone is outrageously sexy or good-looking, instead it's the result of how open and expressive she is. Let me quickly add, by "openness" I don't mean she quickly and indiscriminately shares her innermost thoughts and concerns about her life. What I mean is an uncensored expression of whoever she is at that moment—silly, arrogant, sensitive, humorous, intellectually lively, whatever. People spark chemistry by allowing themselves to be more alive and expressive.

The freer and more spontaneous we can be, even about our fears and anxieties, the more likely we are to have an impact on others. When we can "just be ourselves," we are typically most attractive. It is our real selves that touch people, that move them to reveal themselves to us. Uncensored and unrehearsed expression carries the message, "It's okay to be yourself, I'm not nearly as judgmental as you feared." You create a contagious sanction for expressiveness.

Ultimately, one way of getting off the singles treadmill is allowing the real you to emerge. This means reclaiming the

Forgotten Self that you've abandoned, obscured by desperate quests. Unburdened of self-denial, you create a forum for discovering the love you deserve.

CHEMISTRY AND THE FORGOTTEN SELF

One reason why chemistry is scarce these days is that we were periodically brainwashed by the media to embrace the notion that men and women should be similar. This wish for androgyny almost came true, and we're still paying the price for that naive and simplistic notion. While men and women are similar in numerous ways, we are also very different, and these differences create attraction and connection.

In my experience as a psychologist, I find many men and women, desperate for love, have lost a grasp of their sexuality. Men and women are not grounded sexually. Yes, in the past it was valuable for men to begin exploring their more "feminine traits," such as their feelings and their emotional expressiveness, and it was certainly important for women to reclaim their long-denied "masculine traits," such as their wish for mastery and assertiveness. Unfortunately, however, what it now means to be masculine or feminine is rather unclear.

We've blurred gender differences so radically we have lost sight of some fundamental, even instinctual, energies. We became so fearful of looking at the opposite sex as objects that we've become neutered lovers. Hence, chemistry is nearly extinct. Despite rhetoric, it's no sin to regard the opposite sex as an intriguing sexual being, in addition to their more important and universal human qualities. If men felt more masculine and women more feminine, then perhaps we wouldn't be so deeply caught in our present dilemma of diluted attractions.

When I work with single men and women who rarely if ever report feeling chemistry with the opposite sex, I begin by helping them explore their own conceptions of sex role identity. One of the first questions I ask is how they feel about their sexual identity, when they feel "manly" or "masculine" or "womanly" or "feminine." I ask them to think back to situations when they felt their masculinity and their feminity and then to understand the context that gave rise to it. Fortunately, as I inquire, my patients rarely revert to stereotypes, and their answers often surprise me.

A man may feel masculine when he is being tender and gentle, say with a child. The moment fills him with a sense of inner strength and self-assuredness. A woman may feel feminine when she is skillfully leading a corporate team to a decision, and senses her intuitive and nurturing power.

I have found, however, that singles, caught on their treadmill and brainwashed by trendy notions, don't ask themselves about masculine or feminine experiences. Their attention is focused outside of their own experience and they have lost touch with these basic feelings.

I see single men and women facing dead-end situations because they don't express who they are, sexually or otherwise. Chemistry happens when people are being themselves, not when they are performing. The performer is left with the performance. The free and uncensored individual often finds that in her presence, others become freer and less censored.

Often someone will ask, "How can I be myself when I feel so nervous on a date?" The answer is to be open enough to let that nervousness come out in a light way. Everyone's nervous, whether she admits it or not. When the person we're with reveals her feelings, we often relax and are drawn toward her! When I suggested this to a male patient, he totally rejected the idea. "Sure, you're telling me to show how uptight I am, when every woman I know wants a confident, take-charge kinda guy."

I responded, "If a man really accepts his own very understandable and commonplace nervousness on a date, and he mentions this, the nervousness becomes minor and his self-acceptance comes across as strength. Just try it out."

It was difficult for him to get beyond the notion that he had to perform in a certain way because women expected him to do so. In time, he took the chance to be more of himself, and as I expected, he found that consciously choosing to be more real communicated self-assuredness rather than the weakness he feared.

Another self-deception fostered by the treadmill is the conviction of many single men and women that they rarely experience chemistry because their tastes are so refined. With this attitude their judging stance comes through and they are not open and expressive in a way that tells the other person, "Come on, we can relax and be honest with each other." The other person feels judged and closes down. The singles treadmill makes us anxious, picky, bitter, distrustful, and highly judgmental. And it is this very behavior that kills spontaneity. The irony is evident: When two people with high standards meet, they both feel judged and guarded. They feel alone in their superiority, and disappointed in the other person.

I had a patient who exemplified the power of self-acceptance. She was in her early forties, aggressive and bright. She was outgoing and vivacious, and felt comfortable with men. In time, most men perceived her as attractive, but certainly not in any conventional sense of that word. She had long ago decided that no matter who she was, it was good enough. She wouldn't perform or play games. She would conduct herself with men in the same way she acted with close women friends. Nothing was edited, and nothing was molded or shaped to curry favor with the opposite sex. And men loved her. They gravitated to her because they felt so free in her presence. She would laugh at the old canard that men don't like strong or bright women, for she was that in spades. She wanted to find a husband, but she wasn't desperate. She knew, in time, the person for her would come along. And she experienced chemistry, frequently! Her ability to be herself was a plus and she knew it. Whenever I spoke with her, I always thought, "If only others could learn from her." Her secret wasn't magic, her secret was feeling good about who she really was.

GETTING OFF THE TREADMILL

The primary danger of the singles treadmill is that as you become more anxious, disillusioned, and more certain that the right mate is as elusive as ever, you end up with totally self-defeating feelings and attitudes. Instead of creating an open and receptive attitude, you become cynical and suspicious. Old disappointments create scars others perceive as bitterness and anger. Old hurts manifest greater guardedness and mistrustfulness. Sadly, these negative feelings impel you to close off the possibility of experiencing the chemistry you have been looking for.

As I indicated earlier, chemistry happens when you exude a maximum amount of information and energy for the opposite sex. The more you learn to do this, the more likely that you will experience a meshing of mutual and complementary wishes, hopes, and dreams with another person. But when we are defensive, bitter, and overly cautious, we face negative reverberations. It doesn't matter how justified your negative feelings may be, the treadmill is still self-defeating. The hurt, disappointment, and withdrawal starts a downward spiral, and bitterness leads to rejection, which in turn leads to more bitterness. People on treadmills become their own worst enemies, yet they fail to see how they perform an active role in their own disappointments.

Desperate searching invariably leads to psychological fatigue and a growing feeling of resignation. Shelly is forty-three, divorced and has a twelve-year-old daughter. "I can't stand going to all the different functions I go to," she says, "all I do is stand around with my friends, one eye on them, one eye scanning the room. And all I do is come up empty. Most of the guys I meet are jerks—either they're too young and there's no future with them, or they're these bachelor-type guys who are so rigid and arrogant they make me sick. I'm tired of looking, and I'm tired of getting disappointed. A lot of my friends feel the same way. In fact, a lot of them are deciding to stop looking and resign themselves to never getting married. In a way, they feel a lot better than I do. They're starting to live their life instead of just keeping it on hold."

I felt sympathy for Shelly, who seemed unusually sad as she talked. Instead of trying to give her a pep talk, I agreed that maybe she needed to accept the fact that she might not get married again and begin living life instead of riding the singles treadmill. This attitude was a temporary device that freed her from crushing expectations and ultimately led to her meeting someone when she least expected it.

When it comes to finding a mate, the old saying A watched pot never boils is surprisingly appropriate. Sometimes, I do advocate singles becoming aggressive and goal oriented in their search for a mate. Looking for a mate is in part a numbers game, a networking phenomenon—the more exposure you have, the more contacts you have, the more likely it is that you will meet someone. However, and this is critical, this strategy only works when it's underscored by a solid plateau of self-acceptance. For example, until she found a plateau of self-acceptance, Shelly would attend events and parties or join organizations, only with the intention of finding someone. Even when she went with friends, an underlying desperation always accompanied her and kept her from connecting with anyone. When she let go of her frenzied search and started enjoying herself, her odds went up. Men and women who are able to accept the fact they may not find someone may be surprised when love finds them.

Seemingly not looking, or engaging in desperate pursuits to get off the treadmill, can amount to merely a kind of disguised passivity. But the singles treadmill is not only a physical manifestation of frenetic searching, it is ultimately a mental dilemma. Men and women who opt to not search for a mate are often still crazed with obsessional thoughts about love and marriage. Their dreams are filled with such imagery, although they may feel fully invested in other activities and interests. But you are on the treadmill whenever you find yourself ruminating excessively about your plight, and I'm referring to daily and hourly obsessions. Such ruminations are typically based on the notion that without a mate you are less than others, your self is diminished, or you are not a success in life because you don't have a loved one. You must free yourself from the treadmill's internal trappings, as well as curtail your frenetic activities.

Both pessimisim and passivity are self-defeating. Pessimism keeps us focused on the losers and jerks we keep meeting, allowing us to shirk responsibility for helping generate our own disappointments. Passivity, or withdrawal, can give us temporary relief from our pain, although it doesn't get rid of the causes of that pain.

We can always find a hundred good reasons to justify our pessimism and passivity, but ultimately we have to let go of both if we want to get off the treadmill. You begin by building a plateau of self-acceptance. This doesn't mean resigning yourself to a life without a loving and committed companion. It does mean that you see yourself as a source of comfort and well-being, that you live as much as you can in the moment. I am always surprised at how self-sufficient and contented single men and women can be when they allow themselves to enjoy the present rather than always looking toward the future. As you find a plateau of acceptance, and your pessimism fades, you will probably see and discover valuable people out there, because you don't desperately need them.

DISCOVERING YOUR PLATEAU

Whenever single men and women ask me about the secrets of success in finding a mate, I typically answer, "I'm going to tell you the answer, but it's nothing surprising. Just learn to accept and be yourself and then allow that person and that self-acceptance to be made public." It sounds so simple and yet for so many of us, it's difficult. "Suppose I don't like myself," is a typical response. "Well," I answer, "start working on that. Nobody who's fake, or guarded, or overly concealed is going to have an impact."

Getting off the treadmill requires that you first find a plateau of self-love and self-understanding. There's no way around that. And for singles, the plateau involves not only the acceptance of yourself, but searching your mind for those attitudes and beliefs that helped put you on the treadmill in the first place. In preceding chapters I have dealt with some necessary tasks to help you discover the real you. Now I will focus on some of the attitudes and beliefs that get us on the singles treadmill and some of the truths we need to accept to get off that treadmill.

Some Sobering Truths

Most men and women are bedeviled by false beliefs about what it takes to find someone to love. These brief thoughts may help you open your mind to new possibilities.

1. There are no perfect men or women. Yes, this may come as a surprise if you've watched too many television commercials depicting wonderful men and women having a fabulous time. Perfect people don't exist. Everyone has flaws, just as you do, and you had better learn to accept the imperfection in others. Doing so will help you accept it in yourself.

2. Excitement is not necessarily the same as feeling chemistry. Foolish choices are often triggered by excitement, which often disguise anxiety and apprehension. Too many singles pursue an elusive and unattainable mate because they unconsciously believe that capturing such a prize will bolster their own self-esteem. Their excitement is rooted in self-deception.

3. Don't turn your quest for a mate into a rehabilitation project. Adults don't change very much. For better or worse is a realistic motto for a relationship, whereas trying to reform or rehabilitate a potential mate is a job for a therapist, not a lover.

4. What you see is rarely what you get! First impressions and appearances can tell a great deal, but not necessarily what you think they do. You begin to know another person when you look below the surface. Today, especially, we often confuse style with substance. Some people look as if they have it all from the outside, but offer us little; others disarm us with seemingly hidden attributes. It takes time to know someone. It's worth taking that time. Hasty judgments usually tell us more about ourselves than others.

5. Having fewer expectations allows for more surprise and adventure. The singles treadmill causes us to approach the opposite sex with so many preconceptions that we leave no room for unpredictability. Fearful or grandiose expectations create a small, self-contained world, openness allows for infinite possibilities.

6. Finding someone takes initiative. Once you feel you have a foundation or plateau of self-acceptance, you must aggressively reach out to the social world around you. Nobody's going to just knock on your door. And if they do, having left it all in the hands of fate, you'll probably be in the backyard.

Purging Yourself of Negative Attitudes

As well as accepting positive ideas, you need to purge yourself of various negative attitudes.

1. "I don't want to lose my pride." This usually means false pride, a cover for fear, the fear of dating someone new, or the fear of testing our perceptions of ourselves. Too many singles still think life is like high school, where somehow you're either popular and things come easy, or you have to work at relationships, which means you're unpopular. You must let go of superficial self-labeling. Remember, one deadly cause of the singles treadmill is the basic belief that a mate is a symbol of your personal success. If you embrace this idea, you will spend your time posturing and performing, never allowing your pride to be wounded.

2. "Nobody's out there." This is not a statement of fact, but attitude. Remember, most singles create their own dating experience. When they believe prospects are meager, they in effect get meager returns. Because their attitude is cynical and pessimistic, they fail to bring out any real positive qualities in their partner, reducing her to the impoverished level of their expectations.

3. "I'm angry at men/women." As I've indicated, this is a principal block to chemistry. No matter how much you've been hurt, or how justified your anger might be, anger pushes people away. Anger breeds anger, and rejection invites rejection.

Risking Revealing Yourself

Beyond accepting truths and freeing yourself from negative attitudes, try this experiment. Start breaking old patterns by showing others more of yourself and by revealing aspects of your personality that are only selectively shown, if even that.

A patient of mine, a young woman age thirty-two, had an absolutely hilarious self-effacing sense of humor about the single life, even when she felt sad or pessimistic. One day I asked whether she acted that way with men. She responded, "Oh no, I only do that with you and my women friends. I don't think men like that sort of thing, you know, it's not very sexy or confident sounding." I was shocked that she kept under wraps what was probably her most attractive attribute, one that many men would find absolutely charming and delightful. I finally understood why she was having so much trouble meeting interesting men.

Many of us keep hidden our playful, humorous, even silly behaviors—the very qualities that our best friends may cherish in us—from the people we meet. Sometimes, risking can mean showing more of your intellect or discussing ideas that arouse your passion and conviction, ignoring fears that you won't be liked. It's so odd to hear single men and women try to come across in as sophisticated a way as possible, not realizing that posing or performing is the quickest way to become a bore.

Stop worrying about rejection and humiliation. We all fear rejection, but the fear is usually more paralyzing than rejection itself. And if this fear causes you to suppress your most colorful traits, you wouldn't want to be with that rejecting or disinterested person anyhow. What draws us to others are qualities that are uninhibited. Notice why you are drawn to certain friends or even television personalities. You will find that you are attracted to individuals who don't censor themselves and take chances with personal disclosure. Don't label this a kind of unattainable charisma. Everyone, without exception, who is given a comfortable environment has a uniqueness about her that can be expressed. The problem is that too many of us wait for the secure atmosphere to magically materialize. It doesn't. It happens after you take risks, not before. Cast away incesssant worries about what others will think of you. You will become overly cautious and unavailable to others. Set aside the pretenses you have created and risk revealing yourself. Not everyone will like the real you, and yes, sometimes you will be rejected. But when you do connect with someone it will be based on your true self, which leads to that connection.

CHAPTER NINE

CHANGING YOUR MATE: THE MARRIAGE TREADMILL

Love is union with somebody, or something, outside oneself, under the condition of retaining the separateness and integrity of one's own self.
                    —Erich Fromm, philosopher

Because I have worked extensively with couples, I am repeatedly asked if I know of any happy marriages. My answer is always resounding. "Yes!" I know scores of them, even though some might not appear to be happy on the outside, deep down they really are. Too often we only see conflicts and neglect to see deeper levels of commitment and companionship.

Even after working with hundreds of couples, I am still amazed at the varying bonds that emerge between men and women, and I am no longer arrogant enough to presume to know who should be with whom. The couple that appears to always be in conflict may have a better marriage than the couple that seems happy on the surface. It frustrates me that real contentment is elusive for so many couples. They haven't necessarily chosen the wrong mates, rather they have blindly embraced the wrong beliefs—wishes and expectations that, left unexamined, create a marriage treadmill.

In my work, I have identified this treadmill as an overriding reason for marital disillusionment and grief. The unrelenting need to change our spouse into someone different is a disguised way of solving personal unhappiness. The other side of this compulsion is the exaggerated expectations that society has encouraged us to have about marriage.

The marriage treadmill emerges from a set of unrealistic expectations about what marriage should do for us, many which we seldom acknowledge. For example, we expect marriage to complete us, or give us self-esteem. When exaggerated promises or unacknowledged needs are unmet in the marriage, a vacuum of discontent drives us to demand even more of our marriage. Increased disappointment leads to increased demands, and we are firmly on the treadmill, again, going nowhere fast.

Take Bernard and Carol, two intelligent, aware people, married for thirteen years. They came to me after therapy with two other marriage counselors had failed to help them enhance the harmony in their relationship. Bernard sees Carol as sexually cold and unyielding. "I'm always the one initiating sex, and more often than not, she refuses. It's reached the point where I know she is going to bed earlier and earlier just to avoid me."

While Bernard tells his side of the story, Carol smolders, arms folded. It's obvious she's annoyed with his characterization of her feelings. When I ask her to respond to Bernard, she tells me she's tired of his demands and doesn't feel close enough to him to respond. Moreover, she adamantly denies there's anything wrong with her sexually and asserts that he's the one who is shut off emotionally. She goes on to describe how for years she's tried to get him to be more open with his feelings, to share himself with her. I can tell after our initial session that Bernard and Carol are at a stalemate, common to couples seeking help. They have gone round and round in their fighting, with no resolution in sight.

In later sessions, I discover that in spite of the issues that brought them in, they still enjoy their children together, they have good friends, and they still find time to laugh together. So what's gone wrong? Here are two people, once very much in love, now they find their marriage derailed, and the idea of divorce is being thrown around, although usually in anger.

Each of them feels justified, even self-righteous about his claims: Bernard, because the one who desires sex is naturally the healthier one; Carol, because the person who champions openness is obviously more emotionally aware. But the reality that unfolded, as we probed deeper, told a different story. Bernard had a rather cold unemotional mother and, unfortunately, his first wife was also this way. He is especially needy and emotionally hungry. He deceives himself about his sexual demands because they are really not about sex at all, rather they are about wanting to feel close, about having contact with Carol that will ease his inner loneliness. Bernard, like many men, has no close friends, and he has learned to express his inner needs only in the realm of sexuality.

Carol is a bright woman who never allowed herself to work, to seek out other experiences that would make her feel better and more confident about herself. It turns out that most of her requests for openness from Bernard are directed solely to get him to vocalize his feelings for her. There's nothing wrong with that, but unfortunately, she expected Bernard exclusively to validate her.

In time, each could see they were each looking exclusively to the other for a solution to their own individual problems. Their personal dilemmas became disguised as marital problems. They were unaware they were on a marriage treadmill—making themselves miserable, estranging one another, and inevitably depriving themselves of the love and contact they both deeply desired. They needed to slow down, stand back, and look at their own behavior.

Instead, in this cycle of expectation and disappointment, wives and husbands focus on improving their mates, or changing the way their mate responds to them, wholeheartedly convinced that succeeding will improve their marriage and give them what they want.

Parallel to having a Perfect Self, many people believe they can have a Perfect Marriage. And society offers them myriad images of what such a marriage would be like, if only they could get their partner to shape up. The Perfect Self and the Perfect Marriage go hand in hand, both externally defined, both a mirage.

Just as we must reject the Imperfect Self, we must also reject our obsession with the imperfection in our marriages. We must not allow ourselves to narrowly focus on what's wrong with the marriage and neglect celebrating what is right with it. The quest to improve the marriage too often makes it worse.

A genuine solution to this dilemma is trying exactly the opposite of what we are doing, but the treadmill process keeps us from acknowledging what is good about ourselves and our marriage. Like the Forgotten Self, in the drive to improve our marriage, we create a Forgotten Marriage—which holds those positive, loving, and complementary qualities that brought us together in the first place. In the face of perfection, that which is good is no longer good enough and is too quickly forgotten.

The marriage treadmill skews everything. Part of getting off the treadmill is refocusing. Wives and husbands need to reclaim the self that gets lost in the process of focusing on the other partner. And they need to relieve their mates, themselves, and their marriages of the unrealistic expectations that suffocate them. This frees their mates to love them the way they wanted to in the first place. With the marriage treadmill, as with other treadmills, the paradox of change is the same; by getting off, you may actually find what you were looking for when you got on.

But most couples don't understand this and expend much energy and frustration doing everything to make things "right." Carol read all the relevant books available. She talked to her friends, who gave her their best advice: "Talk to him, let him know what you need, get him to communicate more." She did her best but it didn't work.

Sadly, men and women get on the marriage treadmill not because they're selfish, or unloving, but because the preferred path to marital fulfillment has been wildly distorted in recent years. Mistaken beliefs encourage us to get on the marriage treadmill, buttressed and exacerbated by society's exhortations that we should make our marriage terrific, or super. The treadmill is sustained by the unceasing demands that are made on our mate and on marriage itself, all too often in the name of psychological growth.

Essentially, the marriage treadmill is based on the self-deception that your mate is the solution to your unhappiness. You believe he should allow you to change him so you can feel better. Like all treadmills, it is based on the denial of both the good and the self-defeating parts of our real selves. This denial makes us feel worse about ourselves, and we become more demanding as we look to our mate as the solution. And as you go faster on the marriage treadmill, your mate feels more attacked, gives less and less. As a result, you feel worse and become even more demanding and resentful. As with all treadmills, your marriage goes nowhere fast—you want the best but you end up with precious little!

Like other treadmills, the solution to your problems is to stop getting in your own way, which is of course easier said than done. As you discover a plateau of self-acceptance, which includes an acceptance of your mate, you begin slowing your treadmill down, and then, surprisingly, you begin to receive returns that are more satisfying than your original expectations. You begin to get what you need rather than what you want. But none of these changes can happen until you uncover your self-deception.

But remember, if you are on the marriage treadmill, don't blame yourself entirely. Society's seductions have aided and abetted you. Most of what we want and expect has been shaped by forces outside of us, we have blindly absorbed these notions without questioning their validity or utility. When I work with couples, I first attempt to let them know they have been unknowingly programmed, no matter how bright or educated they are. We may intellectually know these myths—like many about finding contentment and peace of mind—are false, but unconsciously we're still prone to be seduced by the wish to have it all.

IN SEARCH OF A SUPER MARRIAGE

Our expectations of marriage have profoundly changed. In the past, marriage was viewed as a cooperative venture with adherence to traditional marriage vows. Mutual fulfillment and accommodation were taken for granted. But in recent years, we began to see marriage as a vehicle to meet our own needs, to complete and fulfill us. Our role models on television in the sixties were overidealized, simplistic, and conflict free. We expected Ozzie and Harriet. In the movies, romance never waned, and magazines offered a set of tactics for getting your mate to gratify you in the way you deserved. The realistic complexities of marriage were rarely portrayed.

Today, marriage is in vogue after twenty years of a rising divorce rate. Men and women want to get married and stay married because marriage still offers the best avenue to being loved, finding a lifelong companion, and creating a family. The bad news about marriage is that unmet expectations still lead to epidemic levels of disillusionment and disenchantment. For many, these darker feelings are not painful enough to cause divorce, and may not even be fully conscious, but quietly flow beneath the surface of many marriages like a polluted underground stream.

When men and women became preoccupied with self-realization and growth in the sixties and seventies, marriage was one of the first institutions that was scrutinized. Instead of asking, "What am I bringing to the marriage?" we coolly and dispassionately began to ask, "What am I getting out of it?" We became obsessed with trendy and superficial wants, rather than fundamental needs. And we wanted a lot! Slogans such as You do your thing and I'll do mine were in vogue. The concept of monogamy was up for renegotiation if you desired an open marriage. No aspect of bonding or marriage was considered sacred if it interfered with personal growth.

Because personal growth and actualization were viewed as positive and mandatory, it soon followed that each of us had the right, or obligation, to ensure our marriage was also growing. This meant we could demand that our mate grow or change as well. This next, and seemingly logical, step in "shoulds" set in motion a new kind of marriage, which still exists today—one based on looking to your mate as the source of happiness and the cause of your unhappiness. The irony in this is that personal growth became a way to escape personal responsibility.

Everything seemed crystal clear. If we were not fulfilled, it was our mate's fault, if we were not sexually aroused it was because they didn't turn us on, if we were not growing as individuals it was because our marriage was too prohibitive for us to blossom and thrive. The women's movement labeled marriage as a potential prison. In a variety of ways, wives and husbands became adversaries, focusing on demanding rather than giving, blaming rather than accepting.

A mandate to work on your marriage unwittingly became a code word for relentless attempts to get your husband or wife to change! The phrase *For better or worse* was seen as naive, as was its underlying presumption that good things happen when you start with acceptance rather than criticism.

As with so many of the ideas that came from this period, superlatives became commonplace. Instead of satisfying our peaceful psychological states, we focused on the "super" or "creative." The marriage treadmill evolved out of these new objectives, especially the fantasy that you could have a super marriage. Even after the rash of creative divorces in the sixties and seventies, when couples started thinking maybe they were better off staying married, they still held on to the pressured desire to make their relationships better. We were told we could have it all and that's exactly what we tried to force out of our spouses. We mistakenly learned that marital bliss was created out there with them, rather than inside with us.

Today, many of us are staying married, secretly unhappy with what we have. The sad cause of much of this unhappiness is the marriage treadmill and its impossible expectations. Because of it, couples foolishly and unnecessarily create their own disillusionment.

Having more in your marriage—what was offered as the solution to the depreciated marriage of the last two decades—has now become the problem! The marriage treadmill is now pushed tirelessly along, by couples who believe in a number of self-defeating myths that society endorses. Like other treadmills, this one starts out with good intentions. We all want to derive maximum fulfillment from all of our involvements. But when the desire to get more is motivated by the anxiety about having too little, we take false paths to solve our self-worth problems and get into deeper trouble. As we explore the beliefs that shape the marriage treadmill, be aware that the degree to which you embrace these beliefs is also a measure of how fast you are traveling on the treadmill.

THE TREADMILL:
WHY CHANGING YOUR MATE IS SELF-DEFEATING

What are the danger signs? If you find yourself obsessed with blaming your spouse, overanalyzing your mate, or exhausted from endless communication and negotiation, you are on the marriage treadmill. You have embraced values that society, the media, and psychology actively and regularly propagate. You think you're trying to make your marriage better, but in fact you are making it worse, and making yourself miserable in the process.

"But if my mate changed, I would feel better! Isn't marriage supposed to lead me to fulfillment?" These assumptions make us point to our mates as the solution to life's dilemmas. We think to ourselves, "if only" he were more loving, or richer, or sexier ... then I would be happier. That might be so, but attempts to remake your partner will more likely result in the opposite. When our partners sense we are disappointed in who they are, it strips them of the confidence necessary for allowing their positive qualities to glitter.

The forces that propel us into romantic connections—the wish for fusion, validation, a sense of aliveness—are present as emotional cravings in marriage. Childhood leaves us feeling incomplete, so we look to our marriage partner to become the solution to our problems of self-esteem. This overarching assumption about marriage mobilizes all the other self-defeating fantasies that characterize the marriage treadmill.

We have all grown up believing If you really loved me you would do your best to meet my needs. We believe that if our mate loves us he should change his personality for us. None of us may actually insist on a major personality change, but we're unaware that some of what we're asking for amounts to just that! Changing behavior is a lot easier in theory.

Those of us who conduct marital therapy often inadvertently play into this key element of the marriage treadmill—the desire to change your spouse. We counselors contribute to the folly by the ways in which we often conduct the first session. We turn to the husband or wife requesting, "Tell your mate what you need from him or her." We unwittingly set up the notion that fixing a marriage is about getting something from the other person—not to mention the fact that what we want from that person may be very different from what we really need from them to feel better. For example, we may request more communication when we really want more play. People have been taught that negotiation is essential in a good marriage—not realizing that they can negotiate tasks, and certain specific behaviors, but not a mate's personality. There are many facets of who we are that cannot and should not be negotiated.

Trying to change your spouse can make you crazy. You've all seen wives and husbands haranguing each other to the point where the targeted behavior becomes an obsession. I've worked with men and women who persist in trying to change their spouse and who assume when they fail that the continued presence of those irritating qualities is a sure sign their mate hates them. After all didn't you beg and plead for him to change? Doesn't he know how badly you need him to be different? If he loved you, surely he would alter himself for you, right? Isn't that what love is all about? Sorry, no, that's not what love is about. Love is not about meeting your husband's or wife's every need.

What I often find most self-defeating about married people's attempts to change their mate is that they're often terrified of the very differences that are directly connected to things they liked in their spouse. For example, a passive person marries a lively person and then ends up trying to make this lively partner more subdued! Or, a less responsible person marries someone who is stable and conscientious and then tries to get them to be more wild. In each case, the very qualities that attracted you become inextricably linked to what you're trying to change. The underlying reason for such behavior is that differences, especially in a marriage, are often scary. They become signals of potential instability or even abandonment. If our mate is different, maybe they won't like us or appreciate who we are.

A common example of this fear of differences occurs when women choose to break out of the housewife mold and opt for a career or new interests they feel passionate about. Typically, a husband feels some unease as his wife talks about going back to school or pursuing a career. Underlying his thinly disguised opposition or resistance is the fear that she might become bored with him, or even that she will meet another, more exciting man. Rather than confronting their anxieties head on, such men frequently find ways to sabotage their wives' new endeavor. Sadly, they fail to consider the possibility that differences can revitalize their marriage, rather than threaten it.

Opposites do attract. And that's not bad at all. Whenever I work with a new couple, I invariably tell them, early in the therapy, "Try to remember why you were attracted to your mate in the first place. Some of what you may be trying to change is irretrievably linked to many qualities you may love in the other person. After all, these very differences lend surprise, novelty, and intrigue to relationships."

THE PITFALLS OF CHANGE

Change is always more complicated than most of us imagine, especially in a marriage. Even when you are highly motivated to change, it's difficult to actually do so. Years have gone into building who we are, and more than anything it is scary to rearrange our parts. Annoying or aggravating qualities may be your mate's self-protective strategies for survival, a notion supported by the old adage What drives you crazy about another person is what keeps them sane. Besides, we are rarely manipulated into change. It's against our basic instincts to allow someone to change us, and we will do anything to defeat their efforts.

We all fall prey to a certain insensitivity in marriage. We don't understand the various psychological defenses our mates employ, we see only walls that keep us out. We fail to see these barriers are erected for self-protection, not to drive us crazy.

As I discussed earlier, change only follows when a foundation or plateau of acceptance—either by oneself or by one's mate—has been developed. In the absence of acceptance and caring, the request to change yourself can feel like an invitation to skydiving—you know you'll probably survive but you are substantially resistant to the idea.

Affirmation of ourselves must precede change, and we must affirm others if we wish them to change. The demand for change is experienced as rejection. If we pursue a Perfect Self or a Perfect Mate we end up denying who we are or who they are. And we suggest that everything is wrong, not that various features could benefit from a little work. When we affirm ourselves and our mates we start from strength, not weakness, in creating what we need.

I am convinced we need to reembrace the traditional promise For better or worse as the foundation or plateau that must exist for our marriages to thrive. Only when we feel another person loves and accepts us, can we take that great leap of faith and courage necessary to break old patterns.

COMMUNICATION: FUELING THE MARRIAGE TREADMILL

There is a great irony in the fact that the alleged cure-all for marital discord—communication—can propel people onto the marriage treadmill.

I would guess that one out of every two couples that comes into marital therapy declares, "We don't know how to communicate," an often erroneous diagnosis. When I ask what they'd like to talk about, I'm met with blank stares. Often they are really saying, "We don't have a whole lot to talk about anymore," but that's a difficult admission for most couples. Rather than face the fact that their interests and concerns may not be in sync, and that they have grown uncomfortably estranged, one of them seizes the initiative and blames the whole thing on the other person. The one who issues the complaint has the luxury of acting self-righteous, seemingly the more concerned and involved partner. The recipient of the "let's communicate more" request is, by default, labeled the sluggish and oppositional member of the pair. When they enter therapy, the more silent one is typically labeled the "problem" and the more outspoken advocate of communication is self-labeled "healthy." The truth, of course, is somewhere in the middle, which is something I try to make clear from the outset, so that they begin on a level playing field.

As almost anyone who works with couples today will acknowledge, *communication* is one of the most overused, even abused, words in the lexicon of relationship concepts. Communication is an all-inclusive solution to everything is a concept that has evolved out of the mandate that we be open with our feelings, because the more open we become, the more likely we are supposed to feel intimate with each other.

Openness has been another popular concept of the last two decades. It has become the mark of emotional honesty, a measure of the courage to be, and the ultimate risk in self-disclosure. I generally have no quarrels with this equation. The more honest men and women are with each other, the more likely they are to share their deeper feelings about what they find exciting, scary, or stimulating. The man who shares his anxiety about success and failure is more likely to feel close to, loving toward, and caring about the woman in his life. The woman who expresses anxiety over success and independence, or sadness due to a lack of passionate involvements, is much more likely to feel close to the man she loves.

Still, openness isn't always a loving gift to another person, and communication isn't always a milestone on the way to deepening intimacy. Actually, with increasing and dismaying frequency, communication is but a pretense, a disguised way of challenging a loved one to meet your needs. When it masks manipulation, communication is the primary fuel of the marriage treadmill.

Mere openness is not necessarily synonymous with intimacy. All too often, sharing what you feel becomes a form of complaining. Listen to what goes on in a typical marital therapy session. A wife says to her husband, "I feel cut off, lonely, like I could just as well be living alone." What does he hear? "I feel alone, emotionally neglected, and it's your fault." In this example, in the guise of openness, instead of telling her mate who she is, she is telling him about his failings. Statements beginning with "I feel" are all too often met with silence, resistance, and anger because they are not really statements of feeling, rather statements that carry a sharp, but unacknowledged, barb.

The accuser, if he were more honest, might say, "I feel lonely and maybe it's my problem . . . maybe we've both drifted apart . . . maybe I need more than I can reasonably expect from a wife . . . maybe . . . maybe . . ." If the accuser were honest, a number of valuable dialogues could take place.

Too much emphasis has been placed on the mere expression of feelings, as if this automatically leads to a sense of closeness. What binds people together goes beyond the ability to talk about their feelings. Many husbands and wives express love by what they do, not just by what they feel. Talk is important, but the familiar cliché rings true: Actions speak louder than words. Marriages are bound together by what people do and think and share. In strong relationships, people share ideas, thoughts, impressions, and attitudes about a range of subjects. They talk about the world, not just about the relationship.

Interestingly enough, some of us use the demand for communication, and the goal of openness and intimacy, as a way to avoid feeling alone. We assume that we should never feel alone, and if we do, something is terribly wrong.

When Jack and Elaine first came in to see me, I could see why he was as sad as he sounded on the phone. She was angry, aloof, and did not have a whole lot to say to him. He felt they didn't communicate anymore, even though, "God knows, I've read all the books and tried everything," he said. But she had an illuminating side to convey. It seemed Jack was unusually dependent on her. He had no friends and had never been close to other men, even in his youth. "But I want her as my best friend," he insisted. Elaine felt suffocated and found his attempts at communication stifling, especially now that she had begun a time-consuming career. Jack quickly began to see that he was demanding too much of her, needed to make other friends, and most of all, that he needed to understand that many of his attempts at communication really came from his need to feel constantly connected to someone. He finally admitted that when they had legitimate things to talk about, they communicated quite well. When he accepted that it was okay to feel alone sometimes, his incessant demands for communication eased.

In my work, I see both men and women terrified of feeling alone. They demand openness—not as an affirmative act or gesture designed to bring them closer to someone—but to release them from the painful realm of their aloneness. Communication and openness become an antidote to feeling isolated and estranged. These men and women have difficulty with the concept of separateness. This dilemma of confronting who they are when they're alone exaggerates their treadmill mentality in the marriage, as they forever look to their mate as a fantasied savior from a deeper personal issue they are terrified to confront.

THE FANTASY OF NO CONFLICT

Being on the marriage treadmill grows from the wish for a perfect relationship that will solve everything and for many wives and husbands that automatically means no fights, no hassles, no conflicts. It's impossible to achieve this in marriage. The sooner you accept that, the faster you will get off the treadmill and start appreciating what you have.

Marital fights occur not because people are incompatible, but because all of us, in varying degrees, take our spouses for granted. And there's a good reason for this. Marriage is a safe haven, a sanctuary for feeling secure, letting your hair down, and being yourself. When we're married, we don't have to be on good behavior; we don't have to watch everything we say and do. That's one of the delightful rights that exist in the marital pact. If we didn't have this privilege, we would probably feel insecure most of the time. We would lack a sense of comfort and trust that we could be ourselves.

And when two separate human beings are themselves, clash is inevitable. It doesn't have to be damaging or hurtful, but whenever two people are relaxed enough to let their true selves emerge, invariably there will be some rough edges. People on the marriage treadmill are often frightened of these edges, believing that they signify a bad marriage. Superficially other relationships appear more loving. But I remember that we never know what's really going on with another couple in the privacy of their bedroom. That seemingly nice, sweet couple living next door may not have a word to say to each other. Don't use other marriages as a way of depreciating yours.

Passion, too, sometimes creates conflict. People say that love and hate are closely related and they are right. Whenever you need someone as intensely as you do in marriage, you will fear losing them or fear being rejected or betrayed. These darker emotions surface when we love someone and depend on them. Dependency is frightening for many of us, and this fear coexists with love and creates conflict for couples. Passion invites a degree of instability, a lost concept for couples caught on the marriage treadmill. Their idea of the Perfect Marriage has little to do with the unpredictibility and passion that comprise its human core. They want ease, stability, and seamless interactions. And when they encounter something else, they view it as wrong or unacceptable.

One of the dangers of the marriage treadmill is that some wives and husbands will adamantly suppress anger and do anything to avoid a fight. This denial sows the seeds for real troubles. I have seen more people get divorced because they don't ever fight, than because they do. People whose need for perfection makes them fearful of fighting will bury resentments and disappointments, only to find that much like toxic waste, they will resurface and poison the marriage.

The fear of conflict can lead to strange impasses. Janet, forty-four, has been married to Barnett for sixteen years. And for sixteen years, they've had the same fight. Janet is envious of all of her married friends and assumes they all have terrific marriages. Barnett, she complains, gets angry whenever he tries to talk about what's irritating him. As soon as he starts out, she cuts him off with, "Look, don't yell. Let's talk about this reasonably." Barnett tells me that as soon as he lowers his voice, she starts talking for him, so he angrily raises his voice again and they get nowhere. When I asked her why she couldn't just let him blow off steam and suggested she stand back and listen, she became exasperated. "People don't have to get angry. I just hate it . . . and there are other ways to communicate." I didn't disagree with this, but she was missing the point. She was terrified of his anger, and her attempts to diffuse it only made him angrier. In spite of this conflict, they had a good marriage and each admitted they were very much in love.

I told them they had two choices: I could try to change his personality style, or I could help her not be as frightened of his anger, so she could listen beyond his outburst and then communicate. If we tried to change him it might take a year or two, because suppressing behavior is tougher than learning to listen in a new way. If she could tolerate listening to anger for a few minutes and gradually learn not to react to it with such fear, that might take a month or two. Neither answer was right, neither was wrong. Both required compromises. They opted for the quicker fix. At first Janet resented her end of the deal, but in time she was able to diffuse his anger into "noise," that while not particularly pleasant, did not terrorize her.

I have found that any constructive fighting, or conflict resolution, first requires that you acknowledge a fight is in progress; and one symptom of the fight is anger. Most couples jump into fighting so quickly that they never really hear what is being said or, more importantly, never detect the hurt that is usually behind the anger. Most couples can tolerate arguments provided they last only a few hours, and provided they don't equate imperfection with a "bad" relationship.

Finally, most couples don't realize they will probably bicker about the same issues over and over again throughout their marriage. Most fights are not resolved, but set aside until triggered again. It's most essential that we learn to make up, forgive, and forget, without having anyone be right or wrong. In the best marriages, both people willingly make up as quickly as possible without having to point fingers.

THE FANTASY THAT FRIENDSHIP AND SEXUAL DESIRE ARE NATURAL AND SPONTANEOUS

One of the mistaken beliefs that fuels the marriage treadmill is the notion that if love exists, friendship and sexual desire should automatically follow. This isn't the case for hundreds of couples that I have counseled. They may still love each other, albeit in a quietly committed and somewhat passive way, but friendship has waned and the sexual fires seem to be on the verge of extinction. This is not an irreversible condition. But it requires breaking the treadmill habits. When wives and husbands continue to look to their mates for solutions to their own problems and continue to make demands, criticize, and exhibit no real acceptance, love gradually becomes dormant.

We say we've "fallen out of love" or "our love just died." The truth is that love more often dims, than disappears. The cumulative effect of hurts, pains, and resentments build up like scar tissue. To protect ourselves from further hurts, we focus on our all-consuming fearfulness and resentment. Love and mutual pleasure become leaden and elusive. When these negative feelings accumulate, they serve as a layer of insulation that seals off loving and giving. But most often, our love isn't gone, we have just pushed it aside.

When couples attempt to step off the marriage treadmill, they find that the possibility for friendship and the potential for rekindling sexual desire is dramatically enhanced. But even then, it is not spontaneous. The fantasy of the perfect marriage misleadingly makes everything seem effortless. Good things don't magically happen, nor do they happen just because you learn to talk. You can communicate endlessly about a better sex life, and you'll probably just make each other uptight. It takes action, not words.

OVERCOMING SHYNESS

Most people are shy in varying degrees, especially husbands and wives who want to break old patterns and revitalize their marriage. This shyness can become a stumbling block in the way of getting off the treadmill. The treadmill mentality convinces you marriage should be effortless, if you love each other. The truth is that we have to consciously and willingly risk approaching our mate in a new way, which usually makes us self-conscious and shy. To overcome shyness you need to focus your attention outward. If it's friendship you want, you have to be interested in what he likes, or search out common interests. But this takes work, and it doesn't sound romantic, as the treadmill suggests. If you want a better sex life, you had better stop complaining about your mate not turning you on and find ways to turn yourself on and/or learn to seduce your partner. Maybe this sounds like work, but it's work that many couples enjoy, especially when it starts to change things.

Early on in my work with couples, I like to present a challenge—one they initially hate! "Suppose you were dating each other? What would you do differently?" I inquire. I ask them to try and act as if they were still in a courtship period for one month. Usually, their first response is, "We're too angry to do that." They're too wary to take such risks. As one wife said to me after one week of "dating" her husband, "These are such bad dates, we'd probably never continue seeing each other if we weren't married." I encourage them, not because I think magic will occur, but because this instruction awakens them to how passive they've become with each other. As they continue to try, they become aware of the attitudes and behaviors that create good feelings in their spouse—feelings that are invariably reciprocated. As they focus their attention on pleasing the other person, they begin breaking out of their self-imposed cocoon. They forget themselves momentarily, and stop waiting for their mate to take action.

The disastrous effect of the marriage treadmill is that you always look to your mate to be the catalyst for love, sex, and friendship. You think if you can change them, you will feel better, you will feel whole, and you will experience new heights of self-esteem. The truth is that good things happen the other way around—they start with you!

LETTING GO: RESIGNATION OR LIBERATION?

Helping someone get off his treadmill is complicated. The first response of many patients is an anxious one. "You mean I'm just supposed to accept things the way they are? I wouldn't have come to see you if I knew that was the best you could offer." What they don't understand is that acceptance and resignation are separate concepts. To the cynic who says, "I see, I just accept my spouse and I will be happy. It sounds like resignation to me," my response is, "Like all treadmills, there is a hidden paradox; by getting off, and expecting less of others, you end up getting more."

Put simply, you must first examine self-deceptions and confront your own anguish; relinquish unattainable wishes for perfection and accept your mate's imperfections, then you may discover a path that leads to contentment and peace of mind. In the case of marriage, you may find an opportunity for real love in the present, rather than a fantasized love in the future.

You must be courageous enough to recognize and admit that you are indeed caught on the marriage treadmill. If you have deceived yourself into thinking your mate is the solution to life's problems, and if you expect him to be the god you want him to be, you should notice a number of signals alerting you to the fact that you are on a treadmill. Be honest with yourself and see if you recognize these signs. Perhaps you spend a great deal of time secretly blaming your spouse, and these resentments erupt with increasing frequency into vocal complaints. Maybe you spend too much time analyzing your mate's behavior. You may be angry much of the time, feel victimized, helpless, and frustrated with others. Or perhaps you feel hopeless and disillusioned about the future of your relationship.

There are two salient behaviors that should signal to you and your spouse that you both are on the treadmill: You spend an excessive amount of time communicating, which is really disguised blaming and complaining, or you engage in too many endless negotiations, which are often disguised threats and manipulations. If you recognize this in yourself, you are on the treadmill. Now, how about getting off!

A MARRIAGE PLATEAU: STEPS TO TAKE

The first step in changing the pattern of your marriage is to take responsibility for your own behavior and investigate what you can do yourself. You must see yourself as the catalyst for change. But taking responsibility means that you have to experience yourself as alone in a certain sense. As I have suggested, men and women get on the treadmill as a way of avoiding and denying themselves. Getting off means dealing with yourself again, which can be unnerving and even terrifying. Working with couples, I often see attempts at change and communication as a way to avoid being alone. Being alone is one of the solemn givens of life and is quite different from feeling lonely. We can alter our loneliness by filling our schedules, but we can never change the fact that we are alone. For many people, being alone is horrifying and avoiding it was why they got married in the first place. When I ask patients to confront their fear of being alone, they often answer, "If I do as you say, I'm afraid I'll just be shrouded in gloom. I feel disenchanted enough as it is!" I understand their hesitation, but I encourage them to forge ahead, knowing that good things lie beyond their fears. Being alone doesn't mean being isolated.

Take as an act of faith that you will survive stepping back and getting off. Sometimes it helps to remember the good things that happened in your marriage, because they provide a foundation of feelings that helps you make that leap of faith.

Another act of faith is remembering that your mate is not trying to make you unhappy. Believe that whatever he is doing, he is doing for his own protection and survival. For example, the seemingly cold and aloof man may be shielding himself from hurts similar to those he has experienced in past relationships. The seemingly distant woman may be apprehensive that she will lose her identity in a close relationship. If you set aside old perceptions and objectively look at your mate, you will automatically find yourself less angry and accusatory.

The next step to getting off the treadmill is to take charge of your emotions. Holding back feelings of anger and resentment is difficult at first, but soon you will actually feel better mastering your emotions rather than letting them victimize you. Venting feelings often resuscitates them, rather than deflating them. Anger breeds anger, and resentment breeds resentment. The process of letting go of your resentments strengthens and empowers you. Perhaps you will even befriend yourself.

The final step is setting aside the impossible expectations and fantasies I described earlier. It means letting go of those wishes that got you on the treadmill. It means not trying to have a perfect marriage.

Expecting less will inevitably lead to discovering more in your marriage, and there's an important reason for this. By disengaging, you free your mate from implicit criticisms and accusations embedded in your relentless requests. He will feel more accepted by you. From this plateau of acceptance, your spouse will gradually learn to hear what you're saying or needing. Nobody can listen or give when under attack. You know this is true, because put in your spouse's place, you'd react the same way. Best of all, your dormant love will be revived.

Afterward, if you still want to make changes in your marriage, you can do so from these plateaus of self-acceptance, and acceptance of your mate. Love is tested by actions. Love is about what you do.

The heart of love is accepting, liking, and cherishing another human being. Love is both cause and effect. By giving love, acting on loving feelings, you will undoubtedly feel better about yourself and will have even more energy to expend in loving acts. In too many marriages—especially those infected with a treadmill mentality—there is a basic failure to accept the other person. Remember, acceptance doesn't mean resignation, nor does it mean you wouldn't mind if that person were different. It just means that you don't hate him for who he is, nor do you feel it your duty to relentlessly try to remake his basic personality. Love is a power we carry within us. When we withhold our love because we feel hurt, angry, or resentful, we stifle our own being. Love doesn't have to always be reciprocal, or instantly rewarded, for us to express it. When we free our love, we free ourselves. You don't have to wait for someone to love you first.

CHAPTER TEN

RAISING PERFECT CHILDREN: THE PARENTING TREADMILL

Parents wonder why the streams are bitter, when they themselves have spoiled the fountain.
—John Locke, philosopher

Tina and Phil, parents of seventeen-year-old Sean, come in to see me. They're bickering and worried about their son and his seeming "apathy and depression." Sean is a senior in high school, a *B* student, and three months away from taking his SATs for college admission. His parents are concerned because he refuses to take an SAT review course that could help substantially boost his scores. Phil anxiously informs me that without top scores, he won't be eligible for the state university system. "And if not, what then?" I inquire. They tell me he would have to go to a state college or some other less prestigious school. "Well, he's apparently aware of this, so why do you think he doesn't want to take the course?"

At this point Tina, frustrated, chimes in. "Sean is happy the way he is, and even though I want him to take the course, too, I can't stand the way Phil badgers him and tells him he'll never get ahead in life."

I asked to see Sean alone. Bright, personable, and not at all intimidated by being in my office, he told me all about his interests in sports, music, and his concerns about the future; and, yes, his ill-defined academic goals. "I know I'll make it. I'm aggressive, and when I want to go all out, I do." When asked about college, Sean replied, "I've had it with all the pressures.

Maybe I'm wrong, but I can't stand all my friends killing themselves over what college they'll get into. I'll take the SAT like everyone else and I'll get into a good college, but it's not going to dominate my senior year. I'm really tired of my father's lectures. He never even went to college and he still became successful. I know it's different today, but I'm interested in being my own person. I've never followed the pack, doing what everyone else thinks is right, that's why I never even tried drinking or drugs. You'd think my parents would be proud of me."

His parents are proud of him, but they've lost sight of their own psychological boundaries as well as their son's. We all see our children as extensions of ourselves. Sometimes that's good, because that link makes fierce our loving and protective feelings. The old cliché about giving up your life for your child is one most parents take to heart. Tina and Phil are neither cold nor neglectful parents, nor are they interested solely in the ways in which their son glorifies their success as parents. But, they act that way. In spite of their best intentions, they are caught on the parenting treadmill—wanting their child to be as excellent, or as perfect, as he can become.

Phil is a hard-working middle manager at an aircraft plant. His wife is a schoolteacher. Both of them intended to arm their children with every opportunity that would prepare them for life's challenges. But in their zeal—especially Phil's wish that his son become a professional and not have to work for others—they have tried to foist a treadmill mentality on Sean. Tina's wishes are somewhat different than her husband's. As a teacher, she always felt she could give her children a special edge. Unfortunately, as time went on, she regarded each child as a reflection of her parenting and teaching skills. The more they excelled at academics, the more likely they would enhance her own sense of a Perfect Self.

The parenting treadmill arises in one of two ways. First, as with Phil, it can result from a parent's own treadmill mentality being presented as a guide for one's children. Children observe their parents entrenched in a treadmill mentality and come to see the relentless quest for being and having more as the way to conduct their lives. They adopt these values through the process of modeling and identification, even when parents themselves are trying to get off their own treadmills. For example, even if parents are trying to escape the money treadmill, their children nonetheless learn about financial anxieties and the condition of regarding money as a solution to self-worth.

The parenting treadmill is also played out in the home when parents perceive their children as reflections of their own values, including their success as a parent. Children become psychological extensions of parents and are subjected to all the anxieties, wishes, and unrealistic expectations of their parents. Children are, therefore, unconsciously encouraged to act out the same relentless need for self-improvement.

The parenting treadmill, more than any other, has negative effects that are absolutely unexpected and thoroughly unwanted. As parents we get on the treadmill out of love. But because our concern for our children is driven by our own needs, rather than their needs, we forget that love is about accepting and nurturing them, not blindly improving them.

There is a danger point in parenting that is barely discernible until we're past it, where our best intentions shift from hopes to anxieties. This is the point where we begin to focus on what our kids should be, rather than what they are. When this happens, we must realize the difference between communicating our wish to help them, and unwittingly communicating rejection by emphasizing their need to be improved.

Our agenda for molding our kids starts early. Modern seven-, eight-, and nine-year-olds have the schedules of young executives. They go to school, they take ballet lessons, music lessons, or gymnastics, and have scheduled study times. More and more of these kids are showing up at the doctor's office with stress symptoms—they can't sleep at night, their little stomachs are in knots, and their heads ache. They are miniature versions of their parents. And as parents we have passed our dissatisfaction onto them, all in the name of giving them "the best."

Anna, a forty-year-old single mother, enrolls Josh, her seven-year-old boy, in a soccer league. Josh acts excited because it makes his mother happy. But he's fearful because he knows himself and realizes he's not sufficiently coordinated or athletic. Anna hopes this experience will boost Josh's seemingly low self-esteem and, in so doing, help quiet her anxiety about being a single parent. The experience is a disaster. He is the worst player on the team, and after a few Saturdays of waking up feeling sick and missing practice, Anna gets the hint. She is smart and sensitive enough to know that her own perfectionism was determining her choices, and her wish to improve Josh came from her insecurities, not his. When she finally allowed him to quit the team, they both felt a lot better. She realized there was a whole range of other experiences that he could savor without feeling inadequate.

With few exceptions, most parents want to do the best they can for their children. Today, this starts even before they're born. We have excellent prenatal medical care and advanced technology today. We supposedly know more than ever before. So why is parenting so difficult, and why do we so often take the wrong path and grab the wrong solutions? One answer is that we are deluged with more information, which leaves us more confused. As with all the other treadmills, society inundates us with risky prescriptions for success. We are overwhelmed by the message that more is required of us if we are to survive in today's world: more skills, more knowledge, more drive. Soon we'll have computer programming courses for toddlers.

WHEN WISHES BECOME ANXIETIES

As soon as our child is born, we're faced with a desperate wish to do what's right. Armed with books that tell us what to do, consulting with friends and relatives, we set out to help shape the life of our newborn. In the past, when we had doubts, we relied on our instincts. But parenting, like everything else, has degenerated from something natural and commonplace, into a complex task. The guidelines constantly shift, providing fertile soil for mistaken paths and unrealistic solutions.

Take, for example, our theories of child rearing. They're constantly evolving. Many years ago, parents were probably overly strict and even insensitive to the unique needs and emotional requirements of children. But as child-rearing experts came to the fore, armed with Freudian insights about the critical effects of parental behavior before the age of five, we entered an era of permissiveness. This was a time when childrens' emotional needs were placed ahead of a parent's comfort level. If a child cried in the middle of the night, you rushed in every time, fearing she would be enveloped with feelings of dread and abandonment if you didn't. It was believed these feelings could create irreparable scars. It seemed the potential for childhood trauma was everywhere.

Most recently, we have begun to reconsider parents' rights, and the possibility that children may need more limits and guidelines than we previously thought. Our school systems are returning to basics. We believe certain fundamentals must be taught. We believe that adults have lessons to impart to their young. Ironically, some of this return to tradition is part of our national treadmill mentality and our desperate wish to compete with Japan. We are probably at a midpoint in the pendulum's arc—both parents and children have entitlements—and we must learn to accommodate one another in the family context.

Media-generated theories frequently mobilize changes in parenting attitudes. We look outside of ourselves for answers. Perhaps the most fundamental question for parents is "How much of an impact can I have on my child?" Is little Susie a blank slate on which I will write her destiny? Or, are my children programmed at birth to live out a destiny created largely by their genetic codes? For a number of decades, we were convinced that environment played the major role in shaping a child's behavior. Especially in the last two decades, we came to believe that because adults can grow and realize potential, so, too, can children.

Recently, the nature-nurture controversy has been revived—and this rethinking has enormous implications for child rearing, as well as for those on the parenting treadmill. The more we learn about the biochemistry of brain functioning and the under-lying physiology of behavior, the more we see the effects of heredity and genetic destiny. We are learning that while envi-ronment stills plays an important role in molding and shaping emotions, attitudes, and actions, the foundation and limiting factors are set by heredity—what is programmed into us before birth, or the nature of our genes.

Studies of identical twins who were separated at birth indi-cate that much of our identity has been genetically set. Such studies show that regardless of the environment, identical twins are still much more alike in intelligence and personality style than they are different. Our genetic predispositions cannot be ignored. I'm not suggesting that we must, therefore, be passive or resigned in how we respond to our children or about our wishes for them, but it is important to realize that some of their personality is already stamped in, whether we like it or not. For example, we know some children are more active and assertive, while others are more passive. Unable to accept this, the parent on the treadmill can harm her children by foisting unrealistic expectations on them. Put simply, in addition to the child who is *becoming*, there is also the child who *is*, who already has a uniqueness and an identity, and a child that can delight us, but may also sometimes frustrate us in years to come.

Because we all emphatically believe in potential, we proceed as though parents were the primary determinants of their child's psychological evolution. And that's okay, because shaping our children is our parental duty and responsibility. My comments are simply intended to show that imposing our lifestyle values on our children is a complex task, especially when we uncon-sciously but desperately need them to act out our own treadmill mentality. If parents have an image of their child that doesn't fit their child's temperament or inherent abilities and interests, their child is pushed into an ill-fitting mold. In her attempt to please her parents, the child won't discover her own strengths or will learn to devalue them. Such a child will push these dimensions into her Forgotten Self. Children will try to live up to the Perfect Self their parents have created for them, always at great cost.

But before things end up this way, most parents start out with the same basic wish for a healthy baby. But our criteria quickly expand and grow more exacting. Early on, we secretly wish for them to be extraordinarily attractive, bright, and physically agile. There's nothing wrong with wishes, but turned into rigid expectations, they indicate your wishes have been transformed into musts, a classic treadmill symptom. Loving parents allow their children to develop in their own directions. They have a basic appreciation for their child. In contrast, parents on the treadmill see their child as a project.

As I've indicated, our difficulty started with our own guidelines. Whom should we believe? Whom should we trust? The more we read, the more anxious we can become. It's not unlike the cholesterol controversy. The experts are constantly changing their minds. Confused by conflicting information, we lose our parental instincts. As a result, our children get confused also. We hear that they need limits and guidelines, but what exactly are those? Our external guidelines can't take into consideration individual differences. The experts can tell us what to do in theory, but they can't be there for us on a day-to-day basis.

If we allow ourselves to be confused and to feel compelled to pay attention to exterior voices, we infect our children with a similar confusion. If we are geared toward having it all, then how can we deny our child? When we're afraid to restrain our own emotional and material hungers, how can we teach our children to do so? One solution has been what sociologists refer to as a *transfer of functions*, which means abdicating responsibility to other parties. For example, we insist that the school system not only teach the three Rs, but also inculcate a system of values that provides an ethical framework for young people. It's a noble, but clearly unfulfilled, goal.

Some upper-middle-class parents opt to have fewer children. They believe this creates fewer chances to make mistakes and more opportunity to provide for the children they do have. But this equation is fraught with difficulties. Parents with a treadmill mentality can inadvertently create even more pressure when they only have one or two children to focus on.

Evelyn and Roger had their only child somewhat late in life—when Evelyn was forty and Roger was forty-three. Both executives in the movie industry, they decided to have only one child so they could provide him with "quality" time and still keep up with their all-consuming careers. David was seven years old when they came in to see me. Ostensibly, they were fighting about issues of parenting techniques and discipline to the point where they doubted their ability to keep their marriage together. Their family life sounded like a marine training camp. David led a busy, regimented life. Their last fight was prompted by Evelyn's tearful outburst after they left an interview for a new school (naturally, one that was considered the best in town). David was almost noncommunicative with the headmaster and his father yelled at him afterward. Evelyn told me they were almost sorry they had a child because "maybe down deep we just aren't parent types." I suggested they were using the same mind-set or attitudes toward David as they did when they nurtured a movie project along, and a child can't be "packaged" like a movie.

In time, Evelyn and Roger acknowledged that their approach with David was backfiring. In spite of their good intentions, they said they were foisting their conception of a Perfect Self onto their son. To relate to David on his own terms, his parents had to learn to shift gears at home, shedding the perfectionistic mind-set they operated with in their work. This was hard at first. Like so many other parents, they reinforced each other's beliefs to the point where they were convinced they were right. Now they had to let go and rediscover their son. They had to listen to him and not filter his personality through their value system. After some time, they not only became closer to David, but they had a new perspective on their work life and the emotional toll it had taken on them.

Parents are clearly more nervous and apprehensive than ever before. Some of that anxiety may be valuable if it spurs us to be more sensitive and conscientious parents. But much of the anxiety gets transformed into a treadmill that blurs our perceptions of our children. Unfortunately we inadvertently encourage our children to lose sight of their basic personality, because they fail to live up to our wishes for how we wanted them to turn out.

A 1986 Harris Poll found that less than half of all parents believed their children were basically happy. What an unfortunate statistic! And yet, it's hardly surprising. As parents, we have a lot to worry about. Today, we have less control over our own lives and over our children's lives than ever before.

THE END OF INNOCENCE

Only 20 percent of families with children under the age of eighteen are *traditional*, meaning one parent stays home and cares for the children. New traditions are being established. I cite this statistic not to suggest that it is economically feasible or emotionally advisable for most of us to return to the traditional, but to suggest that we need to follow new guidelines to keep up with the ways social change rapidly alters our lives. Gone are the days of Mom making a peanut butter sandwich as her child comes home from school!

Another troubling statistic: The average child watches five hours of television a day! I remember the days when we talked about educational television. No one makes a pretense of that anymore. Clearly television isn't doing much to enrich children's minds, or prepare them for life's challenges. It does prepare children to be seduced by life's illusory and superficial enticements: money, power, and fame. The few shows that do attempt to enlighten are watched by adults, not kids.

Television is an opiate, because it helps us escape from life's pains. And kids, today, have many pains. For example, many children have to deal with divorce. This means they must deal with issues of separation anxiety and instability, often well before they are psychologically equipped to do so. And, new research indicates that the old adage Well, it's better for kids if parents divorce, rather than living in an unhappy home is not universally accepted. That was one of the bromides that emerged from the Me Generation, helping people ease the guilt of marital dissolution.

When some kids feel sad and lonely, they search out quick solutions just as adults do. We all know drug abuse is rampant. And why not? In our society we emphasize feeling good and instant gratification. If children are depressed, booze and other drugs are an easy way to cope. Is it any wonder that high-school kids are becoming heavy beer drinkers when every televised football game is filled with beer commercials? And sex can also be used to ease a sense of isolation. Movies, MTV, and music videos are available for after-school entertainment, and much of this material is sexually explicit. Children tend to model themselves after idealized figures who speak directly to them.

Because television provides us with the images that end up comprising our inner world, the inner world of children is little different than the inner world of adults. Children are barraged with adult concerns. Images of sex and violence predominate, as do our adult solutions to pain. Children no longer focus on real childhood concerns, instead, they become miniature adults. We are stealing childhood from them, as well as their precious inner worlds.

Children no longer look to adults for information or direction when the media offers such seductive and convincing images. They often feel that they know more about the "world" than their parents do. And to the degree that the world comes to them through television, they often do. But they have no context or experience to deal with these powerful pervasive images. And simultaneously, their parents' authority has been so undermined that they don't look to them for help or guidance. We pressure our children into an adult world, but forget they lack the means to deal with it.

The effect of these pressures add up to epidemic childhood and teenage stress. An alarming teenage suicide rate is one measure of youthful despair, as is the general increase in adolescent depression. Young people, just as their parents, are all too often finding themselves going nowhere fast, feeling disillusioned and aimless.

Clearly, parents have a lot to be worried about today. And these worries do one of two things. Either they alert us to the dangers that exist and make us more vigilant parents or they create fertile soil for the parenting treadmill. The more worried we are, the more anxiety we feel, and the more likely are we to stray onto false paths in our attempts to ensure fulfillment for our children. And, as parents, the more anxious we are, the more imperfect we feel, the more likely are we to try to make our children perfect.

Wanting perfect children is an ambiguous goal, because we don't quite know what they should look like. We often have outdated images in mind and our methods are somewhat hit and miss. We try to protect them from an increasingly dangerous world out there, but we use the television set as a babysitter when they are home. We "preach" more to our kids, but we don't set an example that makes much sense to them, or to us.

Still we want to be good parents. We try hard. We read books, watch "Bill Cosby," commiserate with other parents, and consult psychologists. But while we search out the perfect models, we seem to lose our kids. And we grow more burdened with our own sense of imperfection.

Part of our anxiety manifests itself in the pressure we put on our kids to do well in school. We cling to the hope that education leads to the good life. Kids, living in the here and now, question this equation, and we, too, have our doubts. But we still preach it. If our children are doing well in school, we are successful parents. For parents on the fast track, success is a question of whether their kids get into the right college. On our simplistic ladder of success a second-rate school won't get you far. No wonder our kids question the inherent value of education. It's part of the game—you're not really perfect if you aren't sitting on an upper rung.

I detect two coexisting attitudes with today's parents. On the one hand, they hope their kids escape childhood and the teen years alive and intact, without becoming drug addicts or worse! On the other hand, they have a whole set of rarified and often unrealistic expectations for their children. No longer do we hear parents simply sigh with the hope, "I just want my kids to be happy."

These increased pressures have a dramatic effect on children. Consider the following as indicators of the parenting treadmill. Parents are not solely to blame, but these symptoms do indicate how they contribute to young people developing a vivid sense of an Imperfect Self. For as we ignore our own inner resources, we become part of the process that robs our children of theirs.

If you are concerned that you may be on the parenting tread-mill, watch for these symptoms in your kids: excessive concern over appearances as a measure of self-worth, avoidance of school because the pressure is too tough, and test anxiety of epidemic proportions, as though a grade can be life or death. In addition, more children are imitating their parents, consumed by self-destructive measures of envy and jealousy. And finally, in so many kids we sense an inability to tolerate failure and the refusal to see failure as a learning experience.

As parents, we become anxious about these signs. But in our haste to fix things, we create even more anxiety in our youngsters. As with all treadmills, the fantasized solution to enhanced well-being only creates an even greater sense of deficiency.

GOOD INTENTIONS OR PERFECTIONISM?

If you wish to be a perfect parent, you are doomed from the outset. As I've suggested, children have their own unique personalities and predispositions that will thwart your attempt to dramatically remold them. But that doesn't mean parents can't have a strong impact by loving their children for who they are. Love is the most powerful influence on their lives.

But too often we greedily want more than the rewards of loving, we may want children to be the absolute best they can be, and we may impose this wish on them with a vengeance! Mostly parents' wishes come straight from their hearts. "I want my child to have more than I had" or "I want to be a much better parent than I had." Isn't it surprising how often we hold those wishes and yet fall short of our goals? For many of us, we finally learn to accept our own parents when we realize how difficult it is to be a parent. We, too, invariably fall far short of perfection. It is an occasion to forgive and accept our parents and ourselves.

As parents today, we tend to get caught up in the opportunity and enrichment frenzy. We can provide innumerable experiences that will give our children an edge in this competitive society. From the very beginning, we can present them with alphabet flash cards to improve their reading readiness, send them to toddler Gymboree classes to improve their physical potential, and provide them with an array of educational toys designed to stimulate their mental processes. This is only a beginning that leads to computers and lessons and summer camps, and whatever other improving experiences we can think of. Unfortunately, while we are improving them we forget to give them our time and our love. They learn to judge themselves by how much they accomplish, by outward rather than inward qualities.

If we anxiously see our children as a reflection of our worth, we can end up on the treadmill from day one! We can give them a head start, we tell ourselves. We ignore concerned experts who are skeptical about these pressures. Research of all kinds strongly suggests these early attempts for improvement are not all that effective. Children hear only the subtext that says it's essential you learn as quickly as possible. Or it's not what you learn, but how much better you are than your playmates. Thankfully, perhaps our zeal is being tempered a bit. There is a growing body of evidence that pushing children too early can actually hinder them in developing other skills and attitudes that need to emerge in a casual, even leisurely way.

But, fueled by our own treadmill mentality, we choose to ignore some of this new evidence. After all, we think, it can't really hurt. As our children begin elementary school, we are aware that students are put on different tracks and perceived by their teachers in seemingly fixed ways. "Johnny is a bit slow" or "Susie is advanced for her years and should be put ahead." While it is valuable for schools to offer accelerated programs for advanced students, some parents dread hearing their children are left out of such programs. We lack the patience to understand that children develop at different paces. We are afraid that if they don't have a fast start, they will never catch up.

Today, private tutoring is big business. In some ways, that's a good thing, because parents are taking responsibility for their children's learning, rather than passively cursing the overburdened and underfinanced public school systems. But even tutoring can reflect a treadmill phenomenon when *B* students are constantly pushed to become *A* students. Telling a child a *B* is not good enough is a surefire way to encourage her to learn out of fear or competitiveness, rather than from a positive desire for knowledge.

Children pushed and harried by their schedules are trapped in the "hurried child syndrome." Scores of children are pushed, scheduled, and cajoled into making their parents feel successful. Kids are into soccer, Little League, karate, gym classes, dance classes, music classes, and science classes. None of this sounds so bad, but you have to see it to believe it. Harried parents whip around town in car pools, scheduling their children as though the kids were junior executives. The other side of this scenario is our kids' active, and passive, resistance to any kind of pressure.

What's missing is clear: There is no time or space allocated to a child's inner life and inner timetable. What happened to lazy days, when children could just hang around and allow their imagination to flourish? There is no space for surprise and the unexpected. Play is rapidly becoming lost to a whole generation of children. Play implies a lack of structure, even a disregard for progress or mastery. Play is not good or bad, it just is. Play is what children do to derive pleasure or to experience themselves. It is not supposed to be organized and structured, because that is the very opposite of what it means.

Play shouldn't be primarily competitive or taken too seriously. It's always been interesting to me to see how even team sports get perverted when parents are around. You can put children on a playground and they'll compete with all their hearts, but afterward, a loss is easily forgotten. Take that same child and put her in an organized sports league with parents hovering around, and the youngster automatically senses a defeat means a great deal to the parent. The need for a child to enhance a parent's sense of self-esteem, symptomatic of the parenting treadmill, is at work.

Those of you with children undoubtedly remember parents' night at school. Looking back, if you really were tuned into your child's mind, you would have realized she was probably more anxious than you thought. I've worked with teenagers who were deeply hurt when their well-meaning parents talked to their teachers and kept focusing on how their child might have performed better in a particular class, rather than appreciating what they did well.

It's obvious that we live in a competitive society and we believe that our children should learn to act accordingly. But how early should these lessons occur and what does the child need to be prepared? I think it's clear that the parent who enables her child to feel loved just as she is knows the answer. The parent is providing the child with the best preparation possible, even though she may wonder if she is preparing her child for reality. Conversely, the parent who feels anxious and insecure will only transmit a treadmill mentality to her child. Love is a risk worth taking.

The child who falls prey to concerns about competition focuses on externals rather than the expression of who she really is. It's no surprise that the increasing number of schools that now require a uniform dress code find that children love it. It's not just because they don't have to worry about new clothes and competing with the other kids. Children in these schools are getting off the appearance treadmill, and as a natural consequence find themselves concerned about learning and other more fundamental ways of expressing their uniqueness.

A parent's quest for perfectionism robs the child of a gentle and gradual blossoming. Children need to feel capable and need to have some sense of control over their lives. Treadmills undermine such feelings. They only encourage anxiety and a secret sense of inadequacy. Children not only need love, they need to be left alone, left to their own whims and inclinations. The hurried child grows up with a sense of fragmentation and isn't allowed the time to develop and integrate the various parts of her embryonic personality. Perhaps we rush them because we have a crushing sense of running out of time . . . when they still believe in its endlessness.

The bottom line is clear. If, as a parent, you are driven by an Imperfect Self and are striving for a Perfect Self, you end up on treadmills and you subtly encourage the same fate for your children. Just like parents, children end up having a Forgotten Self, which may in fact be the repository of their best ego resources. It also follows that if you can't accept yourself, you won't be able to accept your child, or teach her to accept herself.

PARENTING PLATEAUS

One day in the course of psychotherapy, Agnes, a forty-five-year-old mother, began to speak about her disappointments with her three children. "I know I wasn't perfect, but I was certainly a better parent than I had. And what have I gotten back? Nothing. The two kids in college barely call. My teenage daughter is like a boarder in my house. I'm lucky if she even eats with us."

I listen sympathetically. As a parent, I'm familiar with the refrain. But I also realize that Agnes tried too hard for too many years. She was always so intent on her children excelling and improving that she scarcely knew or understood them on their terms. Fortunately, life gives us many opportunities to build bridges back to our children. I told this to her and made some suggestions to help her find the patience to wait for those moments. For Agnes, this meant making intermittent calls, one every few months, trying to get together for lunch or dinner and, most importantly, not expecting anything close or intimate until at least five or ten of these meetings had taken place. When parents expect closeness right away, children feel pressured and resentful.

Many parents, like Agnes, did what they felt was right, and believed they acted out of love. We do this and then look to our children for a return on this investment of love, and often it seems we get very little. We wonder why they don't give us love in return, but we rarely ask what we have done to deserve such a fate. Sometimes we haven't done anything. But at other times, we fail to see that we have done very little to encourage it. We improved them when we should have nurtured them!

To deal with her disappointment Agnes will have to begin thinking about parental plateaus. To reach a parental plateau we must learn to see our children as individuals in their own right, rather than extensions of ourselves. We must acknowledge the unique qualities and the deficits of our children, and we must come to accept them. From that plateau, a new relationship can emerge—one based on acceptance rather than selfish wishes.

The first step in getting off the parenting treadmill is acknowledging your own errors, your own self-deceptions, and developing a new perspective for seeing your kids. A sense of humor doesn't hurt. Most parents, especially those on the treadmill, are so serious that they are forever communicating a sense of apprehension to their children. Parents who can accept themselves and establish their own life plateaus will find it easier to accept their children.

You can let go of your driving perfectionism and encourage your children to find balance in life between work and play. By giving them the space to be themselves your children can reclaim their Forgotten Selves and you will discover aspects of them you haven't seen. Reclaiming a Forgotten Self may mean engaging in an activity your child enjoys, that has no real payoff except some intrinsic pleasure. For example, the scientifically minded child may get more enjoyment out of messing around fixing an old radio than attending yet another enrichment class at the natural history museum. Children need to relax just as much as adults do. And nothing is better for a child's mind than to allow her imagination to soar. Children need permission to allow themselves space and time.

Parents who wish to establish a parental plateau will find themselves accepting what their child chooses to read, even if it has no cultural value. Kids who enjoy reading will eventually read material that has some substance. But to push for perfection in reading and to assume that everything should be self-improving may forever cut a child off from the world of fantasy and drama.

Parents on the treadmill are dismayed when their child seems to lack competitive feelings. They fear for the child's survival capabilities out in the world. But kids who revel in competition will naturally seek it out. Kids who despise it will feel even worse about themselves, and, therefore, will avoid it even more. Parents who find a plateau of acceptance discover a paradoxical effect. Deemphasizing competition doesn't make kids weaker, it makes them stronger, because when a child is comfortable with loving, kindness, and cooperation, she often develops a powerful sense of self. It is this sense of oneself that supplies the energy necessary to compete as adults.

A patient of mine had a parent who, like many parents, had his own natural sense of a plateau of acceptance. My patient remembers his father telling him, "Look, you're my horse in this race. Win or lose, you're the one I'm betting on." He never felt judged by his father or that he disappointed his father. This was a father who truly championed effort, rather than just praising outcome.

Perhaps the toughest, and the final, stage in getting off the parenting treadmill, is mourning the loss of the Perfect Child. At some point, when we acknowledge who our children are, we are preparing ourselves to acknowledge what they might not be. This is not resignation, but acceptance. In addition, we know our children may not become handsome or beautiful in any conventional sense. We know they may not be major successes in our predefined ways. We get a sense of their limits, as well as what is good and beautiful about them. Children whose parents mourn the loss of the Perfect Child and proceed to genuinely love them are blessed.

A couple, who had struggled for a few years wanting perfectionism from their children, put it well when they told me the child-rearing principle they had most neglected was gratitude. "We forgot to be grateful for how wonderful our children can be. One doesn't do well in school but is full of love and warmth.

The other gets all *A*s but is rebellious and selfish at home. We got our perspective all screwed up when we forgot all the good stuff, and the qualities we wanted to fix were the only things we could see in the kids. We were the problem, but we saw them as the solutions."

Haven't we all had the feeling of a parental plateau, however momentary? Each of you who are parents knows the feeling of counting your blessings even if it's only for a moment. We hear about a child dying or being taken ill, and we look at our own children and say, "Thank God they're healthy." For that brief time, maybe an hour, maybe a day, we have the experience of looking at our child with total love and acceptance. Their goodness outshines what we may have found disappointing. Oddly enough, these are the moments when we feel most loving too—times of acceptance, not times when our children are excelling and achieving. Times of achievement are satisfying, but achievement is fleeting, and our bond, if loving, lasts forever.

· III ·

*LIFE
ON YOUR
OWN TERMS*

CHAPTER ELEVEN

PLATEAUS: THE SECRET TO SELF-ACCEPTANCE

*Give us the grace to accept with serenity the things
that cannot be changed, the courage to change the
things which should be changed, and the wisdom to
distinguish the one from the other.*
                    —Reinhold Niebuhr, theologian

Stacy is a thirty-nine-year-old garment manufacturer's sales representative. She is in therapy because she's grown increasingly distraught over being unmarried and childless, and has no visible love prospects. "I had my eye so far up the road, that I think I missed the last turn off." She laughed nervously, then broke into tears. "My last boyfriend told me I may know how to appreciate great meals but I don't ever slow down enough to have dessert. I guess that's the story of my life."

Stacy has been the proverbial "winner" all her life. Successful at whatever she tries, vivacious and outgoing, she can compete toe-to-toe with any man, even come out on top, and male rivals in her field still love her. So where has she gone wrong? Stacy was a victim of the having-it-all mentality, that elusive promise that can lure anyone onto a treadmill. She was so busy soaking up praise for success that she thought that was the only option worth pursuing. Beside, Mr. Right had to be dynamic, brighter than she was, powerful, yet gentle and sensitive when she needed him to be. She spent years dating to find him, but her search for love had turned into a singles treadmill.

Stacy was bright, had received a great deal of therapy, and had attended many growth seminars. I wondered why she had single-mindedly pursued goals that were not making her happy and left her feeling emotionally unanchored. Cynical about therapy, she told me, "Everyone thinks I'm so strong and so together, that all I have to do is smile and keep moving and something good will happen. Instead, I spend hours crying at night, and I can't handle seeing my women friends who are married and have children because I feel so lonely afterward."

In reviewing her past therapy experiences, I could see that she had missed exploring an important dimension of her successful life. Supported by her therapists, Stacy had focused on her obvious strengths and had unwittingly reinforced the momentum that was carrying her along. Admittedly, it is difficult to see through success, but all of her life she had focused on what she thought she wanted and ignored what she needed. Her success had only taken her farther away from satisfying her innermost needs. I suggested she would have to put her success in perspective so she could find her Forgotten Self.

As we talked it became clear that Stacy had always been ambivalent about being on a plateau—about pausing, taking stock, and concluding "Right now this is enough for me." Her deep-seated ambition prevented her from making her wish for family a deeper and more heartfelt priority, instead of making the search for a mate another big contract to land. The happiest moments Stacy related to me were her visits back home where she spent time during the holidays with her nieces and nephews. When she described these visits, she seemed happy in a way that was strikingly different from the highs she experienced from her work.

Her profession trained her to look for the best deal, the best package, but these skills had no carryover in the search for a lifelong companion. Relating to her nieces and nephews put her in touch with a more loving side of herself. This recognition was a building block for the new directions she would take in her life.

In any session, I find myself inexorably drawn to those tiny positive building blocks that must be solidly in place before any real change can occur. I know psychotherapy is like mountain climbing. I know we all must have a secure footing before we can scan our own particular horizon and consider new options or take risks. I believe my task is to enable people to feel courageous enough to pause and to look at their strengths, foundations, and anchors before they continue. Indeed, much of that is interminable or ineffective in psychotherapy comes from pushing someone or allowing them to move too quickly.

In Stacy's past were moments where she might have acknowledged how much she wanted to feel connected and nurturing both with a man and with children. But she could not envision a plateau that could take her off her ambition treadmill, nor could she imagine a plateau in relationships (that concept only aroused the fear of "settling"). Luckily, Stacy finally put the brakes on. In time, she realized she had met many good men over the years, and in fact, she called one of them to renew a relationship, an invitation that he gladly accepted. It was this man that she finally married and at the age of forty-one, she had her first child!

For Stacy, life meant striving for success and recognition, and those dimensions of life that didn't fit this pattern escaped her. She could barely acknowledge other needs. She had to break this pattern to uncover herself and to find other ways of meeting her needs. She had to stop, to find inner plateaus of love and strength not based on striving, which taught her other ways to approach life and herself.

In recent years I have found that many women and men are unwilling or unable to stop and reflect. As a therapist, I feel an intuitive resistance to this. I want them to slow down. I know they are frightened at my attempts to get them to discover their own basic foundation, but I also know it is time to put on the brakes.

For most of us, slowing down is painfully difficult because of the anxiety it evokes. Halting feels the same as resignation, and we can't accept that. We need to learn that dissatisfaction and relentless searching are not necessarily virtues—that it is okay to take stock and figure out what is truly rewarding, in contrast with those goals we have absorbed without question or examination. We are ready to arrive at our own personal plateaus when we can acknowledge our limitations as well as our strengths. When this kind of self-examination takes place, it eventually leads to a feeling of balance and contentment—a sense of having found the real you. Only then will you finally discover that peace of mind is neither an ideal nor a fantasy, but a real possibility.

Plateaus relating to work, appearance, love, or parenting allow us room for self-appreciation and contentment. Plateaus are states of acceptance that allow us to look at ourselves and sincerely believe that we are enough.

Plateaus are not carved in stone. They are foundations that exist to meet our needs, and when those needs are satisfied, we move on. But sometimes we establish plateaus and abandon them before we are really ready to. The process is often subtle and insidious, but we can recognize it and work to establish another plateau, the way we did it the first time. The real world isn't perfect, but it isn't out of control either.

THE COURAGE TO REFLECT

Rex, a forty-nine-year-old executive, was referred to me because of conflicts he is having with his superiors at work. He is a key senior person in his company, but his superiors suspect he's recently been drinking on the job and having marital problems. Because he's not self-referred, I anticipate some resistance when he first comes in, but it never materializes. "I couldn't wait to get here," he blurts out as he slumps in the chair. "I'm so tired, so exhausted from performing, from acting, from faking it. I'll tell you right up front, I'm separated from my wife, but nobody in the company knows it. I'll tell you something else, whatever I'm going through has nothing to do with her. That's just an excuse. I've been sitting in a depressing hotel room, drinking too much, and thinking about my life. I'm lost and I know it. I've been lost for a long time. When I think back to my relationships with women, with my wife, my kids, my career moves, it seems I'm standing outside of myself. In thinking back, I forgot why I did whatever I did. I had everything going for me, but I've lost sight of myself. I know there must be somebody inside but he's a stranger."

Rex is courageous; although he views himself as confused and fraudulent, he is decisively and honestly looking at where he is. The existential philosopher Kierkegaard called anxiety the "dizziness of freedom," in a translation of *The Concept of Dread*. To confront yourself as self-determining, and to claim yourself as the cause of your life, is frightening. But to free yourself from obsessions, you must first take responsibility for the paths you have taken. This requires moving from a life of safety, to one of risk. Rex was doing this.

We must understand that acts of courage are required if we are to discover plateaus. That may sound like a daunting task, but I have found that individuals will accept such risks if they truly believe there will be a payoff. People will seek an alternative when they believe something positive will ensue. Getting off life's treadmills requires courage, but it also requires a belief that there are alternatives to blind and relentless pursuits.

The alternative to the treadmill trap is creating plateaus—foundations of satisfaction—in your life. There is a process or sequence of actions that will enable anyone to replace repetitive searching with a foundation of satisfaction. Rex has begun this process. He has found the courage to stop and reflect. Maybe he believed he had to, but in a sense this is how most of us come to grips with who we are and how we're living. Most of us don't alter the course of our life casually or even start changing joyfully. We do it because we decide it's impossible to continue conducting our lives in the painful way we have been.

AN INNER PERSPECTIVE

In the beginning of this book, I described how we lost a sense of our inner landscape. I noted that in a society so focused on finding solutions that are external to us, we have lost sight of an inner terrain. When I use the word *inner*, some of you may automatically think of feelings, or emotions. But as I hope I've made clear, while I believe that feelings are important guides, they can more often than not lead us astray. Feelings are reflexive responses dependent on what we do, but they don't necessarily tell us what to do. They are unreliable guides. We have neglected to use our thought processes, our capacity to muse, ponder, reflect, and remember. Our thinking allows for a new perspective.

As a starting point, consider the notion that you have a right to a life of your own, to choose rather than merely react. I believe the moments we act and choose are life affirming. These moments have been characterized as "existential moments," times when we discover courage, just as Stacy did. No matter what prompts this choice, it is still the ability to take self-determining action that creates the possibility of change, of living your life on your own terms.

As you undoubtedly know when you look at your own life, we often stop doing those things that used to make us happy and forget what felt soothing and relaxing. We either work or we passively seek out entertainment. Of course work and play are fine and necessary, but to achieve a gratifying life, we must think about the directions we've taken.

Rex, confused as he was, almost welcomed his crisis. He felt his hunger for success and his vision of a Perfect Self were killing him and only heightening his terrifying sense of imperfection. Like so many people driven to the point of collapse, he viewed the promise of getting off his ambition treadmill as a last chance for an anxiety-free existence. He acknowledged the inner voices and intermingling of thoughts and feelings that were trying to send messages that somehow never surfaced because his life was moving so fast. Achieving an inner perspective meant that he had to start listening to those inner thoughts, however faint they might be. As Rex noted, "I used to believe I took time to 'sort out my thoughts,' but now I realize that I was just listening to a portion of my thoughts and just cast away the ones I found disturbing, not realizing they were even more valuable than the ones I took time to look at."

Like all of us, Rex had a Forgotten Self. Rex began to remember his life when his children were younger and how much he enjoyed spending time with them. This led him into thinking about people in general, friends he no longer saw, but whose company he had once truly enjoyed. He even felt he could pinpoint the time where his ambitions evolved from joyous challenges into grinding obsessions—late nights at the office, hitting the bars with colleagues to unwind, unspoken irritations when his children wanted help with their homework when he got home. He remembered times when he felt sad, couldn't understand why, and then diverted that sadness into affairs, which always left him feeling more sad when the excitement wore off. And finally, he saw how often the path he took to cure this inner sadness became an increasingly vigorous climb up the ladder of success.

One day in therapy, Rex admitted, "Actually, I'm finding this whole process kind of exciting. In the past, whenever I tried to think things through I just went in circles because I never really wanted to look at my basic assumptions about what my life should be. I thought choices meant whether I should buy a Mercedes or a BMW, not realizing that maybe a Ford would actually meet my needs." Rex decided that he didn't have to make CEO. He chose to acknowledge a plateau of accomplishment that was at hand. He knew that he had not been living his life fully, but knew he could start again. Rex also resolved never again to lose sight of what he had now come to value—his wife, his family, his friends, and his long-neglected interests. The enticements of the ambition treadmill will most certainly beckon to him again, but his new awareness will arm him with the emotional and mental flexibility to withstand such seductions.

It is possible to slow down and reevaluate how you prioritize your precious time. It is possible to learn new things, explore new interests, and attempt creative endeavors.

But first, we must become aware of the various facets of our existence. Identifying and accepting our Imperfect Self, letting go of our wishful Perfect Self, and rediscovering our Forgotten Self are the elements in the process of creating plateaus. Each moment of identification is an existential moment, an opportunity to make a choice, to act or think in a different way. And all require faith and courage: Faith that there is a better way to live and the courage to take what I call "not-me" actions. We hear people say, "Oh, that's not me, I can't do that." But you probably can. Embracing these moments is not something you do blindly and desperately. Existential moments are not like jumping over a chasm. They are much more analagous to calmly and willfully opening a new door into an unknown space.

Plateaus enable us to survey our existing terrain and to take those steps into areas that are less rocky, more tranquil, often surprisingly more adventuresome.

Following are the three critical steps toward creating a plateau in any area of life where you are now on a treadmill. I call them Confrontation, Integration, and Liberation.

CONFRONTATION: ACKNOWLEDGING THE IMPERFECT SELF

If what we are doing is self-defeating, why don't we want to change? Why don't we want to let go of those habits that make us miserable? Is getting stuck a sign of stupidity or cowardice? Ask anyone who is married and he'll swear his mate refuses to change and is just too ornery or selfish to do it. You've seen people keep doing the same thing over and over again, never seeming to learn that it doesn't work. Change is difficult, and the first step in change is acknowledging our Imperfect Self. This is the self that propels most of us onto treadmills. But typically, we are unaware of our self-depreciating tendencies. Usually, we are only conscious of our wish to move closer to a Perfect Self. But as I have noted, this only results in feeling even more diminished. It is this diminished, or Imperfect Self, that must be confronted.

One major indication that you are too concerned with your Imperfect Self is how defensive you become whenever a colleague, friend, or mate gives you some feedback or criticism. Whenever you feel shame or defensiveness, it points to an aspect of your personality that you've been hiding. These pockets of self-dislike are constantly stimulated when you are in search of a Perfect Self. Confronting one's Imperfect Self is also a matter of self-honesty, the courage to acknowledge perceptions that lie right below the surface.

There are two basic reasons why most of us have difficulty confronting ourselves. First, we all try to deny the pain we're in and want to ignore just how unsatisfying our lives have become. Second, even when we are aware of our discomfort, we refuse to give up what is familiar to us, because, painful as it may be, it is less frightening than the unknown.

Denial of Pain

Although treadmills create a vague sense of being stuck, the captured person will not often easily admit it. Maybe it's a woman who keeps going after the same self-defeating choices with men or a workaholic male who can't ever seem to let up and find a more fulfilling balance in his life. When challenged, they engage in denial, or manufacture rationalizations that explain why they must persist in doing something that makes them miserable.

They are afraid to admit how unhappy they are. It's as if shifting gears would prompt some unbearable reality. So they act as though the best thing to do is to keep on going and continue to deny those feelings bubbling just beneath the surface.

If you keep moving fast enough, you can deflect any awareness of personal misery just out of the range of your consciousness. Athletes acknowledge that the adrenaline pumping through their body will offset any pain they feel while playing. But after the competition, the pain comes back. Sometimes blinding ourselves to pain is good, because that may be the only way we can accomplish heroic tasks. But a treadmill mentality often involves blinding ourselves to the point of real harm. The self-defeating nature of what we do is real, and it takes a physical and emotional toll.

Some of us look around, see others involved in the same pursuits and say to ourselves, "Well, they seem happy, so why shouldn't I do what they are doing?" If you're a conformist or a follower, you are also more likely to deny your own feelings.

"I'm too far into it to turn back," said one patient when I asked why he couldn't consider another lifestyle—in this instance, letting go of the pursuit of greater amounts of money. He felt he had so much time and emotion invested that to recognize that it really wasn't paying off would mean acknowledging a loss. In fact, cutting your losses is good advice not only in the stock market but in life as well.

The Illusion of Comfort Zones

A comfort zone describes a range of calculable safe interests, activities, ambitions, and social relationships that are familiar and comfortable to you. From infancy onward, we find security in what is familiar. For instance young children cling to blankets or favorite dolls to give them a sense of security.

We invariably experience hurt and pain growing up, along with, we hope, an equal measure of excitement and joy, or the unexpected delight of finding love. But for most of us, life is still fraught with the fear of the unknown, the possibility of abandonment, rejection, or disappointment. If we're fortunate, we learn to cope with these darker elements of our human experience. But when I refer to fear of the unknown, I am talking about surprises that could cause pain. Therefore, staying in our comfort zone is a kind of familiar illusion that we will be safe from greater hurt.

How do you know if you're honestly confronting yourself? Each of the previous chapters describing life's various treadmills contained questions or self-inquiries. If you diligently followed them, you have a pretty good sense of your Imperfect Self, of just how much you have devalued and depreciated your self-worth. Keep in mind that we all find certain aspects of our personalities less than perfect, and we may always feel this way, but we can come to accept them as being part of us, and not more ammunition for self-loathing.

When we face our Imperfect Self, we begin to shift the basis of our motivation from fear to positive wishes about what we really want. One of the reasons why psychotherapy is effective is because, in the sanctuary of the therapist's office and with reassurance, patients will cease avoiding and denying and finally turn inward to take a clear look at how they act, what they feel, and, most important, squarely examine those self-defeating assumptions and beliefs that have made them miserable. Surprisingly, for most of us, this self-confrontation is never as frightening as we thought it would be. In fact, we usually feel enormous relief when we examine in the light of day that which seemed so menacing, lurking in the shadows of our minds. The individual who examines his life and says, "Yes, I am disappointed in how far I've come in my career," will suddenly find that acknowledgment is simply that, an admission rather than a condemnation.

As you begin to look at yourself, keep uppermost in mind that this is just step one of a three-step process to gain self-acceptance. The awareness of this process is necessary so you won't be overwhelmed by negative self-perceptions. There is a way through the pain, and the reward is a renewed sense of life.

INTEGRATION: RECLAIMING THE FORGOTTEN SELF

Most of us lose valuable facets of ourselves as we grow up. We forget what we once liked about ourselves and what gave us genuine pleasure. Sometimes we forget things that we would be a lot better off remembering!

Cliff, according to his wife, is a "miserable grouch"—rarely enjoyable to be around. He's forty-four, a vice-president of a large public relations firm, and a success by popular standards. Father of two boys—one in college, and one finishing high school—he has been a good provider and a reasonably good husband according to his wife, Carol. As a patient seeking help for a lifelong struggle with a domineering mother, Carol urged Cliff to come to see me. She was convinced he was suffering from a mood disorder, because he always seemed depressed or irritable.

When he came in, Cliff struck me as extremely bright, but firmly caught on an ambition treadmill. Every waking hour was spent hustling new clients and catering to existing ones. As our sessions progressed, it became clear that he was terribly lost. He barely put up a fight when I suggested as much. "What else am I supposed to do? Change jobs? Move to the mountains? Get a hobby?"

"That last suggestion isn't such a bad idea," I told him. "Did you ever have one?"

He laughed at me, saying, "This is what I'm paying all this money for? Give me a break." He then changed the subject, telling me that we had probably achieved what we could, that he was trying to slow down at work, find some balance. He also indicated he was playing more tennis, but he also admitted he was so competitive that he got no real enjoyment out of it.

I summarized for him what I thought had transpired thus far. "You're less irritable, you've acknowledged how unhappy you've been, you admit that you have been on a treadmill, you seem to be getting off . . . but something's missing for me. I still don't know who you were when you were happier, before you got on the treadmill." Cliff nodded and sat silent. "Remember when you asked about hobbies?"

He finally said, "That day I remembered how fascinated I was for years with trains. As a kid, I built model trains with my father. In the summer, I would go down to the train yards and spend the whole day talking to the old train men, and they would tell me stories about the days of steam engines. We'd look at the boxcars and they would tell me the part of the country each came from. They even let me operate the switches that maneuvered the trains from one track to another. I was never so happy. It was a secret world of adventure, a world gone by. Even in college, whenever I would get depressed, I would go to the yards and spend a few hours just watching. I've never told anybody about it, not even my wife or kids. It just seems like a kid's thing, like something you put behind you."

During this recounting, I was aware that Cliff was momentarily "centered" and relaxed, and his pleasure in remembering was contagious. I felt I was in a wonderful reverie myself. As

Cliff talked, his face softened and he sounded warmer and more enthusiastic than I'd ever seen him. This was a long-forgotten part of himself that could still arouse deep feelings of satisfaction, and a sort of passion. I commented on this and it pleased him to hear my reaction, to know I took this interest seriously, rather than regarding it as childish. "So what are you suggesting— I should get on the floor and play with trains?"

"Why not?" I shrugged. "It sounds a lot more rewarding than getting all worked up because you just lost a tennis game to a friend who you were treating like a rival."

He ignored my reference to his overly competitive instincts, but he went on to tell me something quite poignant. He described a Saturday a few years before, when he was so stressed out and depressed he couldn't even talk about it. He told his wife he was going to the office and instead went to the library to read books about trains. "It was like greeting old friends of mine. When I moved out, my mother threw out my train books. Reading the old classics on the history of trains was so delightful, that I spent six hours in the library and walked out feeling as though all my troubles were lifted. But I never did it again!"

When I asked why, he said he felt guilty! He felt that he had wasted the day, that he should have been doing something productive! "What could be more 'productive' than feeding your soul, nourishing that part of you that had been so slighted in your quest for fulfillment?" I asked.

Cliff's story is about rediscovering a part of his Forgotten Self, but it is also about rediscovering play. So much of what we regard as play today is just another variation of life's hustling. What most adults call play is either competitive battle or some version of self-improvement. We have lost the child within us because we have been taught that it is inappropriate to keep it.

Cliff not only revived his passionate study of trains and their lore, he joined a train enthusiast society. He felt shy about this at first because it didn't fit into his existing friendships or social activities. But he accepted this part of himself. Moreover, just reclaiming that facet of his Forgotten Self put him on a liberating path to self-honesty. "Now, in everything I do, I question myself as to whether it is really *me* or something I just slipped into. I'm realizing that I'm actually a pretty simple guy in certain ways and am quite easily satisfied."

Cliff had discovered an inner freedom to invest himself emotionally in life experiences that were nourishing. Cliff's wife was the only person who really saw the difference, because change is more often experienced inwardly rather than perceived by others. He still worked just as hard in the office, but the other hours of his daily life were different. Cliff had learned to play and to find peace.

There are many ways to lose important or meaningful aspects of our lives. In my work, I have found that one of the most common areas of neglect is forgetting the importance of genuine companionship. As we get caught up in life's treadmills, we tend to develop relationships that only serve to advance our self-improvement. Men and women too often choose friends on the basis of what they can offer. Oftentimes, we deceive ourselves about this, insisting that we like to be around people with similar interests, but that really means being around those who are useful, such as possible business contacts. Companionship has been eclipsed by social networking, and we have lost a great deal of our humanity in the process. We forget what it was like to just spend an evening having fun, or engaging in something intellectually stimulating. Instead, even our socializing must be productive in some way.

Our past accomplishments are something we often forget. On the ambition treadmill, we have an unfortunate tendency to remember only what is most recent. If we are engrossed with personal turmoil, stress, and the fear of failure, our past achievements fade prematurely. Yet remembering these accomplishments may be the path toward enhancing self-esteem. I like to ask patients, "Tell me about some of your successes, some good things you've done, we all have at least a few. What are yours?" Exploring this question is another way to help reclaim our Forgotten Self, because it puts us in touch with the strengths and interests that led us to our successes.

In marriage and parenting, where we get on relationship treadmills, our Forgotten Self is often the only catalyst left for reviving dormant love. Remembering why we fell in love with our mate, or retrieving memories of moments when we loved our children more freely is also part of reclaiming a Forgotten Self. We not only remember our love, we also remember aspects of our loved one's self that we have forgotten. Whenever parents tell me about their present resentments against a child who is overweight or doing poorly in school, for example, I tell them to look at old pictures of their children to reconnect with the love they once felt. This puts their present distress in perspective and reminds them of their resources for dealing with it.

Reclaiming the Forgotten Self is critical because it integrates our present narrow sense of self with a sense of who we were in the past, which is much larger and richer. This integration has a curative effect, enabling us to tap into positive reservoirs of self-liking and enjoyment that have long been ignored.

Accepting our Imperfect Self, rather than running from it, allows us to also rediscover our Forgotten Self. Who we were in the past may have some painful components that we have suppressed in the process of denial. But denial isn't as selective as you may think, and it often includes good things as well as the painful. When we can integrate both the painful and the good aspects of who we are, we experience a sense of wholeness and continuity to our lives. We also free the energy we were using to deny ourselves and use it for living.

LIBERATION: MOURNING THE PERFECT SELF

A crucial step in the process of creating a plateau is letting go of the quest for a Perfect Self. Unless you do this completely, you will only create a temporary foundation that will last only as long as you can ward off society's seductive prescriptions for how you should be. Unfortunately, many people in therapy get this far and stop. They feel good for a while, may even have integrated old facets of themselves that were forgotten, and briefly experience real self-acceptance. But when they continue to pursue a Perfect Self, this slips away. For without letting go of those illusory life goals that became treadmills, they are merely primed for the next one that catches their eye! Even though the Perfect Self is illusory and artificial, it has been cherished for a long time.

Why is letting go so difficult? Why do so many of us associate plateaus with resignation, rather than contentment or satisfaction? First remember that letting go allows us to stop being victims and allows us to regain control over our lives. We no longer subject ourselves to societal brainwashing. Nevertheless, a loss is a loss, and mourning the loss of a Perfect Self is quite unnerving at first, for a number of reasons.

The Fear of Mediocrity

Staying stuck on treadmills is too often confused with perseverance, even with having the courage of one's convictions. To entertain the idea of stepping off a life treadmill is to acknowledge that it's not working for you. For some that is tantamount to suggesting they quit whatever it is that they were doing, and in our society being a quitter is a shameful thing. It makes you feel like a loser, as if you've lost all credibility.

"I can't stand the idea of stopping," one exhausted entrepreneur confesses to me. "If I stop now, it's like admitting this is the best I can do, so I have to keep expanding. It's part of the game."

"Are you still enjoying the game?" I ask.

He looks at me, wanting to say yes, but he sees I already know the answer and he's smart enough to recognize that lying is self-defeating.

This entrepreneur is trapped by a narrow sense of self-esteem and will find that getting off a treadmill requires taking a fresh look at the origins of his self-esteem. Remaining stuck is one way of not experiencing a blow to your self-worth and a way of avoiding even momentary insights into your limitations. I say momentary, because ultimately there are always ways of enhancing self-respect, and even old abandoned ways could work. The key lies in whether we come from a place of self-acceptance or of self-denial.

The Fear of Disappointing Others

Staying stuck on treadmills is often strengthened by promises we made to others. Losing weight, being more social, making more money, and so on are not only goals for ourselves, but often declarations or promises made to others. We do this to make them happy about us, or to gain their approval. Taking a new path that feels right for you may entail breaking a promise that you should never have made in the first place! Getting unstuck can mean that you will disappoint loved ones, or even hurt them.

Frank, a thirty-two-year-old stockbroker, decided to quit his job because he was so unhappy in his work. He knew his wife, Alicia, was bound to be disappointed. She knew he wasn't happy, but she wanted to believe that he could work it out. Sadly, he couldn't. Like so many of us, he chose a profession based on values and interests that were not his own. It was not in his nature to promote himself and entertain prospective clients. Frank was a rather shy man, and the social demands of his career just didn't fit him. His decision to change created serious conflicts with his wife, but because of their love for one another, the conflicts were eventually resolved.

Those close to us have dreams about who they want us to be. Unconsciously, we try to play the roles they offer us. After all, that is one of the ways we win their love and approval. Sometimes we're afraid to change into who we suspect we really are, because those we are close to may not love us anymore. We may feel we tricked them into loving us, and feel compelled to sustain the illusion of the person they thought we were. It shouldn't surprise us, although it usually does, that when we begin to change we are met by resistance, rather than acceptance. Changes in us are threatening to the status quo. When Frank quit his job, his wife reacted with anxiety not because she didn't love him, but because his decision upset her comfort zone. The same forces that have kept us stuck are also at work in their lives. They are protecting their illusions. When we set out to accept ourselves, we can't always expect others to do the same. Sometimes they do, but it is one of the risks we run.

Denial of pain, the illusion of comfort, the fear of mediocrity, and the discomfort of disappointing others are some of the most critical reasons for remaining stuck on treadmills, underscoring our fear of slowing down and taking stock. On the surface, the treadmill mentality may seem heroic, but it's not. Choosing to get off is what takes courage and honesty. Facing self-deception is heroic.

The treadmill process doesn't bring change; it prevents real change. Instead of something new, each venture becomes the same old thing, under a different guise. Changing treadmills may bring a brief renewal of hope and enthusiasm, but no matter how diligently we apply ourselves, our enthusiasm slowly wanes. With each failure we grow more weary, our hope diminishes and our panic increases. The dark and terrible specter that the fault lies within us, that we just aren't enough, looms ever larger in our beleaguered souls, and we see no alternative but to run faster.

Mourning the loss of the Perfect Self is a liberating experience. It's like the sense of freedom you can feel when you finally decide that it's not important that everyone likes you. When you no longer have to perform for the benefit of toxic life goals that haven't brought you anything but misery, you are ready to begin living life on your own terms. This period of mourning is an unavoidable step in the process of getting off life's treadmills. But once you're off, you will experience genuine self-acceptance and the power that comes from liberation.

ARRIVING AT SELF-ACCEPTANCE

The well-known Eastern notion of being "centered" connotes a sense of focus, integration, and being "together." Perhaps it is only possible when you are self-accepting, when even if you don't like parts of yourself, you can still integrate all the facets of your personality.

The vast majority of us think we are self-accepting, even when we're not. We pay lip service to particular aspects of our personality, believing that a cursory acknowledgment is the same as emotional acceptance. We view these traits out of the corner of our eye, not wanting to take a long look—because if we did, we would immediately feel the shattering self-dislike of the Imperfect Self. We fear acknowledgment will create ceilings or limits rather than plateaus.

Self-acceptance allows you to finally see yourself in positive terms, rather than negative ones. This happens because mourning the loss of the Perfect Self disarms the internal critic that has been telling you that who you are and what you've been doing is not enough.

Plateaus solve the circularity of the self-acceptance problem: "How can I accept myself when I don't like myself?" By taking each step—Confrontation, Integration, and Liberation—you discover that self-acceptance is something you arrive at, not something you anxiously pursue. Relentless attempts to "like" ourself in the absence of taking these steps is a doomed quest even if masked by a momentary and fleeting sense of acceptance.

Letting go of the Perfect Self and integrating our Forgotten Self strengthens our motivation in whatever we choose to do. Only when you experience a plateau in those areas of your life where you previously had no control, can you begin living life on your own terms. This is when you can come to experience a real you. Sometimes the self we come to accept is neither lofty nor noble, but it's who we are, and we must acknowledge it. Imperfection has a reality that perfection never reaches.

After reminiscing about some of our adolescent experiences, a fifty-year-old friend of mine who runs a multimillion-dollar company is reminded of a recent incident in his office. He was listening to various ad agencies pitch their services, trying to win his account. He tells me he sat there thinking to himself, "You guys are all bullshitters, trying to jack me around. I wish I could tell you to get the f——— out of my office."

In recounting his inner feelings, we laugh, but he asks me, "What's really going on? Am I still an adolescent posing as a mature adult or am I an adult who is just in touch with an old, adolescent, and perhaps immature side of myself?"

I believe that his inner voice comes from who he really is, and it is not adolescent nor is it immature. It is real and unadorned by all the pseudohonest layers of compromise, self-deception, and politeness imposed by society's dictates. Mind you, I'm not suggesting we should always speak what we feel inside, because that is not how the system works, but it is important to affirm who we are and what our "voice" is saying.

The real you does exist, because we all possess an essential core that makes up our identity. You may not fully embrace and admire every part of yourself. But the person you have become after years of experience and conditioning, with all your accumulated trappings, is *not* the essential you. Not everything we have taken on fits us. Getting off life's treadmills involves getting in touch with that more enduring and essential you. Learning the difference between the essential you and the conditioned you takes time and attention.

Self-acceptance brings you closer to those things you wanted in the first place. When you stop striving so fiercely, what you may have been seeking will come to you. And finally, it is only from plateaus that further dreams and aspirations can take place. Anything you do using a plateau as a foundation will be motivated by positive wishes rather than fear and a belief that these new aspirations will solve old feelings of low self-esteem.

STOP IMPROVING YOURSELF AND START LIVING

There is a thin but crucial line between genuine self-enhancement and the kind of self-improvement that is fueled by a sense of deficiency and that invariably leads us onto treadmills. How can you tell the difference?

First, ask yourself, if the particular self-improvement you are seeking seems valuable in and of itself? In other words, are you pursuing it for intrinsic reasons, or for extrinsic ones? Extrinsic reasons include how you will be perceived by others. Intrinsically satisfying pursuits work for you, while those involving external reasons are typically illusory and ultimately unsatisfying. We all may harbor wishes to look better in the eyes of others—what is dangerous is when we deceive ourselves about our real motivation. For example, someone who perfects their skiing techniques because he enjoys a sense of improvement and mastery differs in motivation from someone who wants to impress others by looking good on the slopes. Both motivations may lead to the same end, but each has different psychological results. The intrinsically motivated person feels good about himself, while the extrinsically motivated person feels good only as long as he is receiving intensely craved adulation. And, of course, such recognition is either not forthcoming, or fades very quickly—in either event, the person is left feeling empty and disillusioned.

Attempts to move on in a satisfying way only work when you believe in a foundation, or plateau, of acceptance that supports you in the belief that you are enough right now. If you have done what you needed to do to reclaim yourself, you may take on new challenges, but for the right reasons. Remember, you aren't fooling anyone but yourself if you regard this as a game; by that I mean, make sure you are grounded in personal honesty and self-acceptance. Briefly glancing in the mirror won't do the job; superficial actions are only motivated by the anxiety and fear of never being okay.

Whenever patients ask if I'm advocating a status quo, I insist I'm not. I believe that role-playing, visualization, and other techniques to create *possible* selves are valuable, but only when firmly grounded with a sense of plateaus. People who choose to break out of old patterns can do so. It is possible to act as though you are more assertive, for example, and thereby become more assertive. But many people fail at this because they don't have a plateau to support them. They try to be different because they truly can't stand who they are now. Any change built on self-loathing is doomed to be fragile and short lived.

Men and women who take the chance of going through Confrontation, Integration, and Liberation seem to enjoy savoring plateaus. They are not so ready to move on to new things, partly because having lived so much of life driven by desires they never fully or consciously endorsed was exhausting, as you yourself may know. When you take the time to choose the kind of life that fits your needs it is exhilarating.

· CHAPTER TWELVE ·

INDIVIDUALITY:
THE COURAGE
OF YOUR CONVICTIONS

True individualists tend to be quite unobservant; it is the snob, the would-be sophisticate, the frightened conformist, who keeps a fascinated or worried eye on what is in the wind.
                                          —Louis Kronenberger, critic

"I spent years reading biographies of famous men. I never really knew why I would become mesmerized by their exploits. My wife told me, jokingly, that real life was too boring for me. In some ways, maybe she was right, but there's more to it than that. I think I'm finally realizing that I was looking for some answers, some clues as to how people discover their own vision about life, how they create a life of their own without worrying about other people's judgments." Gavin, a forty-two-year-old high-school English teacher, leaned back in his chair, pleased with himself and the clarity with which he now viewed his own life.

Gavin came to see me one year before, shackled by self-doubt and anxiety about a possible career change. When he was in his late thirties, he had gotten on a money treadmill, working in real estate part time in addition to teaching high school. Even though his wife, who also worked, was quite content with the quality of their life, Gavin felt vaguely inadequate about his work and his modest salary. He loved teaching, but grew up in a family and socioeconomic environment that, unfortunately, placed a low premium on his career choice. Because of this, he was considering going into real estate sales full time. As much as he tried to justify why he had chosen to go into teaching, he still felt infected by the opinions of others and never really felt good about himself. In the course of therapy, Gavin learned to value himself and his choices while courageously grappling with the money treadmill he was on. He decided to stay in teaching. He admitted that he secretly hated the real estate work, and he took a long, hard look inside and rediscovered both the dreamer and the thinker in his Forgotten Self. Finally, Gavin could begin a life on his own terms.

Creating a plateau allows you to rediscover the self-acceptance that fuels your individuality. When we don't accept who we really are, we stifle basic aspects of our individuality from ever coming through. Plateaus help us affirm our uniqueness, and confirm and strengthen our individuality by enabling us to say, "This is who I am, and it is enough." By accepting who you are, you let go of the pursuit of a Perfect Self and turn away from external social pressures that tell you what to be and what to do. As an individual, you are certainly part of a larger social structure, but at the same time distinguishable from it, because you no longer simply mirror it.

Plateaus are declarations that we are risking creating our own rules, no longer blindly subscribing to a "right" way to live, which often doesn't nourish our unique personalities. Plateaus require that we learn to say no to pressures we have formerly conceded to. Instead of endlessly pursuing more money, we decide how much money is enough. Instead of finding fault with our mates because they are less than perfect, we focus on what is good about them. Instead of becoming slaves to the perfect body, we learn to take care of the body we have. Learning to say no to societal pressures frees us to say yes to our own needs. We need to do both.

Building plateaus puts us in charge of our own lives and takes us off self-deprecating treadmills. Our attitudes change from doubt and anxiety to a positive affirmation of who we are and what we have. But we face an increasing pressure, which can put us back on the treadmills. We have to remember that just because we want to get off, the world won't come running to assist us. Too much money and power is invested in the upkeep of treadmills. We have to learn how to maintain our new attitudes, and our plateaus, in the face of strong resistance. And this isn't easy.

When I look around, I see either great skepticism about the possibility of living a life on our own terms or blind and dogmatic adherence to external definitions of individuality. Ironically, we feverently preach individuality, but our hypersensitivity to external concerns has forced us to lose sight of the inward qualities that distinguish each of us.

Self-defeating habits die hard. After being on treadmills for so long, we distrust anything that emanates from within, we can no longer recognize our own instincts or we confuse them with impulses. Instincts are built on a personal body of knowledge that we can tap into quickly and surely. Impulses, however, are fueled by compulsions, fears, and urges that we rarely understand or think through. Because we don't understand or trust our instincts, we fall prey to searching for a Perfect Self. In the absence of self-knowledge, we become victims of what is conventional, trendy, and generally accepted. Treadmills exist when there are no other perceived options, and the failure to consider options is a result of our loss of individuality, our fear of standing back and looking within ourselves.

Kristin, a thirty-six-year-old woman who finally has found a career she loves in stock options trading, exemplifies this dilemma. She tried law school, business school, even graduate school in psychology for a brief time. "Every time I thought I found a plateau for my ambitions it was really just another version of a treadmill. I would see one career counselor after another, but it was all superficial. They seemed to ask the right questions, but I kept coming up with clichéd choices that were directions I just took out of magazines."

One day, two realities hit Kristin with absolute clarity. First, she realized she wasn't a people person. She had a few close friends, but liked spending a lot of time alone. Second, she was drawn to making money, not out of desperation, but as a kind of game. Having looked inside rather than consulting experts she decided to work out of her home and trade stock options on a daily basis to see whether she could make a living at it. Thankfully, she eventually did.

We all have resources we aren't utilizing, resources we have forgotten. As I've suggested, reclaiming our Forgotten Self is one of the most important steps toward starting to create a life of our own. We need to learn to hold opposite or conflicting ideas in our minds without quickly attempting to dispel the tension that creates. In our society today, *feeling good* has come to mean a life without pain, and that's impossible because pain is a part of every life.

Without a sense of individuality, we merely run faster on treadmills, or we become passive and dispirited. We have become so accustomed to always growing, striving, and improving, that we have almost forgotten how to simply live.

Often when I first communicate these thoughts to patients or friends, I hear loud protests—especially from those whose formative years took place in the sixties and seventies. So many people today think they're operating from a position of individuality, but I find this is more about posture than substance. I sympathize with their underlying frustrations, because it is difficult for any of us to find our way through our societal mazes. It is worth looking at the substitutes that tempt us.

PSEUDOINDIVIDUALITY

The appearance of individuality and nonconformity is highly valued in our society. We dress with careful attention to style, supposedly to express our uniqueness, we buy cars that we secretly hope will make a statement about us, and we conduct ourselves in ways we hope will elicit admiration and recognition from others. While some of us may be shy about standing out in a crowd, if we're honest, most of us admit we'd like to. Paradoxically, we try to be unique choosing costumes, roles, and actions that are socially accepted! To be a nonconformist or individual is to take the chance of being laughed at, alienated, or even humiliated. So we try to be safe, even as we think we're being daring. It seems as though we don't trust ourselves unless we fit into a particular category.

The advertising industry is forever tempting us with these ambiguous signals. We are urged to buy a particular car because it makes a statement about us. But if we are just one of many buying that car, it becomes a very safe way of communicating who we are and what our value is. It really isn't all that daring to become part of the herd even if that herd is small and select. We call these choices *lifestyles*. We want to be individuals, and yet we want to belong to our select group. If the members of our group are people we value, then we feel secure in belonging and safe in adopting the lifestyles they do. We rarely think to make choices that are not sanctioned by any particular group, but may enrich our own lives.

I regard the adherence to lifestyles as an essential part of living today, and it is often worthwhile. But to call these life-styles examples of individuality is erroneous. Being an individual is ultimately about personal choices and observations. Being open about these decisions may cause us to stand out in ways that might cause embarrassment, shame, and a sense of aloneness. And few of us are willing to take those chances. We have come to distrust our responses to even the most ordinary, everyday experiences.

You may have had the experience of walking out of a movie theater with some friends, and as you discuss the film, become aware that your impression of a particular character or theme is vastly different from theirs. You may hesitate to voice your opinion—not necessarily because you're afraid of sounding stupid—but because you're reluctant to stand out, as if being different devalues your experience. Our silence at these moments is determined by our inability to trust our own responses and our wariness about their reception. Even our sense of belonging rests on shaky ground. Our silence allows us to feel different without risking asking for acceptance of that difference.

Being different, however, is not synonymous with individuality. Some people assert their opinions openly and clearly, but we sense their rigidity. They are disinterested in what other people think or in examining their own ideas. This is a deceptive mask of individuality. Part of our culture—a carryover from the sixties—is the idea that rebellion is a hallmark of the individual. But the rigid or opinionated person is bound by another kind of conventionality. The rigid person is ultimately motivated by fear and an inability to comfortably entertain new ideas or concepts. She is unable to be open to other ideas and finds openness threatening because she doesn't really trust herself. If she really trusted the worth of her ideas, she would not cling to them so dearly and could relax enough to allow herself to reevaluate them periodically.

If you find yourself in either of these roles, what can you do? How can you move toward becoming truer to those beliefs and attitudes you may have discovered in reclaiming a Forgotten Self? While there are a number of things you can do to confirm and strengthen your newly discovered self, there is one essential task for everyone. You must first tolerate, and then learn to seek out, solitude.

SOLITUDE

A common concern of many couples, especially when they've moved past the intense romantic phase where "fusion" and "oneness" are cherished more than individuality, is how to have some time alone, while still maintaining a loving bond with their partner. When I hear my patients struggling with this dilemma, the first thing I tell them to do is to state it in positive terms. Be sure to ask, "How do I find some time for myself?" rather than, "How can I get away from my mate?" Even though people will say they need to get away from something, more often than not they're really feeling the need to become reacquainted with themselves. As I noted in discussing marriage, privacy is a neglected need in most relationships.

But in spite of the essential worth of time alone, married people often have difficulty finding solitude. Men and women often feel guilty taking time out to be alone. They'd rather use excuses like going to the office, running errands, or dropping by the health club. It's strange that we feel guilty about allowing ourselves time alone, when we only wish to rejuvenate. And these breaks are not only good for us, but are also good for our relationships, because we return psychologically rested and with more energy to give of ourselves.

Solitude is not encouraged in our society. In fact, it is suspect, as though enjoying aloneness means you are unable to enjoy being with others. Solitude, as restful as it may sound, still connotes isolation, aloofness, and even detachment. We are taught to regard togetherness as the keystone of mental health. However, just because we are social animals, doesn't mean we must always be together. We invariably find that a balance between aloneness and togetherness is necessary to fully appreciate being with loved ones, friends, and colleagues. When we're alone, we can relax, cease performing, and most importantly, rediscover ourselves.

When we are alone, we often don't use our time to be with ourselves. We approach aloneness as though it were a void to be filled. So we immediately switch on the TV or the radio, anything to fill the emptiness. Solitude can be frightening because it invites us to meet a stranger we think we may not want to know—ourselves. Yet this is the power and the opportunity of solitude. When we risk knowing ourselves, we find in solitude not emptiness, but our most important companion.

Regardless, few people choose to spend a lot of time alone, as it makes them feel lonely, isolated, and unloved. When we're alone, if we are not totally satisfied or contented, this discontent rises to the surface. When it is a respite from our hurried lives and our need to be productive, we enjoy our solitude. But it is often something most of us avoid, for some compelling reasons.

Negative thoughts tend to dominate positive thoughts because of our need to be vigilant and self-protective. That's why, when we're alone, unless we're occupied with television or reading, we worry and ruminate. Indeed, studies on isolation and sensory deprivation indicate that prolonged aloneness can be terrifying and lead to psychoticlike states. In the absence of external stimuli and cues, we are only left with those thoughts that emanate from deep within us. But we must explore those very thoughts if we are to become individuals!

When we avoid solitude or fill it with diversions we neglect ourselves. After years of neglect, the hurts and fears we have tried to keep at arm's length push to the surface, clamoring for our attention. This clamor of unmet needs and unattended wounds can make solitude more forbidding than it really is; remember there is more to who we are than pain and fear. When we learn to take care of ourselves and don't turn away, we discover resources and even a wisdom about our lives that we were neglecting. Only those who take the initial risk find the blessings of solitude.

If your life is guided by a treadmill mentality, you probably spend very little time alone, and when you do, it is usually only a brief respite from your hurried life. It's hard to make time for ourselves, but when we regard solitude as a luxury, we cheat ourselves of vital experience.

Jean, a thirty-seven-year-old dress designer, has been happily married for fourteen years. She first came into therapy because of anxiety attacks that started occurring when her two children became unruly. She was guilt ridden and perfectionistic because she thought she should be a more effective parent. Her solution was to spend more time with her children hoping a stronger bond would cause her children to behave. Instead her anxiety grew. Her children would sense this and become even more undisciplined. One day I asked her how much time she spent alone. It was very little, mostly in the car, thinking about work and things she had to do. She did remember, however, when she was younger, how staying in her room and writing poetry made her feel quite content. I suggested that she had a Forgotten Self that was crying out for attention and that she should take time out and do whatever felt good. She asked her husband to be more involved with the day-to-day details with the children, and she began to take walks on the beach. She became calmer, stopped taking tranquilizers, and, as a result, was more effective with the kids. Jean had reclaimed some of herself. As she became more self-accepting, she was less demanding of her children; therefore, it was easier to discipline them because she wasn't blocked by her guilt.

Solitude allows us to reclaim our Forgotten Selves by remembering—recollecting old, neglected interests, attitudes, and feelings. In a society that emphasizes celebrity, fame, and recognition, we have come to believe that feeling special only comes from external validation. This is false. Specialness and individuality can be confirmed by others, but its source comes from within. We create our own uniqueness and it is born in solitude.

WILL AND SELF-DETERMINATION

We live in an increasingly complicated world filled with new things we think we should know. Regardless of how sophisticated we become, or technologically advanced, all this increased knowledge doesn't make us feel more competent, rather we feel more helpless and frustrated. People feel unable to control their complex world and, in turn, feel they can't control their personal lives. The external world seems even more remote and less responsive to us, and our will seems impotent. We doubt our capacity to shape our lives.

The concept of *will*, or willpower, is an old one. Will is the capacity to choose or act in a particular way. Feeling empowered is our updated way of discussing the capacity for acting this way, but its source differs significantly. Empowerment implies the source as being external to us. This external focus is at the core of the treadmill mentality. Will, on the other hand, focuses on our capacity to determine our lives. It suggests the power comes from within.

Perhaps you have had to make a major decision about a job promotion or relocation, and you're not sure what to do. Some people make the decision and immediately feel remorse over the choice they didn't make. Others make a choice and experience their will at work. Kathleen, a thirty-four-year-old public relations executive, turned down a job relocation and told me she felt exhilarated afterward. "So often, whenever I ask all my friends about a decision, by the end, even when I make up my mind, I forget it was me that did it. I even feel a little depressed later. Now I realize that I didn't 'own' my choice. When I take responsibility for it, it really does make me feel powerful."

If we are to overcome the lure of treadmills, we must affirm and nurture our capacity to choose. We believe in will when we think we are free to conduct our lives on our own terms. How can we get in touch with this capacity? The first step is determining whether you view your life as externally caused or internally caused. Psychological studies have shown that people have specific views about what is called the "locus, or source, of control." Some people believe the locus of control in their lives is external and are passive in the face of their needs. Others acknowledge forces that influence their lives, but nevertheless place the locus of control squarely within themselves. They know that they can choose and act.

In conducting workshops for executives who are under stress, I often probe their underlying belief systems about the directions of their lives. Even the most aggressive and successful executives often will reveal a secret pessimism about their life path. They may have enormous confidence about particular areas of mastery and control in their work, or even in their personal life, but if you ask them whether they really feel in control of their destiny, most will admit they feel driven by forces they no longer can identify. Much of this pessimism is a by-product of the treadmill mentality—in this case, the ambition treadmill—but the way they describe this feeling suggests they are out of touch with their inner reality. Because they have lost touch with themselves, they try to "control" everything. But this is different from making choices—it is a kind of resignation. We do have the power to choose, but it won't come from outside. We need to learn to think about ourselves in a new way, believe that there are more options than we now recognize. We are all equipped to reconnect with our will and our willpower.

Unfortunately many of us see using willpower as an activity we engage in with clenched teeth. We try to force ourselves to do something we either can't or won't do. When we fail, we hate ourselves even more than before, because we believe we are weak or lack willpower. This becomes a vicious circle in our lives.

There are some things we can control and some things we can't. We can control the expression of our anger, but it doesn't help us to deny we feel angry. We can control the way we express our passions, but we aren't going to make them go away. We can influence other people, but we can't control them. If we attempt the impossible, we are going to come away defeated.

Recognizing and using our will involves accepting what we can't and shouldn't control. We invest too much energy into denying who we are or denying who other people are. When, for example, we accept fear, we can find ways to deal with it. But if we try to control ourselves by denial or by simply ignoring our obstacles, we actually undercut our ability to act.

Using our will requires acts of acceptance as well as acts of assertion and discipline. When we accept ourselves we accept our will, and we can begin giving positive direction to our lives. When we accept ourselves and begin to nurture our will, we open the opportunity to think for ourselves because we aren't pushing important areas of our life out of sight. Our self-possession gives us a perspective for knowing our own minds. This is what it means to move the locus of control within. We know it and believe it from direct experience. It is more than a philosophical assertion.

THINKING FOR YOURSELF

When you finally understand how you can have a self-determining impact on your life's direction, you are then ready to expand this belief into action. To move away from conformity—after allowing yourself some solitude—you must still learn something new: to think for yourself. Now perhaps that sounds easy, but it's not. A treadmill mentality leaves you unaccustomed to using your own mind in new and original ways.

Thinking for yourself is a neglected activity, especially in an era where the psychologizing of everyday life is taken for granted. We don't think for ourselves because we have not allowed ourselves to have a self. To compound the problem, in the last two decades we have been taught that thinking is bad, that access to our feelings is more important than our rational thoughts, and that thought is actually an enemy of feeling. For example, the emphasis on right and left brain processes is heralded because we can now allegedly delve into feelings and intuitive processes. There is value in that, but we've neglected using the mind, which is still critical for decisions and actions. If we focus only on our feelings, we are guided by impulses, which can lead us astray. Rejecting our intelligence is not the way to becoming intuitive.

While it may be true that people on treadmills use intellectual processes to rationalize their actions or to avoid their feelings, it is absurd to conclude that all thought is rationalization. Actually thinking and feeling are closely connected. If we deny our feelings, we inhibit our power to think clearly. But the opposite is also true. If we don't think clearly, we muddy our feelings. The attack on thought puts us farther away from our feelings, not closer to them.

Our heads are filled with unexamined ideas that come to us from outside and may or may not fit our actual experience. This is one of the reasons we are so susceptible to all the social myths that work to put us on our treadmills. Some of our ideas come from the mistaken conclusions we draw from our own experience. After two or three unfortunate relationships, we may conclude that "all women are takers," or "all men are scoundrels." These conclusions profoundly influence how we approach our next relationship. Unless we examine our ideas, they run through our minds like invisible renegades, directing our attentions, shaping our expectations, and limiting our options.

We test our ideas in the crucible of our own experience, and we remain open to the outside perspective of those who know us and care about us. The key word here is *test*. We need to be aware of what we think, articulate our assumptions, and test these ideas against the other things we know about the world and about ourselves.

Today, much of our difficulty lies in the fact that we forget or ignore what we already know. Most of what we learn from our examined experience is sound. We have the inherent ability to make sense of our experience. But when our focus is outward and our cues are from the world around us, we forget to check if what we are accepting really makes sense for us. The less we check ourselves, the less we trust ourselves and the more we move in step with the latest fad or export judgment on the meaning of our lives.

Learning to think means taking some time (this is where solitude comes in) to find out what we think. And it means learning to trust ourselves. Paying attention to our intuition means tapping into what we already know, listening to it, and using it to test the latest information the world has given us.

Intuition is based on knowledge that can be accessed and utilized, seemingly without thinking. But if we don't think first, we have nothing to access! Thinking about what we want and what we need to do to reach particular goals is a necessary first step. Thinking means we pay attention to our experience and learn from it. We take note of what works and also stop doing what doesn't work. Intuition taps into our storehouse of experience and is flexible and responsive, not patterned and rigid. I use the phrases *trusting your instincts* and *using your intuition* interchangeably to describe this process.

Instincts are thought to be inborn and natural, but I'm not claiming that our knowledge is innate. We learn things through experience—for example, don't touch a hot stove—and subsequently these lessons seem ingrained because they become habits and are no longer conscious decisions. But they were still learned the first time. Intuition is the capacity to draw on this knowledge, which is no longer conscious, but forms a part of our Forgotten Self. In choosing to let go of treadmills, and to stay off them, we must draw on the truths that lie within us. Doing this involves thinking about what we know and bringing it to our conscious awareness.

When we look exclusively outside for our directions we forget to check in with ourselves to see if these directions make sense for us. As a result, we have no touchstone for judgment, no basis for evaluating what we have been told. Becoming an individual means that we become conversant with ourselves. We consult ourselves. We remember who we are and what we know.

When I work with patients who are attempting to break old patterns and search out new directions, I may offer alternatives. But I hope I encourage the patient to look within for his own options. When a therapist asks a patient, "What feels right for you?" the patient immediately senses he should look within rather than cast around in the external world for guidance. Unfortunately, this can arouse great anxiety, when he believes he's too far along his particular path to risk changing it.

When we are excessively anxious about changing a path we have taken, coupled with a sense of fatalism, this is a crucial clue that we have stopped being responsive to ourselves. Old patterns that drive us may undermine our individuality. Reclaiming our individuality requires that we break those compulsive responses that keep us rigid, frightened, and driven. Then we begin to experience the satisfaction and peace of mind that comes from trusting ourselves.

THINKING AHEAD

Most of have a tendency to think too late! We act as though we can make decisions at the last minute. For example, if we are desperately striving to realize a new ambition, and we are driven by a treadmill mentality, we often don't think clearly enough. We start a new business venture with a partner, but forget to evaluate our compatibility with that partner until it's too late. After we're well into the project, we typically encounter some personality clashes, and only then do we start to ponder our choice. Or, like single people caught up in their passions, we wait until our erotic desires take us into someone's bedroom before we begin to think about the choice we've made.

We do this all the time. We fail to think for ourselves, we fail to ask ourselves, "Is this something I really want to do?" Decisions are easier to make early in a process, before we are up to our necks in what we are doing. If we make ourselves aware of our motives and think ahead we can usually see where our decisions will take us. If we really don't want to be involved with someone, it is easier to choose not to meet for a drink at all than it is to decide to go home after a few beers. Or it is easier to decide to never smoke than it is to break a smoking habit. Thinking ahead makes our choices more manageable and allows us to avoid those white-knuckled situations. Reclaiming our individuality means we get clear about what we are doing, and getting clear requires that we do some thinking. In getting off life's treadmills, it is essential that you begin to make choices earlier rather than later, because it is then that the odds are in your favor. Having the courage of your convictions enables you to make these choices at the right time.

The ability to think ahead enables us to maintain and sustain plateaus. Individualism requires vigilance. Temptations abound, and we must preserve our self at the same time we're being open! But it is possible to maintain these rhythms of our attention throughout life.

AGE IS NOT THE ENEMY

If there is one fact about people who do not become obsessed with self-improvement or get caught on life's treadmills, it is that they have a sense of balance in their lives. I'm not referring to that compulsive balance so prevalent today among men and women who are trying to have it all. I mean *balance*, not juggling, and there is a difference. These people have a sense of humor, take time out to play, and don't take themselves too seriously. They are more interested in living than in self-improvement and are more likely to talk about play rather than pleasure and more likely to be interested in others rather than working so hard at being interesting themselves. Put simply, they are self-accepting individuals rather than conformists. They know life is too short to be involved in self-loathing. And they believe they have some control over their lives.

Achieving this is not all that heroic, sometimes it simply comes from having the good sense and the self-honesty to recognize when other people have some worthwhile suggestions. In many marriages, one person is the catalyst for this in his mate. I often rely on my wife to keep me on the right path. She is aware of just how much of a workaholic I can be and has the energy to remind me who I am when I'm overly obsessed with one project or another. Those without such guidance will often develop their own inner gyroscope that tells them when their psychic equilibrium is off. They don't compulsively schedule play and work so that it all becomes work, they just listen to a little voice inside that says it's time to play. We all have that voice; we just don't trust it.

Having said many negative things about desperate searching and always needing to be more, I would like to share something I have learned from observing my patients, my friends, and myself. The older you get, the less important it becomes to heal the narcissistic wounds of the past and the easier it is to accept yourself. One reason is quite simple. At a particular age, somewhere between forty-five and fifty-five for most people, you become instinctively aware of the end of life, rather than its stormy beginnings. You are leaving mid-life, rather than entering it.

Mid-life crises are often about what you didn't accomplish and how you suddenly become aware that your life, as it has been, has no meaning. It is a turbulent time for both men and women. Much has been written about it, because it catapults men and women into despair, disillusionment, and divorce. But we never hear about the end of such crises. Many of us realize that our lives haven't been so bad after all. In fact, if you accept who you are and what you've done, your life seems pretty good, even terrific sometimes, because you are starting to discover peace of mind.

When I get together with friends and reminisce about old times and adventures, I'm always vividly aware that I am happier today than I have ever been. Why? Is it that life is so good? Not really. I have just as many problems to confront now as I did then. What has changed is that I am more self-accepting, and so are many of my friends. As we enter our fifties, we no longer feel the need to strive for so much and to be so heroic and so risky in our ventures. Getting older allows us to be more confident, indeed, wiser, especially when we stay aware of all that has transpired and all the illusions that we entertained along the way. As we age, we talk about the difficulties of child rearing, of accepting who and what our children have become. And we talk of accepting how far we have come in our careers, regardless of whether such progress matches our earlier dreams. Indeed, middle age is in itself a plateau, if we choose to see it that way. There is a saying that before the age of forty, you have the face you want and, afterward, the face you deserve. Mid-life is the springboard to beginning a genuine acceptance of your individuality.

Even though we associate youth with the capacity for great accomplishments, it is actually easier to achieve things as we get older. As we mature, and modify our expectations, we can become more productive. Anyone who has let go of treadmills and discovered plateaus has experienced the paradox of getting more by demanding less.

The tincture of time is a phrase used in medicine that means that time, in and of itself, heals both physical and psychic wounds. So often, I wish I could communicate this hope to patients who are locked into their present obsessions. They have no faith that maturity will cast their concerns into a kinder light than now exists. Adolescents fear that the heartaches of youth will never end; individuals in their twenties and thirties worry that they may fail to become successful; people in their forties grieve over lost opportunity. If only we knew what each decade ahead of us knows and trust that the future holds good things for us, we could live in a much more peaceful manner.

In an age when we adore youth and dread the prospect of aging, it becomes even more important that we acknowledge the rewards of growing older. Age can bring us perspective, and from the vantage point of time and clarity, it is often easier to be happy with what we have.

As we grow older, we can gain perspective on all those expectations we have accumulated about what life should be and who we should be. The contrast between what we have accomplished and what we expected of ourselves can sharpen our awareness of our expectations. Reassessing and changing our expectations aren't automatically concessions to failure. Many of our expectations have had little to do with who we are. We have been seduced by media images of success, or we have simply internalized someone else's expectations. Readjusting our expectations can lead to a renewed commitment to the possible.

These processes of reassessment—of sorting out the valid from the invalid, looking at expectations, looking at accomplishments, making adjustments in where we want to go—are all part of building, or discovering, plateaus of self-acceptance. Age doesn't require that we do this, but sometimes it makes it easier for us. When you are young you can, and should, question your expectations and dreams, and build plateaus in your life. But it can be more difficult to get these issues into focus. Difficult or not, by refusing to discover a plateau you can inadvertently resign yourself to a kind of nonliving and deny yourself a life!

With age, we become wiser and more at peace with ourselves and this is something to look forward to. Getting older can be a blessing, especially for those who have been searching to no avail. As the time between life and death shortens, life becomes more precious, and hopefully lived more fully.

As we get older, we are more vigilant about the choices we make. We know that it is all too easy to get swept up in what is trendy and what seems to promise fulfillment at little cost.

Nathan, a fifty-four-year-old college professor, has discovered some of these truths. "I remember in the past how every major decision or choice I made was agonizing. The implications loomed so large, and I had so much apprehension as to whether what I wanted was going to fit in with my life plan. Would I succeed? Would it set me back? And now, living is so much more fluid, easier, maybe organic is the right word. I know that if I'm not true to myself, I end up cheating myself. When my wife suggests socializing with couples that I really don't care for, I find it easy to tell her. Not that I'm more snobbish, I'm probably less so. I just know myself, what I need, what is really gratifying, and I make my choices based on that rather than what's going to enhance my ego or image."

Those of you reading this who are relatively young should not hear this as a message to passively wait for this wisdom of middle age. I'm suggesting that knowing how life can become easier rather than more burdensome is often an encouragement to discover plateaus now!

With age, we worry less about passages and more about life in the present. Being more successful may be less important than being open to the unexpected and the surprising. True individualists don't dread old age, not do they revere youth. I find that as we age, we find ourselves less self-rejecting, less prone to being caught on life's treadmills. When we find plateaus, when we are self-accepting, we begin to trust ourselves in ways that to others may seem instinctual, but we know they are the product of our thinking and of our will. We choose not to give ourselves away, because we believe in ourselves.

And finally, claiming our individuality is the only way we can break out of our isolation. As individuals, we feel less frightened, less threatened, and more open to others. We can ask for help, acknowledge our hunger for contact, and recognize our wish to love.

CHAPTER THIRTEEN

BEYOND THE SELF: SPIRITUALITY AND CONNECTEDNESS

The person who tries to live alone will not succeed as a human being. His heart withers if it does not answer another heart. His mind shrinks away if he hears only the echoes of his own thoughts and finds no other inspiration.

—Pearl Buck, novelist

I'm waiting for Chuck, my last patient of the day, a thirty-nine-year-old executive with an advertising firm. He's late and I'm worried. I know that he was scheduled to meet with the president of his largest account today, and he expects to be told that they are dropping his agency. Although he had anticipated this, it would nonetheless be a major setback; one that may even cost him his job. Fifteen minutes late, he comes in looking quite calm and relaxed. "Good news?" I ask.

"No," he says, "they're quitting the agency." He doesn't seem distressed. Puzzled, I wait for him to speak. "After the bad news, I left the meeting devastated. I thought of stopping by a bar before I went back to the office, but I couldn't find one open. Back in the office, I couldn't talk to anyone. I didn't even tell my partners. Then I left to come here, even though I was an hour early. I was just going to sit in the waiting room. But you know that church up the street, on the next block? Well, I found myself walking in. It was almost empty, just two older women sitting near the front. I sat in the back and suddenly I just started crying. I haven't been in a church in twenty years. I wasn't thinking about God or religion, I started thinking about Caroline and the kids, how much I love them, how much I need them, how little time I've spent with them in the last couple years. Thinking about them I soon felt so peaceful, so removed from what had just happened."

Chuck smiled and shrugged his shoulders. "Look, I don't even know what I'm saying. I don't know what this means. I certainly don't see myself becoming an avid churchgoer . . ."

Touched by his story, I didn't say anything for a while, then I smiled back at him and said, "I guess you had a real blow today. You felt terribly wounded, and your instincts took you on a path toward healing. There was a time, I think, when you would have bounced back by hustling up more business. And that isn't a bad response, either. But this time, you knew that you had to put your life in perspective, you had to find what's important, and thanks to your instincts, you did."

Chuck did not become a different person. He and his family did join a church in their neighborhood, but he only went on special occasions. Outwardly, he didn't look any different to his friends and colleagues. He was still a shrewd and aggressive businessman. But something did change in his life. He discovered that loving bonds with his family kept him integrated and whole—not success, not money, not things—but love. When this truth hit him, it was not a surprise, for like so many of us, he had at times been familiar with the richness of love and connectedness. But also, for so many of us, this awareness often resides in a Forgotten Self.

In a secular age it is difficult to speak about spirituality. It touches so many tender areas of doubt and disillusionment. Psychologists have learned to skirt the subject, wary of the pitfalls. Yet we return to it, for we know the spirit is a crucial part of being human. We speak of being dispirited, or we speak of having our spirits lifted. If we don't want to avoid the experience of being human, we have to risk, at times, stepping into pools of uncertainty, as Chuck did, to find out that our spirit often takes us to more fertile fields.

We talk of love and we talk of values, not as dogma, but as a focus in our lives. We don't need to arrive at absolutes. Chuck had a revelation. He may not have seen God, but he saw what he truly valued, and he saw what connected him to life. This new clarity helped him put things into perspective: He was still disappointed by his loss, but it didn't threaten his core. Knowing that was no small matter, because many of us allow outside values to determine our deepest sense of inner worth.

GETTING BEYOND OUR SELVES

If the frustrated social idealism of the sixties narrowed to concerns with self-improvement, the focus of the seventies and early eighties was even more circumspect. We have been making money and looking for financial security in a time when economic limits are increasingly restrictive. We have become more self-absorbed and concerned with personal survival. Our social conscience speaks faintly if at all. But there are many indications that the pendulum of concerns is beginning to swing in the other direction. What then will be the motif of the next few years? What will be the dominant quest? Many experts have already taken stabs at answering this question. Some say we'll be staying home more, others suggest that more of us will marry. I am convinced that in the coming decade we will return to spiritual values, and strive to make sense of our lives in ways that will foster peace of mind. If this happens, we will break the bonds of self-absorption, because spiritual values lead to connectedness.

Those who became overly concerned with materialism as a path to happiness have discovered that path affords little genuine fulfillment. The signs of spiritual awakening are everywhere. We hear people talking about volunteerism, helping others who are less fortunate than we are. More people are returning to religion and attending church and synagogue, especially those who are beginning families. While new parents may have difficulty embracing religion, having rejected it when they were young, they consider it for their children. When I talk to new parents about why they send their children to religious schools, they initially attribute it to the superior education that they offer. But then they often cite the role of value-centered education that weighs heavily in their decision.

I see another indication of a spiritual awakening in the attitudes of an increasing number of my patients. In their first session many will blurt out apologetically, "You know, I feel sort of indulgent doing this. There are so many people out there with real problems." I reassure them that personal emotional distress requires attention, but I know what they mean. They sense that if they had a larger perspective, their concerns might not be so consuming, and they're right about that. They realize they are living side by side with alarming levels of poverty and homelessness, issues that cry out for their attention, and they feel some guilt for their self-absorption.

Many people are groping for a way to feel better. Many people have latched onto the so-called New Age movement. While much of the New Age movement seems odd, if not bizarre, the important question to me is, "What underlies this particular path?" While I am uncomfortable with the amount of magical and wishful thinking it encourages, the New Age movement is a spiritual quest and points to the wish to make sense of what seems mysterious and out of our control. As one patient said to me, "I've got to know there's a bigger picture, a larger frame to my life. I'm not sure where I'll find it, but I know I need it."

Two aspects of this search for a larger frame to life are unquestionably positive. One is the search for connectedness—with family, friends, community, and, yes, with ourselves. The other is the reaffirmation of the importance of ethical values such as love, honesty, humility, and tolerance in our lives. We must not simply focus on the content, we have to learn to see the form of how we are living.

The search for values and connectedness, like any other search, can become a treadmill. This search becomes a belief treadmill when it is rooted in the assumption that an absolute truth exists out there that will finally put your life in order. If a spiritual quest becomes rigid, as sometimes occurs in organized religion, then we can fall prey to the notion that something magical out there will save us. This same notion underlies all treadmills—a seemingly simple and foolproof external solution to inner dilemmas.

Those looking for easy salvation or automatic peace of mind cling to rigid belief systems that don't work. Too often people invest their belief systems with a kind of magical power, which is, of course, easily disappointing. Disappointment incites them to quickly search for another belief system in the hope that this time they will find it. We all know people who frantically run from one set of answers to another without ever stopping, always searching in vain.

It is difficult to reach out beyond ourselves. In many ways we have been taught that we can become proverbial islands unto ourselves, that the fully realized individual is someone who has learned how to psychologically feed herself. An old Spanish saying reminds us, You can discover almost anything alone except character. False pride isolates us and makes us forget we need other people.

Self-reliance is only part of the picture. When we carry it to an extreme, we cut ourselves off from others and from the nourishment we need from them. Self-reliance can mask the fear of looking vulnerable, of having to ask for help; we erroneously think we should always be able to take care of ourselves.

Our treadmill mentality is spiritually depleting because we invest all of our energy in self-improvement and self-enhancement, ignoring larger truths about love and connectedness. Creating plateaus allows us to reconnect with people and experiences outside of us. On a treadmill we are filled with self-doubt and don't have the energy to give. And if we don't give to others, we get nothing back.

Spirituality is about transcending ourselves, about setting aside material concerns, about broadening our concerns beyond the self and reaching out to others. When we allow ourselves to be concerned about those who are close to us, we are ultimately affirming ourselves on a higher level. This spirituality may be connected with a religion, and for many it is, but is central to all of us, religious or not.

So many of us are lonely today, although most of us have a great deal of contact with others. The legacy of life's treadmills is that they leave us no real time to enjoy other people. They simply become part of the paraphernalia that helps us further our aims. This isn't intentional—we are just too busy, too driven, and too hurried to be alone with ourselves, or really be with others. Our loneliness is born from our disconnection.

Ultimately, it is love and connectedness that can be realized when we reach plateaus in life. And that is what I want to explore in this chapter. I want to examine what happens when we look beyond ourselves.

GETTING BEYOND ENVY

One of the ways to break a cycle of self-absorption and the depletion caused by treadmills is to begin relating to the world around us. I don't mean mastering or manipulating it. I mean understanding and examining what is going on with other people and creating real relationships with them. This reaching out to others, without envy or resentment, is as important to finding ourselves as our solitude is. It isn't something we do after we know ourselves and love ourselves. We do it now, we choose to do it, and this reaching out becomes a crucial part of the process of finding ourselves and ending our isolation.

Reaching others and connecting with them, rather than just using them, requires that we treat them ethically. This is difficult because we have so often set aside ethics in our quest for the expedient. Our habits of practicing dishonesty and manipulation, engineering our appearance, and ignoring others' needs have become part of the defensive maneuvers by which we protect ourselves. The same protection that has led us to even treating ourselves unethically.

When treadmills consume your time and you are self-absorbed without being self-aware, you become bored with yourself and spiritually empty. The more depleted you feel, the more self-absorbed you become, and there seems to be no end in sight. In time, the truth may hit you—you cannot be replenished by feeding on yourself. Boredom comes from a diminished spirit, not from the lack of external excitement.

Self-improvement has emptied us. One of the key signs of our self-deprivation is that we begin to envy others. Because we aren't connected with them, and don't empathize with them, it looks like they have everything we want, but don't have. Instead of connecting with them, we compare ourselves to them, and end up envying and resenting them. Sometimes the people we need the most become our secret enemies.

Without awareness of the process that has trapped us, our feelings feed on themselves. We become more envious and resentful. It isn't enough to be aware of our feelings—we need to understand what they mean. Without this understanding, we are driven by our feelings and become their pawns.

Envy is especially instructive in helping us understand our isolation because it points both outward to our misjudgments of others and inward to how little we value ourselves. We overcome envy by learning to value ourselves and by learning to appreciate other people, not just comparing ourselves to them.

The treadmill mentality is always associated with feelings of envy, resentment, rage, and a hunger for power that gets us nowhere. In recent years we have become so focused on external solutions and rewards that we have been conditioned to always look outward, but not in the positive sense of embracing our external world or reaching out to others in love, companionship, and extension of friendship. Too often our external reality is darkly colored by envy, the painful belief that others have more than we do or, worse, are better than we are. Envy is a primary fuel for treadmills. It is natural that we feel envy every now and then. Sometimes it is even a clue as to what we want. But treadmill envy is corrosive, incredibly painful, and the source of blind and misguided behavior designed to put other people down, so we can escape envying them. Identifying and examining our behavior is the first step toward changing it.

Envy is a prevalent problem because we are so enamored of our highly publicized lifestyles; We envy what others wear, what they drive, and where they live; We envy their successes.

Having it all means embarking on a clear path to making yourself miserable with envy. Treadmills are always associated with envy because, in the absence of establishing plateaus, our relentless pursuits make everything that is elusive seem all the more desirable. We don't question the source of this emotion, we just feel it like a sharp stab in our hearts. Envy is so powerful that it becomes a reflex that reacts before we can even think about it or label it. In fact, most of us never label it, we simply allow ourselves to become overwhelmed by it. But when we name it, we find we can free ourselves from it and knock down the barriers and begin to feel like a connected and integral part of a community, instead of feeling secretly alienated.

Chuck, the patient I described at the beginning of this chapter, was all too familiar with this poisonous emotion. "I used to feel slightly bogus whenever I gave pep talks to junior executives. I would tell them all the right things—to keep focusing on the positive when they went after new accounts, not to bad mouth the competition because that never worked. And I used to believe what I was saying. But in the last few years, all I ever thought about were those agencies doing better than we were. I'd stay awake at night, thinking about a conversation I had with a friend who just landed a big account for another agency. I felt awful, even when it was an account that wasn't suitable for our shop. I couldn't stand his success. If I could allow myself a moment of real honesty, I really wanted him to do poorly—as if that would make me more secure! What a joke! I used to tell my wife everything, but I was so ashamed about my feelings, I started keeping them to myself."

Such feelings aren't uncommon. You and I may have had them ourselves. Envy becomes so painful we wish others ill so we don't have to envy them. This tendency is one of the dark aspects of who we are, and one we must acknowledge and put into perspective. Once we acknowledge this darker aspect of ourselves, and learn to understand and control it, we can begin to disarm the power envy has over us.

Envy has a secret companion—one that I regard as a blessing in disguise—guilt! People often say, "Well it doesn't do any good to feel guilty, the damage has already been done," as if guilt were an archaic emotional appendix that should be cut out when it becomes inflamed. Some guilt is misplaced and crippling, but some guilt is a clear signal that we are acting unethically. Ridding ourselves of painful feelings is like killing the messenger who brings us bad news.

If we pay attention to the guilt that accompanies envy, we can acknowledge two truths: We wish harm to those we envy and we are treating ourselves as if we had no worth. We should respond to guilt as we respond to the pain that tells us to take our hand off the hot stove—we should change what we are doing.

Guilt over envy—a friend's success, another colleague's promotion, or a neighbor's new possession—is a sign that we will be unable to care about these people unless we rid ourselves of envy. Envy is a barricade for almost all of us at one time or another, I have found that once we recognize it and forgive ourselves for being human, we can move on. And the reward for moving on is that it frees us to love. When I explain this to my patients, they initially feel I'm merely foisting a moral judgment on them, but I'm not. I'm in fact promising them a psychological pathway to the healing, replenishing, and life-affirming freedom to love.

When envy consumes us, we are unable to love, unable to appreciate others. Envy opens the floodgates to our darkest emotions and our most mean-spirited inclinations. Envy becomes a catalyst for treadmill behaviors that lead nowhere and, therefore, only trigger more envy. When we're envious, we lose sight of ourselves and what is good about us.

You must accept the presence of envy in your heart to get beyond it. I have found that envy followed by guilt is healthy, but only when that guilt is then followed by an acceptance that allows you to move on. Too often, people feel envy, then guilt and shame, and they stop there, feeling awful about themselves and resenting the people whom they envy because they triggered these terrible feelings in the first place! Without acceptance, envy is like an endless feedback loop that keeps you feeling awful and, therefore, keeps reinforcing itself!

Acceptance is particularly difficult because we're afraid that we will be stuck feeling overwhelmed with both envy and guilt with no way out. But genuine acceptance rather than exacerbating negative emotions tends to quiet them long enough for us to take a step in a different direction. Allowing others their wins is less painful when we find ourselves on a path toward a win of our own. And, as you undoubtedly know, releasing yourself from painful feelings is a real win.

When we begin to value ourselves, and begin to treat ourselves ethically, we affirm our worth. We stop comparing ourselves to others and become free to love them. Loving them frees us from the guilt that comes from using and resenting them. Self-acceptance is a powerful force in our lives.

Confronting our guilt may require a radical shift in our perception of ethics. In childhood, we were told what was good before we could really understand it. So, at times it felt like a burden. Doing our duty or meeting our obligation sounds ominous. A heavy spirit compels us to painfully try to be "good." When we open ourselves, set aside crippling defenses, forgive ourselves, and stop putting impossible demands on others, we begin to lighten up. Affirming our spirituality gives us wings, not new burdens. Perhaps this is why laughter is one of the most spiritual things to do.

LOVING BEYOND THE SELF

Given all the paths to happiness that have held sway in recent years, love is the most-often neglected one, although there are good signs of its being revived. I'm speaking not of the erotic or romantic kind, but love of others, given freely and unselfishly. We find so much written about romantic love, passionate love, and erotic love. Love has so many faces—longing, infatuation, and excitement—but many of us come to believe romantic intensity and love are synonymous, rather than understanding that love manifests itself in many ways. Love's ambiguities are so painful yet intriguing, that a simpler version has been lost or buried. Love's passionate expectations make it sag from weariness, but left unburdened it can soar.

But how do we unburden our love? I would like to focus on love as unselfish giving, when another person's happiness is as important to you as your own. Whether we call this adult love or mature love or love for one's neighbor doesn't matter. What I believe is essential today is that you see love as something you give rather than receive. Love is an activity of our will.

In recent decades, we have viewed love as something that happens to us—we "fall in love." The emphasis on this self-centered love comes not from some inherent selfishness in us, but largely as a by-product of self-improvement industries. You have heard the saying, You can't love others until you love yourself. And, of course, there's truth there, but the self-improvement movement has misplaced the emphasis. It has focused on *getting* love, rather than *giving* love.

Because of our obsessive concerns with self-gratification, we have obscured the fundamental truth that love is both cause and effect. We have focused for too long on love as effect, as a reward for the way we act or what we are. But love as "cause" must be brought into our consciousness. The only way you come to love yourself is to love others. The more you actively love others, the better you feel about your basic worth. You love yourself in the process of loving others—you don't have to wait until you have all the love you need to start.

Norman, who has seen and done it all, found his own version of self-enhancement by getting beyond his own narrow concerns. He is a successful figure in the entertainment industry. A few years ago, he was at the height of his success, but was overwhelmed by a sense of meaninglessness and he became a serious cocaine abuser and eventually had to be hospitalized. While attempting to rehabilitate himself, a nurse suggested he go to the Braille Institute and do some recordings for the blind. He told me, "At first, I felt this was one of those suggestions we all hear, but never follow up on. I didn't try, either, until this nurse pushed me. Now I go every week for three hours, and when I leave, I feel satisfied and have a greater sense of accomplishment than I ever had before. It was the first concrete thing

I did alone to help others. Oh, in the past I'd go to Hollywood fund-raisers, but that was different, easy. This was probably the only time I really made a commitment to help others without a lot of fanfare and publicity."

Too often people look for unnecessarily grandiose and dramatic ways to change their lives. Small steps are not only feasible, but they may be the only way we really change. There is wisdom in attempting to do what is possible, rather than attempting the impossible. That's certainly true when it comes to love.

Love as cause is something those with a treadmill mentality need to heed. With the parenting and marriage treadmills, the way off those mistaken paths involved loving others. By trying to extract love from others, we create our own frustration and disillusionment. Getting our mate to love us by employing disguised criticism and blame rarely works. Getting our children to enhance us doesn't work either. We must first accept and love without demanding that we get anything back. Although for better or worse and unconditional love sound like bromides, and certainly cannot be absolutes, they at least point us in the right direction.

Loving is a life-giving activity of our spirit. It's not a bargaining tool we should use to get what we want. But we often wait for others to act first. We wait in our isolation, feeling lonely and unloved. We wait for someone to save us. We don't need to wait. Our spirit can reach out.

MAKING FRIENDS

The one holiday many of us would like to avoid is New Year's Eve. One reason, which few will acknowledge, is that this is a time when our "friendship status" is measured—who will we be with and how many parties, if any, have we been invited to? This is a time when we are reminded of high-school anxieties, "Am I popular?" and "Who likes me?" On this holiday we are supposed to be with good friends. But, as a recent poll noted, more than 70 percent of us are dissatisfied with our friendships. Some people merely have acquaintances, others don't even have that. Loneliness is an unspoken dilemma for many of us, including married men and women.

Because of our frenetic lifestyles, we don't have time to savor friendships, to cultivate them, or to make new ones. If we're going fast enough, we don't allow ourselves to miss not having them. But down deep, we all do. In my work, I see loneliness as a deeply felt but rarely voiced concern. Because popularity and social approval are so important, people are terribly shy about discussing their loneliness.

If you're working sixty hours a week and if you have all the new leisure-time diversions such as a VCR, you're spending free time unwinding and relaxing. Who needs friends when the TV set can fill in the gap? We unknowingly allow people to drift away. After a while it becomes difficult to make new friends. It may even become something you've forgotten how to do.

Making friends is not an art, but it takes more than mere intentions. Friendship is a spiritual issue. If we are closed off, if we manage appearances and manipulate outcomes, we aren't really interested in other people. We are too focused on the game. At the same time we don't trust our own worth, and we don't reveal who we are. We remain hidden behind the wall of our defenses.

Some people are deluded into thinking friends result from our attractiveness. This delusion leads to people thinking friendship should be effortless, that if they're externally successful or interesting then others will automatically flock to them. These things may draw people together, but it is the stimulation, lively dialogues, and the comfort of having a confidante to share woes with that keeps friends together. We must remember the value of friendship and commit the time, effort, and attention needed to create it.

Our treadmill mentality may have prevented us from fully enjoying those friends that we do have. We become overly choosy, naively thinking that friends are status symbols and we should be careful about the people we publicly let into our homes and our hearts. We are all discriminating in our own ways, but just as we use the wrong criteria in looking for love, we may do the same thing when we look for companions. We must learn to choose friends based on how they make us feel, and how they awaken and touch parts of us that we instinctively need and treasure.

LEARNING TO REACH OUT

From the time we were children playing in sandboxes, we learned unshakable lessons about friends. Some of these lessons—like loyalty, acceptance, and trust—were positive. Others, such as rejection, abandonment, and hurt, were terribly painful. Maybe we said, "Will you play with me?" and the other kid did, a bond was established and we had a friend. But sometimes our social value was not held in high esteem; we weren't one of those kids that others were drawn to. Maybe we were too shy. Or maybe we were too picky and didn't want to belong to any club that would have us as a member! Regardless, our social worth is often set by these early experiences. It is hoped that as we get older we will allow old hurts to fade and we will gravitate to those we like and those who like us in return.

We must prevent early lessons from haunting us. All of you have had the experience of telling someone you just met, "Let's get together some time," knowing neither of you will go far enough out of your way to actually initiate a get-together. It's not because you're too busy, although, superficially, it's a believable excuse. It's actually because in varying degrees everyone suffers from just enough shyness to hold her back. Sometimes having the confidence to explore potential friendships is all we need to overcome the difficulty of reaching out, because, given a chance, we will inevitably find friends among those we encounter.

There are various levels of friendship, just as there are varying intensities of love. We have casual friends, acquaintances, good friends, and best friends. As adults, we like to mention our best friends, although we toss the word *best* around because we think it makes a good impression. In today's society, most people have casual friends, even though they may see each other regularly and over many years. What keeps it casual is the degree of honesty and emotional sharing that we allow. We keep it safe.

When we shed false pride, we are able to deepen our friendships. If we are prone to envy, we are reluctant to share the emotional difficulties we're experiencing. We keep our hassles with our mate secret, we keep business or financial anxieties secret, and if we're feeling lost or adrift for no reason at all, we keep that secret as well. False pride occurs when we are so concerned about the front we put up and are so envious of the comparisons we make with others that we cannot bear to reveal our vulnerabilities. We are so fearful of looking less than others, of being judged as weak or as a failure or simply as "just not enough," we never risk deep friendships. But, of course, we only cheat ourselves of the joy of sharing, of the relief of unburdening ourselves, and of the experience of feeling known, understood, and accepted for who we are. Often, the first step toward sharing the comfort of real friendship is simply admitting your fears. This often frees others to admit they, too, possess similar fears. And fear, once exposed and verbalized, loses much of its destructive power.

We must seek out the rewards of friendships, instead of settling for only the semblance of it. I know people who monthly go out to dinner with the same people, have the same conversation, and go home relieved the evening is over. Out of habit, we hang onto the same acquaintances. We see them, but we don't know them. We've all had the surprise of hearing one day that couples we've seen for years are getting a divorce. I'm not suggesting that we all share our every intimacy, but never really letting the people we call friends know what's going on inside us makes a mockery of the word *friendship*.

We don't trust ourselves and we don't trust others. This is a spiritual issue because our lack of trust keeps us disconnected. We have experienced a thousand good reasons for not trusting. We have a hundred betrayals to confirm our isolation. But all the good reasons in the world, can't conceal the fact that we choose to stop trusting. We can choose to trust. This is a spiritual challenge. Yes, we will be vulnerable. Yes, we will sometimes get hurt. But we will free ourselves from our carefully orchestrated isolation.

As a therapist, I am privy to people's secret lives. I am always surprised how everyone thinks everyone else is doing so well, especially in the area of companionship. How little we know. We think nobody else needs our friendship. But we are not beggars in a world of abundance. People need and desire our friendship. Just as we must risk knowing ourself, we must risk offering ourself to others and trusting the reception. We might be surprised. Such risks take us out of ourself, and we find that living is more valuable than avoiding pain. Our spirit, with all its scars, will thrive.

THE REWARDS OF CONNECTION

There are rewards for breaking away from the false security of isolation or abandoning the more subtle but equally illusory security of looking for mirror images in those we get close to. When we only seek out friends who are just like us, we deprive ourselves of new ideas, attitudes, and interests. What starts out safe can very quickly become boring. If you want to take some risks, use differences as possible catalysts for reconnecting with others. Instead of sameness, allow yourself to be open to surprise, to the unexpected. With friends, we are less demanding than those who are more intimately tied to us such as husbands and wives and children. As a result, we can be more emotionally accessible to them. Friendships should evoke a sense of trust, ease, and pleasure rather than stabs of envy and the anguish of secret inferiorities.

One of the great rewards for having a diversity of contact is that aspects of your Forgotten Self will be restimulated. Wishes, interests, and attitudes you may have set aside years ago will rise in your consciousness so that you may embrace them again as part of yourself.

Men and women who have declared themselves as individuals find they are less frightened of differences and of change. They are aware of a more expansive world than one that only mirrors themselves. They see that the opportunities are everywhere.

Over the years we can become pessimistic about the warmth and camaraderie we want with others. But, we all have acquaintances we take for granted. When I talk with patients who express loneliness, I'm surprised how often they do have people around them they could turn to. But oddly, because of familiarity and old habit patterns, they don't believe they can deepen these bonds.

Recently, a male patient in his late forties was complaining about not really having someone in his life he could confide in. Yet he would also talk about one male friend with whom he jogged and another with whom he played tennis. When I asked him what they talked about, it became clear to me that there were many openings for each man to be more open and honest. In fact, when one of them talked about the future and life's meaning, I was convinced it was really a disguised way of trying to talk about some things that disturbed him. I told this to my patient and suggested he seize these opportunities. He did. He overcame a moment of shyness and pushed the conversation one step deeper and made a genuine pal rather than just a jogging companion.

If you crave friendships, first look within yourself at attitudes and predispositions. Establishing friendship plateaus requires that you clear yourself of self-defeating biases. In some ways, it's no different from finding a mate. Chemistry happens between friends as well as between lovers. With friends, we may demand less than we do of lovers, but we also do less courting than may be necessary.

Reaching out to others means risking rejection or indifference. Finding those with whom we "click" is not easy. But just as in dating, the more open you are, the more you reveal yourself, and the more you withhold quick judgment, the more likely you are to find those with whom you're compatible. Often we don't like someone when we are first introduced, but if we get to know each other, a liking develops because we both let down our guards. This is especially true of men, who have more difficulty than women in bonding with the same sex.

Friends fight, too. The person who is determined to overcome inevitable disagreements and clashes and forgive and forget is the person who establishes stronger bonds. The key is staying focused on what you like and allowing your dislikes to fade somewhat into the background. Often this is not easy. We've all experienced the joy of feeling someone could be a best friend. But when we discover they already have one or two best friends, we feel we're in a triangle and many of us find this uncomfortable. Some of us have difficulty sharing friends just as children do. If you feel this, don't chastise yourself, it's quite normal. But you can get beyond it. When you have a firm sense of yourself, you won't feel diminished when your friends have other friends in addition to you, even if you never get to really know those people.

Couples have special difficulties with friends. Trying to get four people to connect with each other is hard. You must accept that this doesn't often happen. Sometimes, you must let a friend be someone you see alone and not get together as couples. Again, focusing on what is good and positive is the secret to friendship rather than trying to get friends to fit into your life exactly as you want them to. Remember, it was rigidity and myopia that got you on the wrong path. If you've conquered that problem, don't let old ways of thinking prevent you from living well.

Getting off life's treadmills creates space for friendships. Having plateaus creates the desire and energy to reach out to others. Indeed, I have found that companionship may be one of the most effective ways of staying off treadmills. Our friends are often the ones who remind us when we've gone astray.

THE QUESTION OF VALUES

We have all drifted away from a sense of values, we no longer have strong moral codes or standards of conduct. This is why "values," or "value clarification," are emphasized in the school system. As I have suggested, our wish to reach out beyond ourselves is the intention that provides the adhesive for our values. Once we choose to love others and to give more freely, the question of values begins to come into sharp focus and move toward clarity. In other words, the problem lies within us, not out there in a valueless society. Ultimately, our society is only a reflection of who we are.

But there are also personal values, less lofty perhaps than the others but no less vital. Personal values—including how you care about your children and your friends and your dearly held interests and involvements—all require awareness to be sustained. Moreover, I believe we all have them within us. For many of us, they reside in a Forgotten Self, obscured by our illusory quests.

We don't have to look for values, because we already have them! We must simply strengthen them. We have to clarify and reaffirm our commitment to our own values and that requires discipline, which seems harder to acquire than compulsive actions. But it's not really. Discipline, a vigilant consciousness, comes relatively easy when we trust the outcome, when we believe that our commitment will enrich our lives. The person who reclaims forgotten values will hang onto them tenaciously when he finally understands that they are a precious part of who he is.

In a sense, trusting that we can learn to accept ourselves and then moving beyond and loving others is the final stage in getting off life's treadmills. This trust, this belief, can serve as your personal code of conduct, as an inner gyroscope keeping you on track. Just as infants begin life needing to develop a trust of the world around them, we must vigorously embrace a trust that peace of mind is indeed possible and that there is an inner terrain, an inner journey that leads there.

EPILOGUE: PEACE OF MIND, JUST THE WAY YOU ARE

I began this book by questioning the paths we take to find happiness. The search evolved out of my own frustrations as a psychotherapist. The longer I work as a psychologist, the more I see how easily we overlook the trustworthy signposts that can guide us toward well-being. Durable truths that have stood the test of time are now obscured by seductive and simplistic beliefs about what life offers.

As you are undoubtedly aware by now, I believe that too many of us fail to perceive the possibility of choosing a life we can call our own. Driven by inner dissatisfaction, we reject true individuality and instead live our lives mesmerized by society's unrelenting siren call to always be and have more. Seductive beacons and tedious prescriptions for fulfillment fail to deliver their illusory promises, and they gradually, but inexorably, become life's treadmills. I instinctively sensed there must be a better way to live and set out to identify how life goals can degenerate into deadly traps.

Reflecting on and scrutinizing what I do as a therapist, I realized that fundamental change required more than minor adjustments in my theoretical point of view. What seemed to work with my patients demanded a dramatic new perspective, a rather daring change of focus. I recognized that if a new approach was unsettling to me, it would be even more upsetting to my patients. So, if at times, I have sounded overly harsh or judgmental, it is knowing how difficult it is to halt our momentum, to stop and reexamine the beliefs and assumptions that govern our day-to-day existence.

Complacency usually masks undiscovered challenges. So when I finally wrote this book, my insights and conclusions came not only from my patients but from my own life. I struggle with these forces just as you do, and my desire for contentment is undoubtedly as compelling as is yours. And, I know all too well how loath we are to explore the unexamined facets of our existence and to thereby risk encountering the diminished sense of self-esteem we have so desperately been avoiding. I know we are more compelled to quest after self-improvement, the seemingly easier or more clearly defined path to happiness. I also know that it frequently leads nowhere.

As I was writing, I was always aware that I might seem naive, as though I was yearning to go back to simpler times that may have only existed through a soothing veil of nostalgia. But in the past, there are truths we forgot and I know they yield powerful insights and values that are immune to facile theories and fashionable trends.

While ressurecting old and valuable maxims, I have determinedly explored more contemporary views in a harsh light, exposing enticing psychological illusions. We must forgive ourselves even while we explode these illusions. As I have described, in every area of life today, tempting socially endorsed prescriptions keep us on life's treadmills. The truth is more painful. But if there is one lesson I hope you have absorbed, it is that self-honesty is not self-condemnation. Forgiving ourselves for being human is necessary to move forward.

At my core, I am an optimist. I believe our will to survive is much more powerful than our understandable, but self-defeating, leanings toward darker emotions. In attempting to illuminate our capacity for self-determination and reclaiming our individuality, I've revealed how even my own profession has inadvertently contributed to our illusions. In struggling with these issues, I've sought out counsel with my peers. My colleagues essentially agree with my assessment and insist, as I do, that our advice is ultimately meant to enrich lives, not to make them more frustrating and complex. We all wonder as we question how we serve society, whether we have told the whole story. We ask ourselves if we have unwittingly focused on instant gratification and the elevation of immediate feelings above developing a philosophy of life. In my view, the answer is a resounding, "yes!" We try our best but are nonetheless guilty of a serious sin of omission. We have neglected perhaps the most fundamental state craved by so many of us today, and that is allowing for peace of mind to triumph over the more nebulous goal of self-realization.

We all value self-acceptance, and we acknowledge its urgency. But what has been neglected in our work is the emotional state that accompanies it. Peace of mind is a state of inner contentment, quietude, tranquility, and serenity—these are feelings that have been overlooked, even in this age of "getting in touch with feelings."

Peace of mind is an interior sense of well-being that finally enables us to reconnect with our world without fear, envy, or greed. Valued many years ago, we abandoned this concept probably because it connoted a contentment with the status quo. Remember, we have all been living in a more revolutionary time when acceptance has been suspect. In recent years, tranquility has been viewed as a flaccid rather than robust objective —as though tranquilizers and tranquility are synonymous. Regardless of our recent past, as we go about life today, harried and desperate to conquer chronic inner unrest, I'm sure you will agree that peace of mind is a state to be coveted! And it is attainable.

In revealing those strategies necessary to step off life's treadmills and create plateaus of contentment, I have attempted to show you that you can achieve peace of mind just the way you are. Instead of reaching toward trendy external guidelines, we can pause, allow moments of solitude, and rediscover a trust in our inner lives. I have attempted to outline those processes that lead us back to our inner resources and to reveal how they can be revived and enlivened to shine bright enough to illuminate directions that will enrich our lives.

Men and women today wander toward peace of mind awkwardly and by trial and error. I witness this daily and hear about it from my colleagues. Whether people follow the path I've outlined, or stumble on it on their own, they are nonetheless finding direction. The need for contentment—the desire to affirm that who they are and what they have must finally be enough—is so powerful that they are destined to achieve this state of contentment. Indeed, it is the only goal that makes sense anymore in this era of intense wish fulfillment. Studies show how animals seek out that which will propagate the species. Our present-day quest for serenity and self-acceptance is just as instinctual. It's almost as though we have explored everything else and finally know what we must do.

Honoring and renewing our respect for our inner life and subsequent reaching out to others is, I believe, what people are talking about when they speak of balance in life. What has been missing in our search for balance is an understanding of each side of the equation denoting work and a personal life. The search for balance is an attempt to solve the perplexing problem of pursuing life's goals joylessly and relentlessly. Its answer illuminates how we can reclaim a self that is courageous enough to find plateaus of satisfaction.

As you have finished reading this book, I hope you have sensed my optimism about reclaiming forgotten parts of yourself. I hope you can enthusiastically trust your inner courage and take the necessary steps. We all have an inner self we can give voice to, and when it is allowed to speak, it will affirm our ability to shape our reality and conduct life on our own terms.